I0127508

Anonymous Anonymous

The Golden Rule

The Book for All

Anonymous Anonymous

The Golden Rule
The Book for All

ISBN/EAN: 9783744660105

Printed in Europe, USA, Canada, Australia, Japan

Cover: Foto ©Thomas Meinert / pixelio.de

More available books at **www.hansebooks.com**

The Golden Rule.

OR:

The Book for All,

BY

A Member of a Religious Order.

BALTIMORE:
KREUZER BROTHERS, PUBLISHERS,
1871.

Entered, according to Act of Congress, in the year one thousand eight hundred and
seventy one by
VERY REV. JOSEPH HELMPRAECHT, Provincial,
in the Office of the Librarian of Congress at Washington.

IMPRIMATUR:

MARTINUS JOANNES,

Archiepiscopus Balto.

Die 25 Sept. 1871.

"Nunquam ab adolescentia aut legere aut doctos viros, quae nesciebam, interrogare cessavi, aut meipsum habui magistrum."

St. Hieronymus. Praef. in Epist. ad Ephes.

AUTHOR'S PREFACE.

My dear Reader, I pray you to read this Preface for our mutual satisfaction.

AMONGST all the Institutions of Holy Church, designed by Almighty God for the salvation and sanctification of mankind, that of religious Orders and Congregations stands out, no doubt, in bold relief. However the preservation of primitive fervor, the maintenance of good order, the general well-being and usefulness of religious Communities to all classes and wants of the Church and of Society, depend in a great measure, on the wisdom and prudence of those who govern them. Experience teaches that subjects easily imitate the example of their Superiors in virtue or in vice. "What manner of a man the Ruler of a City (of a religious Community) is, such are they that dwell therein."[1] The conduct of Superiors is, as it were, a law for their subjects. It was on this account that the holy founders of religious Institutions took particular care to qualify the Superiors for their duties; and that they preferred not to accept any new foundations rather than to entrust the Superiorship to subjects who were not qualified.

[1] Eccl. 10. 2.

The art of governing well is a divine gift, consisting in grace and prudence rather, than in holiness of life. For this reason it is more advisable to elect for Superior, one gifted with prudence and discretion, than one, who, though holy, is destitute of these gifts. Moreover, to be qualified for the Superiorship, it is necessary to be a man of prayer, of humility, of detachment from everything in this world, of true paternal charity for every one without exception, with a heart full of compassion for the sick, the afflicted, the tempted; a man who does not easily believe fault-finding characters; a man who knows how to master his passions, who excels in punctual observance of religious discipline, in firmness of mind and ready obedience; and finally he must also be surrounded by virtuous brethren. If any of these qualities be wanting, there is danger, because, without these virtues, a superior may be an excellent political, but not a good religious Ruler.

Men endowed with these virtues and qualities are very scarce indeed. "It is far more difficult," said St. Francis de Sales, "to find good Superiors, than is generally believed." "Nay, there are many," said St. Alphonsus, "who are not fit to be Superior for one hour." "My brethren," said St. Francis of Assissium, on his death bed, when asked which of his brethren he thought was possessed of the proper qualities to be his successor, "my brethren, I know no one who is possessed of the qualities requisite to be the leader of so grand an army, and the pastor of a flock so widely scattered." Such men are gifts of

God Who alone can raise up good rulers. "In His time He will raise up a profitable ruler over His people."[1] "If the rulers of a city are wise," wrote Plutarch to Numa, "then the citizens must believe that they have received one of the greatest of divine benefits;" for, "of the benefits of God," wrote Pliny to Trajan, "there is none greater and more desirable, than a ruler, who resembles God by his great sanctity and wisdom."

Taking then into consideration, both the great necessity of good Superiors and the extreme difficulty of finding them, it is a matter of surprise that, amongst so many books published in every language for the instruction of religious, there is so little published for the instruction of those who have charge of religious Communities. Such a book would undoubtedly prove very useful to many Superiors, at least to those who enter upon their office for the first time, perhaps without ever having received any practical lessons on the subject. Being thus destitute of experience and practical knowledge of the most difficult of arts and sciences, their methods of governing will, of course, vary according to their characters, dispositions and education. A Superior of a peaceful and gentle character, will govern with all possible mildness; one of an austere disposition, with all possible rigor; one of an impetuous character, with more indiscreet zeal than common sense, while a Superior of a timid disposition will remain inactive, where he should show his firmness and zeal for the glory of

[1] Ecclus. 10, 4.

God and the welfare of his neighbor, all being under the fatal necessity, of learning the art of governing, by an experience that proves often prejudicial to their subjects. For if subjects notice, that the divine authori y, invested in Superiors assumes so many forms and changes they say, that their faith is too much tried, that they cannot accommodate themselves to every kind of government, and thus show themselves less ready to obey and to carry the yoke of the religious life.

As the art of governing is no more an infused science than any other, it must, like all the rest, have its wise rules and sound principles. A book, then, containing these rules, and treating of the chief duties of Superiors and the principal faults into which they may easily fall, cannot but be most desirable, especially, at a time, when religious Communities are increasing day by day. Such a book will be not only a great means, to prevent or correct many considerable mistakes, but also a great preserver and promoter of the true religious spirit.

It is with this intention, that the present work has been published. The compiler hopes, that it will prove very useful not only to Superiors of religious Communities, but also to directors of souls, to teachers, to heads of families, and to all in authority; nay, competent judges both of the clergy and laity have assured him, that the perusal of this book will prove very beneficial to every reader; for, generally speaking, parents must be to their children, pastors to their flocks, confessors to their penitents, teachers to their pupils, all in authority to their subjects, and in general, one man to another, what Superiors of religious Communities should be to their inferiors ; what is praiseworthy and blameworthy in Superiors, is so too in subjects, though not in the same degree.

The book bears the title "The Golden Rule, or the Book for All," a title which I trust, dear reader, you will find fully justified, because, in compiling this work, I have but done what the Wise Man has said : "Seek out the wisdom of all the ancients."[1] "Stand in the multitudes of ancients that are wise, and join thyself, from thy heart, to their wisdom, that thou mayest hear every discourse of God and the sayings of praise may not escape thee. And if thou see a man of understanding, go to him early in the morning, and let thy foot wear the steps of his door."[2] Now in reading this book you will always stand, as it were, in the multitudes of ancients that were wise, and see yourself joined to their wisdom ;— the golden rule of every one's conduct ;—for you will learn in this book, nothing but the sound maxims and instructions, as well as the wise manner of acting of such prudent and holy men as have excelled in the art of governing.

Hence, "despise not the discourse of them that are ancient and wise, but acquaint thyself with their proverbs. For of them, thou shalt learn wisdom and instruction of understanding."[3] Let not the discourse of the ancients escape thee, for they have learned of

[1] Ecclus. 34, 12.   [2] Ecclus. 6, 35-36.

[3] Ecclus. 7, 9-10.

their fathers; of them thou shalt learn understanding and to give an answer in time of need.''[1]

May, therefore, God bless this work; and may all those who peruse it, ''keep the sayings of renowned men,''[2] in order that the compiler may be able to say with the same Wise Man: ''See that I have not labored for myself only, but for all that seek truth and discipline.''[3]

[1] Vers. 11-12.   [2] Chap. 39, 12.

[3] Chapt. 24, 47, and 33, 18.

PROTEST OF THE AUTHOR.

N obedience to the decrees of Urban VIII. of holy memory, I protest that I do not intend to attribute any other than purely human authority to all the miracles, revelations, graces and incidents contained in this book; neither to the titles 'holy or blessed' applied to the servants of God not yet canonized, except in cases where these have been confirmed by the Holy Roman Catholic Church and by the Holy Apostolic See, of whom I profess myself an obedient son; and, therefore, to their judgment I submit myself and whatever I have written in this book.

CONTENTS:

CHAPTER I.

ON THE DIFFICULTIES OF GOVERNING.

Ars artium est, et scientia scientiarum regere hominem.
Gregory Nazian. Apol. I.

(The art of arts, and the science of sciences is, to govern man.)

T happened once that a young Carthusian Abbot, had great trouble and difficulty, with some of his subjects. In a letter which he wrote to St. Bernard, he says, "That, had each one done his duty, he would have found no difficulty in governing them, or in being their Superior." The young and inexperienced Abbot said nothing that was surprising ; for, should every one do his duty, a statue might, as it were, be capable of being the general of an Order of fifty thousand religious, having need of eyes only, to behold the good done by them of their own accord. But, alas ! ever since the beginning of the world, there have been two elements continually combating each other — the good and the bad. "There must be scandals," said our Lord, a fatal though divine decree. St. Michael and Lucifer combat each other in heaven ; Cain and Abel in the family of Adam ; Isaac and Ismael in that of Abraham ; Jacob and Esau in that of Isaac ; Joseph and

1

his brethren in that of Jacob; Solomon and Absalom
in that of David ; St. Peter and Judas in the company
of our Lord Jesus Christ ; the Apostles and the
Roman emperors, in the Church of Christ; St. Francis
of Assissium and Brother Elias, in the Franciscan
Order ; St. Bernard and his uncle Andrew, in the
Cistercian Order ; St. Alphonsus and Father Leggio
in the Congregation of the Most Holy Redeemer ;
orthodox Faith and heresy and infidelity, in the
Kingdom of God on earth ; the just and the wicked,
in all places ; in fact where is that country, that
city, that village, that religious community, or that
family howsoever small it may be, where these two
elements are not found in opposition. The parable
of the sower and the cockle, is everywhere verified ;
even should you be quite alone, grace and nature
combat one another. "And a man's enemies shall
be they of his own household."[1] Strange to say, not
only the good and the wicked are found in perpetual
conflict ; but God, for wise ends, permits that even
the holiest and best of men are sometimes diametrically opposed, and even incite persecution, each against
the other, though each one may be led by the purest
and holiest of motives.

St. Epiphanius disputed with St. John Chrysostom, saying, that he never would tolerate the disciples of Origen. St. John Chrysostom, not so hasty
in his conclusion, said, that he would never confound
the innocent with the guilty. St. Epiphanius replied,
that the heresy was so impious, the crime so enormous,

[1] Math. 10, 36.

that true love for the faith should force him to expel this brood of vipers from the Church without delay. St. John Chrysostom answered : "A good judge condemns no one without a hearing." St. Epiphanius exclaimed : "You are too punctilious in the matter." In reply St. John Chrysostom complained, that Epiphanius was too zealous, not having patience enough to listen to the truth. "Patience," answered St. Epiphanius, you mean sympathy with the cause, and hypocrisy !" "Say rather violence and precipitation," answered Chrysostom. "But," said Epiphanius, "are you afraid to condemn heretics ?" "And have you no fear of condemning the innocent as guilty ?" asked St. Chrysostom. "I clearly see," remarked Epiphanius, "that you favor Origen." "And I," rejoined St. John Chrysostom, "fear that you side with the enemies of truth." "Be it so ! But I say to you in the name of God," replied St. Epiphanius, "that you will not die in Constantinople ; you will be banished, and will end your life upon a distant shore." "And I also tell you, on the part of God," answered St. John Chrysostom, "that you will not reach your diocese, and that you will die at sea."[1] Both were saints, both prophesied truly, both were right ; and yet there seemed to be sufficient cause for dispute and opposition between them. Similar contests and differences of opinion occurred between St. Peter and St. Paul, the Princes of the Apostles ; between St. Augustine and St. Jerome, and many others great and eminent in learning and sanctity.

[1] Annals of Baronius.

Who does not see how difficult it is to govern men so strange in their views, so whimsical in their characters, and differing as they do so widely in their opinions and intentions. It might be asserted without exaggeration, that it is more difficult to govern one solitary man, than to rule the whole universe. The course of the material world is so regular, that he who should direct it for one year, would find no difficulty in governing it during a whole life-time. But the little world-man — changes every moment : — he turns like a weather-cock with every wind. One is of a hasty temperament, and does everything with impetuosity ; another has a sluggish mind, and troublesome disposition ; he is as dull as lead, and as inflexible as iron. If he be urged on a little, he begins to despond. This one is as restless as quicksilver ; he can scarcely be kept quiet ; that one is melancholy and always looks upon the dark side of the picture. Another is ambitious and selfish, and strives to draw the eyes of all men upon *himself*. Again, one desires to be flattered, another, on the contrary, assumes an attitude of distrust when treated kindly, and puts himself on his guard. What is too indulgent for one, is to severe for another. What is illiberal in the eyes of one, is deemed too great freedom in the eyes of another. One prefers a spirit of freedom and liberality, whilst another is displeased at such a spirit, and complains of the want of rigor and discipline. One is controlled too much, the other too little. This one considers a command, a regulation, too arbitrary and despotic, that one looks upon it as unwise and unseasonable; both criticise the directions and actions of the Superior, though they do not, and often cannot know, the motives which prompt him. It often happens, that the orders of a Superior, are interpreted in a manner which is entirely foreign to his thoughts and intentions. This is very painful to a Superior, particularly when fraternal charity is in question. Now and then, he is also grieved to see, that his subjects are not always sufficiently sincere towards him; some approve of his course of action in his presence, whilst behind his back, they murmur and complain among their brethren, manifesting their discontent, nay, even exciting others against him. They seem to expect the Superior to be above all the miseries of our fallen nature, and therefore his faults find less excuse in their eyes, than do those of any other person.

"But no Superior," says St. Vincent of Paul, "must be surprised at meeting with this kind of cross; for from such crosses our Lord Jesus Christ Himself was not exempt. How many have there not been, who have found fault with His actions! "John the Baptist came," said our Lord to the Jews, "neither eating bread nor drinking wine, and you say: he hath a devil. The Son of Man is come eating and drinking, and you say: Behold a man that is a glutton and a drinker of wine, a friend of publicans and sinners."[1] Some admired and believed the miracles and words of our Lord, whilst others rejected them as proceeding from a sorcerer or, a man possessed by the

[1] Luke vii. 33—34

devil and as calculated only to cause disturbance amongst the people.''

"There must be scandals.'' The permission of these evils is not the least of the mysteries of God's Providence. According to St. Vincent de Paul, the Lord permits them to show us the wretchedness of human nature, and to keep those in fear who are not as yet firm in their good purposes. According to St. Alphonsus, God permits these evils to serve as occasions for the practice of patience. According to St. Francis de Sales, the Lord permits them for the practise of passive humility, one ounce of which is of incomparably greater value than many pounds of active humility. According to Father Binet, S. J., God permits crosses of this kind to remind us of our common weakness and nothingness which, if left without contradictions, would soon degenerate into pride, self-elevation, self-complacency, vain-glory in our actions, into attachments to offices, and forgetfulness of our Lord's saying: "When you shall have done all these things that are commanded you, say, We are unprofitable servants.''[1] Moreover God permits these crosses as a means to purify our intentions; to supernaturalize our love for our fellow-men; to acquire a disinterested charity; a meekness similar to that of Jesus Christ; a constant conformity with the will of God; the happiness of finding God as well in the bad, as in the good; the dominion over our own passions; the perfection of a true Apostolic man; a heart seeking nothing but God, and faithfully co-

[1] Luke 17, 10.

operating with all the designs of the Lord, even at the cost of its own contentment. The Lord in His wise Providence permits even the holiest men to fall into errors of judgment, without any sin on their part, thus often causing great troubles and trials to each other, to their Superiors, and to their fellow-men; all this happens for the manifestation of the greater glory of God, and to make the Saints distrust themselves and humble themselves before God, acknowledging their misery and avoiding obstinacy in their opinions; ever fearing lest they deceive themselves, and seek not the honor of their Sovereign Lord. According to Cornelius a Lapide, God permits such evils, nay scandals even, in order that the impiety of one, or of a few, may by way of antithesis or contrast, set forth the virtue and holiness of others in greater splendor, as light in the midst of darkness, gold amidst lead, the sun among the planets, the wise among fools: for, if two things of different natures, says the Wise Man, are brought into opposition, the eye perceives at once their difference. "Good is set against evil, and life against death: so also is the sinner against the just man. And so look upon all the works of the Most High. Two and two, and one against another."[1]

Hence St. Bernard was right in writing thus to a Superior: "Take care," he says, "to make a good choice of your Religious; but take as an infallible rule that those, who in the eyes of men work most against you, do you most good in the sight of God.

[1] Eccl. xxxiii, 15.

Far from diminishing your merits they will only increase them : nay, should there be a Community in which no such characters could be found, one ought to be purchased at the price of gold, so incomprehensibly great is the good that this evil, if well managed, will afford." To live with good brethren, is, of course, more agreeable to poor nature; but to have to deal with touchy, susceptible persons, and those with whom, as we say, it is difficult to get along, is a thousand times more profitable and meritorious. Is it not then extreme weakness, on the part of a Superior to do all in his power in order to rid himself of so precious a gem, and to think that he will do wonders after it is gone? Is it not great self-love to complain that his life is a martyrdom, the reward for all his troubles being only ingratitude—a burden for his weak shoulders too heavy to be any longer borne? Is it not a great want of practical faith in God's wise Providence, without Whose permission and disposition, our Lord Jesus Christ assures us, nothing can happen to us, in so much, that to those who love God, all things work together unto good, even the sins and faults of their fellow-men? Is it not to have, as little sense, prudence, and judgment as those servants of the good husbandman, who wanted to gather up the cockle before the time of harvest, not understanding that, at the same time they would injure and root up the wheat? "The good would soon cease to be good," says St. Augustine, "were they not kept up and strengthened by the sufferings which the bad cause them to endure." Does not a Superior, by such conduct show less interest in the spiritual and temporal welfare of his Community than does a merchant in his affairs? The man of business does not on account of difficulties shrink back, nor break up his establishment, nor transfer it to others. Is it not to show less affection for his own brethren, than that of a physician for his patient, who always tries to help him, and to be useful to him to the very last moment of his life? Finally, is not a Superior who desires so much to get rid of his office and to make all possible efforts to be discharged from it chargeable with great infidelity towards God? Did St. Paul renounce his Apostleship, on account of meeting with contradictions and troubles from the Jews, the Gentiles, and his own brethren? Did St. Peter give up the government of the Church in order to escape crucifixion?

"You tell me," writes St. Frances de Chantal to a Sister, "that you can no longer bear the burden of your Superiorship: O my dear daughter, let me never hear again such an expression! Do you wish to render quite useless the talents and gifts which the Lord has given you? And all this for want of determination and resoluteness and your timid and narrow-hearted disposition and of keeping your soul above yourself! Trample upon all this, and looking up to God and His good pleasure alone, abandon your days to Him that He may dispose of them for His honor and glory, in the manner He pleases and not according to your desire. As to the fear of risking your salvation and that of others in your charge, you will try to guide the Community according to the spirit of the Institute, that is in the spirit of humanity and charity, and then you have nothing to fear, for the Lord will be with you and assist you. Your humble submission and acquiesence to the will of God in this office must be greater than the pain and reluctance for it. To think and act otherwise is a mere temptation. Think rather of the blessings which the Lord has prepared for you if you are faithful in trying to preserve by your maternal care and charity, peace, union and the exact observance of all the rules and customs of the Institute among our Sisters."

But, such a Superior will reply: "The Saints themselves have tried to rid themselves of their burdensome Superiorship; what fault can there be in imitating their example?" It is true, we read this in the lives of some; but, are you a Saint, and guided by the same spirit? You allege perhaps, the same motives which the Saints would urge; but tell me, do your motives spring from the same pure fountain of true humility which was the source of theirs? Alas! the manner in which you complain and set forth your reasons for resigning your office, the uneasiness of your heart when you are not listened to, evince but too evidently that your motives flow from a quite different source. They proceed from self-love; from attachment to your own ease and comfort; from the want of a proper intention in your actions; from your own unmortified heart that cannot wait for the time of harvest. "Excuse me, Sir," I one day said to a gentleman, "for troubling you so often." "Never mind, my dear friend," was his reply, "we have to live on trouble." Great truth ; but little understood, and still less loved by many of those calling themselves servants of God ! Troubles are indeed the daily bread of Superiors ; they must feed upon this bread ; it is the Lord Himself Who gives it to them, according to the words of Jeremias : "I have set thee to-day, to root up and to pull down, and to waste and to destroy, and to build and to plant !¹ And according to Ezechiel "to strengthen the weak, to heal that which is sick, to bind up that which is broken, and to bring back again that which was driven away, to seek that which is lost."² Great courage indeed, great generosity, prudence, and heavenly wisdom are required, to bring about so many difficult, nay, wonderful things. "Truly, he who assumes the government of others," says St. John Chrysostom, "must be among them, like man among irrational creatures, or like an Angel among men, or like the sun amidst the heavenly bodies ; that is to say, he ought to be so pre-eminent in virtue as to cast into the shade the perfections of his subjects, even as the sun by its brilliancy, eclipses the surrounding luminaries." Indeed, one may exclaim with the Prophet Jeremias : "Ah, ah, ah, Lord God : behold, I cannot speak for I am a child !"³ Alas ! what must one do considering all this ? "As we know not what to do" said King Josaphat, "we can only turn our eyes to Thee, O Lord God."⁴

¹ Jeremias i. 10.   ² Ezech. 34, 4.
³ Jeremias i. 6.   ⁴ II. Paralip. 20, 12.

CHAPTER II.

ON THE NECESSITY OF PRAYER FOR A SUPERIOR.

SUPERIOR on entering upon his office, is placed in a position similar to that of Solomon when chosen King of Israel. He should therefore say to our Lord : "O Lord God, I am but a child, and know not how to go out and come in. And Thy servant is in the midst of the people which Thou hast chosen. Give therefore Thy servant *an understanding heart to judge Thy people, and to discern between good and evil.* For who shall be able to judge Thy people?[1] God of my fathers and Lord of mercy, Who hast made all things with Thy word, and by Thy wisdom hast appointed man that he should order the world according to equity and justice, and execute justice with an upright heart, give me Wisdom that sitteth by Thy throne, and cast me not off from among Thy children ; for I am Thy servant, a weak man and of short time, and falling short of the understanding of judgment and laws. For if one be perfect among the children of men, yet if Thy wisdom be not with him, he shall be considered as nothing.

[1] III Kings 3.

Send her out of Thy holy heaven, and from the throne of Thy majesty that she may be with me, that I may know what is acceptable to Thee. For she knoweth and understandeth all things, and shall lead me soberly in my works and shall preserve me by her power. So shall my works be acceptable and I shall govern Thy people justly. For who among men is he, that can know the counsel of God? or who can think what the will of God is? For the thoughts of men are fearful, and our cousels uncertain. And hardly do we guess aright at things that are upon earth ; but the things that are in heaven, who shall search out? And who shall know Thy thought except Thou give wisdom, and send Thy holy spirit from above : and so the ways of them that are upon earth may be corrected, and men may learn the things that please Thee.''[1] Solomon knew but too well, that, to govern men, was the art of arts, and the science of sciences. He knew, that in this art and science, no one can excel unless the wisdom of God be with him. "Wherefore," he says, "I wished, and understanding was given me, and I called upon God, and the spirit of wisdom came upon me."[2] Thus Solomon obtained this admirable gift by most fervent prayer. Indeed, in this science every one remains more or less blind until he is enlightened from above. "Yes," exclaims St. Augustine, "I should always have been blind hadst not Thou, O Lord, vouchsafed to enlighten me.''[3]

[1] Wisdom ix.   [2] Wisdom vii. 7.

[3] Solil. c. v.

Solomon asks of God this light of holy wisdom and obtains it. "Because thou hast asked this thing," said our Lord to him, "and hast not asked for thyself long life, nor riches, nor the lives of thine enemies, but hast asked for thyself *wisdom to discern judgment*, behold, I have done for thee according to thy words, and have given thee a wise and understanding heart, in so much that there hath been no one like thee before, nor shall arise after thee."[1]

If God has called you to be Superior, rest assured, that He will not fail to grant you wisdom enough to govern aright; "for the Lord does not call," says St. Bernardine of Sienna, "without giving at the same time, to those whom He calls, all that is requisite to accomplish the end for which He calls."[2] But remember, that this wisdom is granted only, on condition, that you, like the wise man, ask for it. "If any one of you want wisdom, let him ask it of God, Who giveth to all men abundantly . . . and it shall be given him; but let him ask in faith nothing wavering."[3] "Hence", according to Balthasar Alvarez, S. J., "that Superior will exercise his office most successfully, who understands best how to treat with God about his spiritual and temporal affairs, although for the rest, he be a man of no merit." Being but too well convinced of this truth, St. Vincent de Paul wrote to a Superior in the following terms: "What must you do, in order to instil into the

<hr />

[1] III Kings 3. 11–13.   [2] Patroc. St. Joseph Noct. III.

[3] James i. 5, 6.   Lesson II.

hearts of those whom God has already intrusted, or will, in future, confide to your care, priestly dispositions and virtues, and to help them to attain perfection and salvation? This is not indeed, the task of man, but of God and a continuation of the Mission of Jesus Christ. Mere human care, then, will only injure the work, if the blessing of God is not upon it. No, Sir; it is neither philosophy, nor theology, nor eloquence, which moves the heart. Christ, our Lord, must necessarily labor with us, and we with Him. We must labor with Him, and He in us. We must speak like Him, with His spirit, and teach only that doctrine which He taught. It is, therefore, necessary for you to divest yourself of self, in order to clothe yourself with Jesus Christ. Every cause produces an effect similar to itself. When, therefore, he who guides and forms souls, is animated by the human spirit, what else is to be expected, than that those souls, influenced by this spirit, instead of practising true virtue, will assume the bare appearance of it. No matter what he may do and say, he will communicate to them that spirit only, by which he himself is animated. On the contrary, if he is deeply grounded in the maxims of Jesus Christ, all his words and actions will be so many exhortations to the practice of virtue. However, before you can attain to this state, Jesus Christ our Lord must transform you into Himself; for, as a wild tree bears sweet fruit after it has been grafted with a good branch, so it happens with us. Of ourselves, we are miserable creatures, thorny wild trees:

but when our Lord imprints upon our souls His own
perfections, when He communicates to us the sap, as
it were, of His own spirit, when He becomes united
with us, like the vine with the tendril, then we can
do what He has done, our actions will become, as it
were, divine and we also "shall bear children to
Jesus Christ our Lord," as St. Paul said of himself.
Hence to be in constant communication with God by
prayer, is a most important point, to which you
ought most seriously to apply. It is in prayer, that
you will find the instruction you need for the exercise
of the duties of your office. If a doubt arise, go to
God and say to Him: "Lord, Thou Father of Light,
teach me what to do in this circumstance!" This
practice I recommend to you not only for important
matters, but also for all those things in which you
are obliged to instruct others. First go and ask
counsel of our Lord, after the example of Moses, who
announced to the people nothing but what he had
previously heard from God. You must, therefore,
have recourse to God by prayer, so that you may
keep your own soul in His fear and love; for it is my
duty to tell you, and you ought to know it, that
many a one who leads others to salvation, ruins himself. Whilst Saul yet lived in his father's house, he
was found worthy to be king; but when he sat upon
the throne, he fell into disgrace with God. Even
St. Paul chastised his body, lest after he had preached
and pointed out to others the way to heaven, he
should himself become a cast-away. In order to
avoid the misfortune of Saul and Judas, you must

keep yourself closely united to God, often raising your heart and mind to Him, in the following words: "Permit not, O Lord, that whilst I am trying to save others, I myself be lost ! Be Thou my Shepherd and do not refuse me those graces, which by virtue of my office, Thou dost bestow through me on others." However, you ought to ask also what is necessary for your subjects. Be assured that you will do more by prayer, than by any other means. Christ, our Lord, was not satisfied with preaching, laboring, fasting, nor even with the sacrifice of His blood and life. To all this, He added prayer. He did not need it for Himself. It was on our account that He prayed so much, in order to teach us to do the like, to pray, not for ourselves only, but for those also whose redeemer we ought to be." This He so touchingly taught His disciples in His last discourse, "I pray for them," He says, "I pray not for the world, but for them whom Thou hast given Me, — Holy Father, keep them in Thy name, whom Thou hast given Me: that they may be one, as We also are one. I do not ask, that Thou take them away out of the world, but that Thou preserve them from evil. Sanctify them in truth. And not for them only do I pray, but for those also who through, their word, shall believe in Me : that they all may be one, as Thou, Father, in Me, and I in Thee, that they may be also one in Us ; that the world may believe that Thou hast sent Me. Father, I will that where I am, they also whom Thou hast given Me, may be with Me ; that they may see My glory, which Thou hast given

2

Me.''[1] And, again He says: "Behold, Satan hath desired to have you, that he may sift you as wheat: but I have prayed for thee, that thy faith fail not.''[2]

The venerable Father Hoffbauer, C. SS. R., when asked on his death-bed, who, in his opinion should be appointed his successor as Vicar-General, "The tall Frenchman," he answered, meaning Father Passerat; and the reason he gave for his choice was, because this Father knew how to pray well.

St. Frances de Chantal, wrote to a Superior: "Be humble and love to hold intercourse with God; and then He will work wonders in you and your daughters;" and in another letter she says: "Be not troubled at the charges imposed upon you; but fulfil them with humility, meekness, and simplicity of heart without considering your incapacity. The less there is of self, the more there will be of God. Look straight to Him in all your actions, and do not stop at creatures. Often ask the assistance of the Holy Ghost, and be faithful to follow the lights and inspirations He will give you.''

"A Superior," says St. Francis of Assissium, "ought to be a man of prayer and a lover of this holy exercise: but he should divide his time in such a manner, as to have certain hours set apart for himself, and others for his flock. He ought to offer up the Holy Sacrifice early in the morning, giving himself a long time for this sacred action, so that he may devoutly implore the protection of God for him-

[1] John Chapt. xvii.   [2] Luke, Chapt. xxii. 31-32.

self and his flock,'' according to the example of Job who "rising up early offered holocausts for every one of his children : For he said : Lest perhaps my sons have sinned and have blessed God in their hearts. So did Job all days."[1]

"Yes," said St. Vincent of Paul, "give me a man of prayer, and all things will succeed well with him. He will be able to say with the Apostle: "I can do all things in Him who strengtheneth me." The Congregation of the Mission will prosper only as long as its members, particularly the Superiors, persevere in the exercise of prayer. Prayer is an impregnable bulwark, which will protect the Priests of the Mission against every assault. It is a spiritual armory, a tower of David, from which they may supply themselves with every kind of weapons, both offensive and defensive. With these arms they will conquer all the enemies of God and of His kingdom.

"It is most desireable that the Priests of the Mission devote themselves in a particular manner to prayer ; for without it, their labor will be of little or no avail, whilst, on the contrary, with prayer they will touch hearts and convert souls. Little good is to be expected from a man, who does not love to commune with God, and all failures in the performance of duty, proceed from the fact that prayer and familiar intercourse with God are neglected." — "Without the practise of prayer, every Religious Order is sterile, imperfect, and bordering on its downfall," says St. Bonaventure.[2] Woe to Superiors who

[1] Job i, 5.   [2] De Progr. Rel'g.

do not possess the spirit of prayer ! Woe, to them, "because they are in great danger of dying under the torture of so many crosses, as martyrs without merit and without a crown."[1] Woe to them, because through them, religious Communities commence to become barren and imperfect, and take the first steps towards their downfall. As the shepherd is, so is the flock. If Superiors be wanting in love and zeal for prayer, their subjects will also be deficient in this point. Where there is no prayer, everything goes wrong. Tepidity creeps in, the soul becomes despondent and weak, and loses that strength and vitality which it once possessed. All its good resolutions and dispositions suddenly disappear and the passions begin to awaken and clamor. Then man perceives, that he is again a lover of idle pleasure and talk, of mirth, dissipation, and the like. What is still worse, the inclination to vanity, anger, envy, ambition and passions which had appeared to be dead, spring up again. For this reason, St. Francis of Assissium says : "A religious ought to aspire, in a particular manner, to the spirit of prayer ; for, without it, no fruit can be expected in the service of God. But, with the gift of prayer, all else may be hoped for."

Father John de Starchia, Provincial of the Friars Minor in Lombardy, introduced forced studies, and made regulations more favorable to science, than to the spirit of piety and prayer. St. Francis of Assissium upbraided him for it ; but in vain. So the great

[1] Father Torres.

servant of God cursed the Provincial and deposed him at the ensuing chapter. The saint was entreated by some of his brethren in religion to withdraw this curse from the Provincial, a learned noble man, and to give him his blessing. But neither the learning nor the noble extraction of the Provincial could prevail upon St. Francis to comply with their request. "I cannot," said he, "bless him whom the Lord has cursed;" a dreadful reply which soon after was verified. This unfortunate man died, exclaiming: "I am damned and cursed for all eternity." Some frightful circumstances, which followed after his death, confirmed his awful prediction. Such a malediction which pride, the natural consequence of the want of the spirit of prayer, brought upon this Superior, should strike terror into the hearts of all those Superiors, who are filled with the same spirit of vanity and self-sufficiency.

On the words, "If Moses and Samuel shall stand before Me,"[1] Cornelius a Lapide remarks as follows: "Samuel and Moses are named here, in preference to others, because they were very holy, and the leaders of the people. Their power with God was so great and their prayers were so efficacious, that they stayed the anger of God, by praying for the ungrateful and rebellious people. This was, because they were the leaders and judges of the people, and the mediators between God and them. They were the faithful friends of God and loved the people with burning charity, nothwithstanding their refractory and rebel-

[1] Jeremias xv. 1.

lious behaviour. For, these two virtues, prayer and
charity, particularly when exercised towards rebels
and enemies, become those who direct others ; they
move and, as it were, compel God to hear their prayers." St. Jerome, St. Thomas, Theodore, Hugo, and
others speak in like manner.

"You have not gone up to face the enemy, nor
have you set up a wall for the house of Israel."[1] God
blames the false prophets for not having mended the
vices of the people, and turned away the wrath of
God by prayer. "Hence learn," says Cornelius a
Lapide, "how great the spirit of prayer, the zeal and
piety of a Superior and preacher ought to be, .that he
may stand like a wall before an angry God." Moses
acted in this manner when he said : "Either forgive
them this tresspass, or if Thou do not, strike me out
of the book that Thou hast written."[2] And St. Paul
says : "For I wished myself to be an anathema from
Christ for my brethren"[3]. . . In like manner when
the wrath of God was raging against the murmurers,
Aaron offered up incense, and standing between the
dead and the living, he stayed the anger of the Lord
and the stroke.[4] "Therefore thus saith the Lord of
Hosts the God of Israel : There shall not be wanting
a man of the race of Jonadab, the son of Rechab (the
Superior of a religious Order, the son of his holy
Founder,) standing before Me forever."[5] but let him
"Arise, give praise in the night, in the beginning of

[1] Ezech. xiii. 5.   [2] Exod. xxxii. 32.
[3] Romans ix. 3.   [4] Numbers xvi. 48.
[5] Jerem 35, 19.

the watches : let him pour out his heart like water before the face of the Lord : let him lift up his hand to Him for the life of his little children, that they may not faint from hunger."[1]

[1] Jer. ii. 19.

CHAPTER III.

ON THE SPIRIT OF HUMILITY.

IN order to obtain more effectually the divine assistance in his office, a Superior must practise exterior and interior humility. The following considerations will greatly contribute to make him practise this two-fold humility.

"It is the duty of a Superior," says Balthasar Alvarez, S. J., "to serve souls, for whom Jesus Christ has shed His blood ; for the love of God, he must serve them as a servant serves his master. Although his services, in themselves, may be of trifling value, yet He will win Heaven by them, if he renders them cheerfully and promptly, and without any expectation of gratitude. Let him, therefore, consider that God, when He made him Superior, did not appoint him to be a master over his brethren ; that God placed them upon his shoulders rather than at his feet ; and gave them consequently a right to his services. This is a truth of our holy faith. "Even as the son of man came not to be ministered unto, but to minister."[1] "Have they made thee ruler ? Be not lifted up : be

[1] Matthew, xx. 28.

among them as one of them."[1] "He that believeth in Me, the works that I do, he shall do also, and greater than these shall he do."[2] Let Superiors learn from this to leave to their subjects what is more honorable, and to keep for themselves what is less esteemed in the eyes of men. This manner of acting will gain for them the esteem, submission, and gratitude of their subjects and the applause of seculars: It is thus that they will do more good through their subjects, than if they were to do it themselves; for that which is done by the subjects, is looked upon as the work of the Superior."

After St. Ignatius of Loyola was made General of his Order, he publicly taught the Catechism, nobly yielding the pulpit to his companions and subjects. He made it a rule, that the Rectors of the Society should teach Catechism in public, when they entered upon their office.

"I could never act as some do," said St. Francis de Sales, "who as soon as they are raised to any dignity, try to enforce the honor due to them, and who will not deign to sign themselves in their letters: "Your most humble servant," unless they are writing to persons above them in rank. As for myself, it is hard for me to make any difference between those to whom I write. All bear the likeness of their Creator, and I subscribe myself to every one: "Your most humble servant;" unless, indeed, my letter is addressed to Peter or Francis, my servants, who might think I was making fun of them, were I to use this expression."

[1] Eccl. xxxii. 1. [2] John xiv. 12.

3

"I have remarked," says Peter Canus, speaking of St. Francis de Sales, "that when any one, even of the lowest rank, visited him, the holy Bishop assumed the demeanor of an inferior in the presence of his Superior, receiving his visitor with the greatest kindness, listening to, and conversing with him, without any regard to the loss of time or the little utility he might expect would be derived from the conversation." To submit to Superiors, is justice, to submit to equals, is friendship and politeness; but to submit to inferiors, is the peculiar characteristic of humility, which tells us, that, since we are nothing, we ought to cast ourselves at the feet of every one.

St. Jane Frances de Chantal relates, that St. Francis de Sales appeared to her after his death, and thus addressed her: "My child, God has sent me to tell you, that it is His will for you to be exceedingly humble." — One day when something that had been said in praise of her Order, was repeated to her, she exclaimed: "Were it to come to my knowledge that vanity had crept into any of our houses, that it boasted of its connection with distinguished persons and was puffed up with pride at the favor of the great, I should be tempted to beg God to send down fire from heaven, to destroy that Convent. Perhaps, it will be said, that I know not of what spirit I am: but, if it were known what humility God requires of the members of our Order, and how much those resist the spirit of God, who love the vanity of the world, every one would be of my opinion. Nothing would sooner shorten my life, than to see vanity and disunion among the children of the Blessed Virgin."

St. Vincent de Paul, also speaks the same language. Writing to a Priest, he says : "I do not at all agree with a certain person, who said a few days ago, that in order to govern well and maintain our authority, we must show by our demeanor that we are the Superior. Ah ! no : Christ, our Lord, did not speak in this manner. He taught the contrary by word and example, saying, that He had come not to be served, but to serve others, and that he who wishes to be the master, must become the servant of all. Let such be your sentiments, and act towards your subjects, as if you were one of them. Live affectionately and simply with them, so that when you are seen together, no one will be able to tell which is the Superior. Tell them, at once, that you have not come to rule over, but to serve them. You will do well to act in this matter, not only towards the members of your own community, but also towards visitors.

"Moreover we must ascribe to God the good which we do by our means ; whilst, on the contrary, we ought to attribute to ourselves, the evil that occurs in the community. This will really be found to be the fact, if we only consider the matter well, for all disorders proceed from Superiors, either on account of their negligence or of their bad example ; for, if the head is not healthy, the other members of the body will also suffer. In like manner should humility preserve you from that vain self-conceit,

which is apt to glide into honorable offices. Ah!
how many good works are tainted by it! For God's
sake, then, be on your guard against this fault,
which I believe to be the greatest impediment to
progress in perfection. Accustom yourself, therefore,
to have humble recourse to Jesus Christ ; and openly
confess that what you teach, is not your own doctrine,
but that of the Gospel. In your instructions, make
use of the simple words and comparisons, with which
Jesus Christ spoke to the people. Oh ! what wonders
could He not have taught, how many mysteries of
the God-head could He not have revealed, since He
was the Eternal Wisdom of the Father ! And, yet,
see how wisely He spoke, what common comparisons
He cited ! For example, that of a father of a family,
of a vine-dresser, of a grain of mustard-seed, &c.
Learn from this how you ought to speak, in order to
be understood, when you deliver the word of God."

Blessed Balthazar Alvarez says : "Acting in
this spirit of humility, the Superior will do well,
when he first enters on the duties of his office, not to
make any prominent use of his authority, but to let
things go on in the usual course, so as not to impress
his inferiors with the idea that he is a severe discipli-
narian. If he does not act in this manner, he will
run the risk of displeasing his subjects and of closing
their hearts against him."

"Be careful and solicitous," writes St. Frances
de Chantal to a sister, "to see that every rule and
custom of the Order may be observed, and that nothing be neglected how little soever it may be ; also

that no novelty may be introduced under any pretext whatever, and that nothing be done that might be in the least contrary to our customs; never suffer any other interpretation and explanation of the spirit of our Institute to be given than that which has been embraced and followed to the present day. What I say is not without reason and fear: for there are but too many persons who, by their wrong conception, pervert Scripture, as well as customs best established. By the name of God, let us never succumb to this misfortune."

In effecting this, however, the Superior must begin with himself, giving the example, particularly in humility, not being ashamed to undertake readily the lowest offices and most menial works of the Order, like a novice, who having just left the world, is animated with great zeal, and after the example of Jesus Christ, "Who began to do and to teach."

St. Charles Borromeo was accustomed to rise early, wake up his servants, and carry a light into their room. St. Francis de Sales also arose in the night, to make his fire, so as to spare his servant this trouble. "What we see," says St. Alphonsus, "makes more impression upon us than what we hear. Let a Superior inculcate humility ever so much by his words, if he does not by his example, by his manner of treating others, by forbearing charity and patience, put in practice his on precepts, he will make but little impression and do but little good."

After St. Francis de Sales, was made Bishop,

the Abbé Déage, his old preceptor, continued to live with him, and urged by unreasonable zeal for the perfection of his former pupil, he used, on every occassion, to reprove the Saint, with his customary dictatorial tone. If the holy Bishop happened to let a pleasant word escape from his lips in order to enliven the conversation and create mirth, Mr. Déage immediately reminded him that every word uttered by a Bishop, ought to be serious and important. If he preached, Mr. Déage always found something to blame in his sermon. If he received visitors with a warm welcome, Mr. Déage quoted the proverb: "Familiarity breeds contempt." At other times, the old gentleman was offended, because Francis did not become vexed ; he thought himself injured, because the man of God forgave injuries ; he was constantly reproaching him with being too kind, saying that his kindness spoiled everything ; and the humble Bishop cheerfully bore with this continual chiding, as if he were a little child.

"Pride," says St. Alphonsus, "makes a Superior odious to every one. It hinders his own sanctification as well as that of his subjects, and prevents the maintenance of religious discipline. It is from a spirit of humility that the Superior should practise an heroical degree of patience ; that he should know how to endure all kinds of labor, trouble and contradictions, and always be gentle and kind to every one, trying to steer the little ship of his community as well as possible."

Blessed Balthasar Alvarez used to say : "Superiors should, for the love of their brethren, forget themselves, sacrifice their rest, neglect their health, and in every thing, be harder on themselves, than on others. They should also love a life of anxiety, and know how compassionately to sigh and weep over the misfortune and misery of their subjects, when these do not faithfully comply with their duties. Murmuring and dislike will often be their reward. Moreover, they should, before God, weep over and bear with, the faults, imperfections, irresolute conduct, and sins of their inferiors. But to grieve too much over the faults of others, would be no sign of true zeal, but rather an indication of want of patience and forbearance, and would betray a narrow cowardly heart. They ought to wait for the moment of grace, and in the meantime, pray, encourage, endure, compassionate, instead of showing displeasure, indignation or ill-humor. Thus they will imitate the manner of proceeding of Divine Providence: "Knowest thou not that the benignity (goodness and long-suffering) of God leadeth to penance?"[1]

When Father Martin Gouttierez, S. J., was, one day, reasonably, as he thought, grieving and complaining to God, that he was unfit to correct certain imperfect religious, his subjects, it pleased our Lord to undeceive him in the following manner. He saw a silver vessel containing a very small heart, which was drowning in a few drops of water, and near this vessel he saw another, filled with water, and containing so large a heart, that the entire mass of water

[1] Romans II, 4.

scarcely sufficed to wet it. Whilst he was thinking, what this vision meant, he heard the following words: "The heart that you see sinking in a few drops of water, represents your own, which at the slightest occurrence immoderately grieves ; but the large heart that does not sink in spite of the quantity of water in the vessel, represents the Lord's heart, which, without being discouraged, bears with idolaters, heretics, schismatics, the impious, and all sinners, awaiting the happy day of their conversion with the most admirable patience. Now this patience must be your model." Corrected by this vision, the Father became more lenient, and changed his conduct towards his subjects. He had soon good reason to congratulate himself upon the change, since God made known to him shortly after, that all those whose imperfections had caused him so much sorrow and grief, were predestined to eternal life and would be saved.

Now a Superior will preserve himself and be strengthened in the above sentiments of exterior humility, in proportion as these sentiments are joined with, and proceed from interior humility, to nourish and increase which he has but to make the following reflections in his daily meditation : "Much will be required of those to whom much has been given." Now according to venerable Bede : "Much is committed to him, to whom, in addition to the care of his own spiritual welfare, is entrusted the duty of feeding his Master's flock." From such a one Jesus Christ, will require much, that is to say,

He requires Superiors to take particular care of the spiritual welfare of their subjects, whose salvation and sanctification will be in some measure his own. "It is affectionate *care* for his subjects and not their cure," (cura non curatio) says St. Bernard, "that God requires of the Superior."

The latter is often impossible, on account of the nature or mental indisposition, imperfection, or obstinacy, of the subjects. "This account," says Titus, "which is to be rendered by teachers, pastors, and others in authority, is not a matter of little importance, but a most serious and fearful affair. Wherefore let them not take pride in their rank and office, but let them rather discharge their duties and feed their flocks, with greater humility, zeal, and diligence." In the place above cited, St. Gregory says, "He who knows, that he has to give a stricter account of the gifts which he has received, ought to be so much the more humble and prompt in the service of God."

The care of souls which Popes, Bishops, Pastors, and Superiors undertake, is an immense and terrible charge, says the Council of Trent. Let them humble themselves and fear exceedingly ; for they carry a great burden and live in a state of servitude. It was for this reason that St. Gregory called himself the "Servant of the servants of God," and succeeding Popes have followed his example. Speaking of Popes, Adrian IV. said: "No one is more worthy of pity than the Roman Pontiff: no condition do I compassionate more than his. The joy and happiness of his whole life, is nothing but bitterness. His throne is a thorny seat ; his path is sown all over with briars, and so great is the weight of the burden he bears, that it would oppress and bend the strongest shoulders.''

Upon the tombstone of Adrian VI., we read the following inscription : ''Here lies Adrian VI., who never thought life more unhappy, than when he had to govern.'' When Pius V. was elected Pope, he turned pale and trembled. On being asked the cause of his agitation, he answered : ''Whilst I was living in the Monastery, occupied alone with God and myself, I had the greatest hope of my salvation ; when I was made Bishop and Cardinal, I began to fear for it ; now, I almost despair of it.''

''A nation,'' said our Lord one day to Blessed Balthasar Alvarez, ''is always good, when it is governed by a good ruler. A shepherd is a model for his flock ; *it is this very thing that makes his office so awful.* His flock keep their eyes fixed upon him and adopt his habits. A good shepherd promotes the welfare of his flock ; it is, therefore a great blessing, when God gives a good ruler to His people. Let a Superior then, says Alvarez, in order to keep himself humble, bear in mind, that, the care of a religious Community, and particularly of a Seminary, is a heavy burden, and that all his efforts to direct it according to the spirit of the Church, will be of little avail, unless he is strengthened and guided by the grace of God. Indeed, what is more difficult, than to govern men of different dispositions, and at the same time, to keep them humble and faithful in their duties ? Truly this is no human task ! God Himself must put His hand to the work ; for He alone can break the will of man and keep it in subordination.''[1]

"Be then humble,'' writes St. Frances de Chantal to a Sister, "and you will be strong enough to bear your burden ; "for God giveth grace to the humble,''[2] He is their light, their courage, their strength, their support, their counsellor, and their all.

[1] Life of Blessed Balth. Alvarez.   [2] James 4, 6.

CHAPTER IV.

AN EXAMINATION, AS TO THE COURSE TO BE PURSUED BY SUPERIORS IN THE GOVERNMENT OF THEIR SUBJECTS.

THERE are some who think that a Superior, in the discharge of his duties, should be severe; others, that it is better for him to be mild, kind and full of paternal affection.

However, the more experienced say that both kinds of government should be united, and used with proper discretion. Unfortunately, every one thinks and flatters himself that he has discovered the most excellent mode of governing. Every one imagines himself to possess meekness enough not to be a tyrant, and firmness enough to enforce the exact execution of his commands. If you tell him that he is not yet walking in that golden mean, so difficult to find, he looks upon you as blind and ignorant; he openly asserts, that any man of sound jugdment must acknowledge, that he has discovered that judicious mode of governing in which there is found as much severity and meekness as the person, and occasion require. But who is it, that believes this? No one but himself or some miserable flatterer, who pretends to believe it. Such uncommon perfection cannot be attained in a few months with so little care and effort. All that he can have, is a good intention. An almost infallible sign that he deceives himself is, the fact that he so firmly believes and supposes that he has acquired this excellent art of government; for those who possess this valuable gift, generally acknowledge freely their want of it, they daily strive to acquire it, and, because they are conscious of their own weakness, they seek the sweet yoke of obedience, fly from the cross of the office of Superior, and decline the difficult and arduous task of steering a ship which is so easily tossed about by so many contending minds.

It is the general opinion that the most perfect manner of government is that which is mild but firm, or, in other words, that in which severity and mildness are judiciously blended. If he who guides others, sometimes becomes displeased, his anger should, be the anger of a dove or lamb, which does not injure any one. If he has recourse to soothing marks of kindness, he ought not on that account to neglect the strict maintenance of discipline.

It is, however, very difficult to find any one, who knows how to keep in this, the golden mean, that is, it is very difficult to find any one who is not inclined more to the one side than to the other. We may venture to say, that there is scarcely any one, who is not a little too much inclined either to severity or to mildness. It is therefore a question, which is the better, to incline too much to meekness, or to severity? To inspire fear or love? whether it is not better to be a little too kind, than too strict?

Those who are in favor of severity, which they call firmness of mind, courage, zeal for discipline, bring forward the following arguments in support of their manner of acting.

1. Human nature, they say, too easily relaxes: a little rigor is, therefore, necessary to keep it up to duty, and if it turns aside from the path, a strong bridle must be put upon it and a few strokes of the spur given, which it will feel, even though it bleed.

2. If a somewhat strenuous exertion is not made, the evil is only plastered over and a relapse is the probable consequence, so that it may be said that meekness only keeps the wound open and feeds the ulcer, which will finally burst and discharge the putrid matter it contains.

3. The Apostles themselves are called the children of Thunder, in order to show, that it is impossible to heal sick souls, unless you rouse them from their state of sluggishness by a little rigor and some sharp words.

4. In order to render the acts of subjects more meritorious, it is necessary, that the Superior should command in an authoritative tone rather than by entreaty — otherwise the subjects will lose half the merit of obedience.

5. It is true that love is necessary, but a little fear judiciously mingled with it, keeps the heart up to its duty. Does not our Lord say of His Apostles,

that they are the salt of the earth? If salt is not pungent enough, it does not cure meat well.

6.   The rod which Moses carried, as well as that with which St. Paul threatened the Corinthians, show that the rod was not less needed than the manna, in order to guide the people of God; so, neither would meekness bear any fruit, unless severity were mingled with it.

7.   Say what you will, it is, nevertheless, a sweet necessity, which forces one to do good, and those inferiors who are a little roughly treated, are at the end of their lives, thankful for it, and acknowledge that they stood in need of it.

8.   Experience clearly enough shows that fear is the beginning of wisdom, and many would, perhaps, give too great liberty to nature, and thus ruin themselves, if they were not restrained by a salutary fear and reasonable severity.

9.   Could any one guide the world better than God Himself does? And yet, although He is goodness itself, He makes use of threats; He lets His thunder be heard; He allows Himself to be called the terrible God, the Lord of hosts, and a fire which consumes all who are not obedient to His laws and commands.

10.   The Ark of the Covenant, contained not only the commandments of God and some manna; it also contained the rod of Moses; if the sweet manna contributed towards the observance of the law of God, the severity of Moses' rod did not less so.

11.   If a Superior yields too easily and accepts

the slightest excuses of his inferiors, he will never accomplish much. Every one will excuse himself. The negligent and slothful will gain the ascendency, and the good and obedient will be over-burdened. Murmuring, discontent and disunion, will constantly arise.

12.   Has not the Holy Ghost said, that he who spares the rod, spoils the child and ruins his house? How then can the strict observance of rules be maintained in a Community without the application of a moderate severity, which keeps every one within the bounds of strict religious discipline?

13.   Heli lost his children, the ark of the Covenant, his life, his reputation, and the priesthood; and he was thus punished, because he had spared his children too much, and admonished them too gently.   God Himself gave no other reason for the fall of this patriarch, than that he had been too indulgent to his children, allowing their faults to go unpunished.

14.   Superiors are called shepherds: but who ever saw a shepherd without a crook? Does he not always hold it in his hand to be in readiness to strike the sheep which wanders from the flock? These innocent animals tremble at the very shadow of it and keep within the sheep-fold.

15.   It is daily to be seen how some abuse the too great kindness of their Superiors. They always want too much, and they ask for dispensations which are injurious to the Order, knowing that to them nothing is refused. They become bold and insolent,

and do what they choose. On the other hand, those
who are modest are obliged to perform the lowest and
most laborious functions, whilst the others exult and
laugh at their simplicity.

16. It frequently happens, that the too great
indulgence of the Superior excites contempt, which,
by degrees passes from the person to his commands
and causes disorder in the Convent. Then it appears
that the tepidity with which obedience is practised,
can be looked upon in no other light than as the ruin
of the religious, who become so spoiled that they
have to be treated like glass which cannot bear the
slightest strike without breaking.

All these arguments and many others which
might be adduced, clearly show that in order to
govern well, it is better for the Superior to use
severity — that gentle severity, which understands
how to maintain religious discipline in its primitive
vigor.

Those who are in favor of mildness in governing,
have more numerous, more convincing, and more
solid arguments, than those adduced by the advocates
of severity.

1. One of the strongest arguments may be
drawn from the common sentiment. Let every man
in the world be asked whether he prefers mildness or
severity, and it will soon be seen that all are in favor
of the former.

2. And this is so true, that the very persons
who, whilst in office, deal severely with others, cannot bear with the least severity in their Superiors;

4

and they would consider themselves very unhappy, were they to fall into the hands of Superiors who would treat them as harshly as they themselves have treated others. They are forced to acknowledge openly that mildness is more powerful and influential with men than severity, and that its reign is a thousand times happier.

3. More courage and virtue is requisite to govern with mildness, than to rule with severity. Mildness is, indeed, not a mark of weakness, but of strength ; those who exercise it from supernatural motives, prove that they have perfectly overcome themselves ; and thus achieved the greatest of all victories: "He who prevents his neighbor, with the blessings of his sweetness," says St. Francis de Sales, "is the most perfect imitator of our Lord." In fact, man is imperious only because he can bear with nothing. The proud spirit which sways him, is nothing but the weakness and impotency of nature, which, under the false mask of zeal, gives play to its own passions, and listens only to self-love which cannot endure anything. A noble heart is surprised at nothing and applies the remedy with ease ; but a narrow heart, a weak mind, at once kindles up, and under the pretext of zeal, gives vent to bitter words and has recourse to threats. A wise man never allows himself to be surprised by anger or mastered by his bad humors.

4. Even those who are severe do not like that others should consider them so, nor are they willing to believe it of themselves.

5. Were there no other argument, it would suffice to cast a glance at the different modes of government. It may be said that he who is more feared than loved by his subjects, is hated by all ; for it is natural to hate what we fear. Because he is hated, he is obeyed only with a reluctant heart. His inferiors find all that he ordains, difficult; they have a thousand excuses wherewith to justify themselves ; they never submit their judgment; they murmur at everything, and approve of nothing. Their hearts feel chilled ; the yoke of the religious life appears insupportable. They say, that they do not find, under his direction, the hundred-fold promised by our Lord, to His servants even in this life. By his harsh treatment, he gives them reason to think that all the boasted advantages of the religious life, are but pious exaggerations and snares laid for the credulous. What wonder, if they should turn their thoughts again to the world, and seek there what is unjustly denied them in the house of God. "My sheep," says the Lord, "have wandered in every mountain and in every high hill, and My flocks were scattered upon the face of the earth, and they became the prey of all the beasts of the field." Why? "Because there was no shepherd."[1] And yet there were shepherds in Israel at the time ; — but they were such as were highly displeasing to, and rejected by the Lord. "Son of man," said the Lord to the Prophet : "prophesy concerning the shepherds of Israel :—The weak you have not strengthened, and that which was

[1] Ezechiel chapt. 34.

sick you have not healed ; that which was broken
you have not bound up, and that which was driven
away you have not brought again, neither have you
sought that which was lost. You ruled over them
with rigor and with a high hand."

The subjects count the days of such a Superiorship, and when the end of them comes, they all
rejoice. If such a Superior remains any longer in the
house, he will soon find out how little he is loved and
how much contempt is manifested, for his person,
and how much all desire, never again to see him appointed Superior, or, at least never again to be under
his direction. They think, say, and write a thousand
things to his disadvantage. At last he sees evidently, that, instead of having won the hearts of his subjects, he has but filled them all with fear, so that
nothing remains of his government except hatred and
horror of his person.

Quite different are the consequences of a mild
government. Every one desires to be under a meek
Superior. His inferiors weep, when he is removed,
when he dies—to judge by the general outburst of
grief—all is dead with him. It is in such a Superior
that the subjects find, even in this life the hundred-
fold, not indeed so much the hundred-fold of temporal
goods and honors which they despise, as rather the
hundred-fold of that which is never renounced,
although all else should be given up ; viz : the hundred-fold of love and affection, on the part of their
kindred and friends ; for, he truly supplies the place
of father, mother, sisters and brothers, so that his in-

feriors may justly apply to him, the words of our
Saviour when speaking of a man who does the will of
God: "He is my brother and my sister, and my
mother."

By his affectionate treatment, he indemnifies his
subjects for having renounced all that was near and
dear to them ; he dries up the tears, forced from them
by the painful separation, from their parents and
friends ; he prevents the sad and regretful thoughts
which the remembrance of all the devoted attention
and marks of love received from their own, would
naturally awaken in flesh and blood. His subjects
acknowledge that they have nothing to regret in the
step which they have taken, but that they daily
experience how greatly preferable is that supernatural
charity which is based on the love of God, to that
love, which nature alone excites in the parent's
heart.

6. It is true, that the kindness of a Superior
will sometimes be abused. But as it is only the spider
that draws poison out of flowers, so it is only the bad
that will abuse his mildness and kindness. With
regard to severity, however, the good become provoked at it ; the wisest take offence, and every one
murmurs.

7. It is to be observed, however, that those
who abuse the kindness and mildness of their Superior, easily return to their duty ; because they are
aware that his fatherly heart is ever open to receive
them ; whilst on the contrary, those whom too great
severity forces to lose their self-command, feel incap-

able of retracing their steps ; there is need of a miracle almost to bring them back.

8.   It cannot be denied that faults will be committed, and mistakes made under any Superior ; but, they occur less frequently under a Superior whose mode of governing is mild. Besides, faults committed under his direction, are more easily corrected, because the delinquents find the return to duty less difficult.   If the guilty do not amend, they have no excuse and they have to attribute their misfortune to themselves.

9.   Every one can play the Master.   Nothing is more natural.   It is always easy to command and to desire unhesitating obedience, and to give vent to our displeasure, and to show our authority, when any one disobeys.   These lessons can be learned without a teacher : enough of this knowledge, to drive inferiors to despair, may be acquired in less than a week.   But to bear with the faults of others with a truly apostolical heart, to subdue the passions, to appease the storms of the troubled soul, and to allow the fire of anger to die out before an attempt is made at correction, so that there may be no spark of revenge in the admonition, is manly virtue ; is something that can proceed only from a heart entirely devoid of self-love and which knows how to conquer itself.   I say still more : calmness and equality of mind are divine virtues, and according to the testimony of Seneca, a heathen writer, mildness and kindness are the only virtues which possess the power of transforming, as it were, man into God, and of effecting

in a wonderful manner a participation in the divine nature.

10. There is nothing more true, than, that no difficulty is found in obeying one who commands with the kindness of an Angel, rather than with the severity and passion of a mortal. Every one desires to be under a Superior whose kind conciliation places him beneath all. He who is feared by all must necessarily be afraid of every one; he who is sincerely loved, also loves without mixture of fear. Every one would rather suffer himself, than see such a Superior suffer. His commands are anticipated, and, could his wishes be guessed, he would be spared the trouble of commanding. His subjects try to do even more than he commands; so true is it, that obedience has no limits, when meekness gives the order. For this reason, St. John Chrysostom says: "When the Jews saw David's forbearance towards Saul—whom he might have killed—when he met him alone in the cave, but whom he preferred to caress and to pardon, they obeyed David from that time forward rather as a being descended from heaven than as a man."

11. We cannot doubt that God knows the dispositions of men, and that He is aware of the wickedness of those who are ever ready to abuse great kindness and love : but, neither is He ignorant of the fact, that these very men would be much worse if they were treated with severity. Hence, He commands those, who have to direct others, to prefer mildness to severity. Certainly, God does not wish, that, for the sake of a few ill-disposed men, all the rest should

be treated harshly. Let such troublesome, restless beings be governed as well as they can ; but it is unreasonable to make all the others suffer on their account. Among those two millions of men, of whom Moses was the leader, there were no doubt some obstinate and perverse characters, who caused the Jewish people so often to rebel. Yet, God commanded this great patriarch to direct them with the greatest possible meekness, and to carry them, as it were, in his bosom, as a nurse does her little child. Could a better mode of direction be given, than that which God Himself taught Moses, His faithful servant, and the model of all perfect Superiors ?

12. It may seem contradictory to say that meekness accomplishes what the greatest severity cannot effect. This, however, is a truth announced to us by the Prophet Isaias. Speaking of the coming of the Messiah he says : "The wolf shall dwell with the lamb ; and the leopard shall lie down with the kid ; the calf and the lion, and the sheep shall abide together and a little child shall lead them."[1] That is, the wildest animals will flock with the tamest, and will be as easily guided by a little child, as if they were lambs.

In every religious Community there is a mixture of choleric and gentle dispositions. If they be treated harshly, there will be neither peace nor harmony. The bad will become worse ; and the good will be deeply afflicted at seeing lambs treated like wolves, children like slaves. But if the spirit of meekness

---

[1] Isaias ix. 6.

prevails the bad will, sooner or later, become ashamed of, and acknowledge their faults; the good will be encouraged to strive after still higher perfection, and charitably to bear with the faults and weaknesses of their brethren.

13. In the Old Testament, God has taught us this truth in the most wonderful manner. Eliseus sent his staff to restore the son of the Sunamitess to life: but in vain. He was obliged to go himself, lay himself upon the little corpse, and by his breath bring back the soul into the body. St. Peter Damian makes the following reflection upon this miracle. His remarks suit our subject admirably. He says that severity and the rod never raise those who have fallen: they rather kill the living, than restore the dead to life. But, when a Superior, makes use of his power and authority like another Eliseus, when he acts kindly and condescends to the weakness of those who have fallen, and who, in this state, resemble a dead body, he will be able at once to awaken them to a better life, and to restore them to their good mother, the Order, and to the way of perfection. When the disciples of our Lord were about setting out to preach the Gospel, He forbade them to take either staff or stick with them; 'bidding them go bare-footed, and to speak nothing but peace and mercy.

14. What one day befell Elias, is worthy of notice. This holy man possessed sincere and burning zeal. If what he desired, were not done quickly, he listened to nothing but his zeal. He even went so far, as often to wish himself dead: Now, God once

5

allowed him to see something, which might serve as
a most wholesome lesson to him.   On a certain occasion in which his zeal was at its height, and at the
very moment he had wished for death, God commanded him to keep himself ready to see His Majesty.
He immediately heard so great a crash, that it seemed
as if the elements were let loose, and the mountains
were moving from their places.   But the Prophet
was told that God was not in this awful crash.   Then
he heard the stormy whistling of a furious north-wind
which appeared to uproot everything.   Again was
the Prophet told that God was not in the storm.
This was followed by a fire which threatened to lay
everything in ashes.   Once more was he told that
God was not in this destructive fire, that the Divine
Majesty took no pleasure in such violent, stormy
things.   At last the Prophet perceived an East-wind
blowing gently and evenly, with a slight and extraordinarily sweet rustling.   "Ah," said Elias, "this
is certainly the Lord God."   He cast himself upon
the ground, and veiling his head with his mantle,
worshipped God, and gave Him thanks for having
made known to him the workings of His Divine Spirit,
and what was most pleasing to Him upon earth.

15.   The power of meekness is also most beautifully illustrated in the Apocalypse.[1]   St. John relates, that after God had shown him an almost
incalculable number of Saints in the kingdom of
heaven he saw, only one single lamb leading them
all.   From this we learn that since a lamb, the sym-

[1] chap. xxi.

bol of meekness, governs paradise, no other virtue
should be raised to the throne on earth. Should any
one, unfortunately, abuse such a mode of governing,
should the wickedness and perverseness of an individual, serve for some to blame the conduct of such
a Superior, let him have recourse to God, and thus
address Him : "If this manner of acting is displeasing to Thee, my Lord and Master, why hast Thou so
repeatedly and so expressly commanded us to direct
others in this manner ? I have followed Thy example : hast Thou not given it to be imitated, and even
confirmed it by miracles ? Yea ; even those among
Thy Saints who have been the most zealous for Thy
glory, have not acted otherwise."

16. It is said of Moses, that he was the meekest
man of his time ; that the people would rather speak
with him than with God Himself, Who only spoke
in thunder ; and that his manner of treating every
one was so attractive, that he was the king of hearts,
and the god of Pharaoh himself. For this reason
St. Ambrose does not hesitate to say, that the forbearance and kindness of Moses, won for him more
hearts, and were more effectual in keeping that large
number of men in awe, than the very miracles, which
he so frequently wrought in their behalf. Notwithstanding the frequent murmurs of the people, their
calumnies, their reproaches, apostasy, and other in-
dignities, he acted towards them with the same kindness, taking no other revenge, than to pour forth his
prayers for them. Justly, then, did our Lord honor
him with this eulogium : "For Moses was the meek-

est among men.'' Hence Tostat says, that God Himself assists those whose moderation seems to put
an obstacle to the success of what they have undertaken, and He brings about, by His own power, what
they themselves cannot accomplish. When Moses
was ridiculed by Aaron and Mary for having married
an Egyptian woman, his meekness was so great, that
he uttered not a single word of resentment, nor expressed any desire of revenge. But, says Tostat,
when God saw his meekness, He turned all to the advantage of His servant. He first admonished Aaron
and Mary of their fault, and then punished them for
it. From this we learn, that God, Who forbids His
servant to take revenge on his enemies, becomes Himself his protector when He sees the virtue of His servant abused, and does for him, what his extraordinary
meekness would never have allowed him to do for
himself.

The text of the fact above given, says that God
became indignant at the fault of Aaron and Mary, in
order to show us, in an impressive manner, that nothing is so intolerable in the eyes of men, of Angels,
and of God Himself, as to see too great kindness
abused, and to perceive that a person is ill-treated,
merely because *he* never treats any one unkindly, nor
knows what vengeance is.

Here, however, it may be objected, why did
Moses, who is held up to us as a model Superior,
have a number of the people of God killed, and why
did he praise those who laid their hands upon their
own kindred? This awful butchery ought surely to

be looked upon as great cruelty. To this we may
answer, that we do not say that meekness should allow sin to go unpunished, and that it should not be
troubled at anything.   That would be too great
cowardice, by which one would become guilty before
God and man.   But what we insist upon is, that we
should chastise as Moses did.   On the one hand he
was willing to die for the people ; for, when God
was about to destroy them, he offered himself as an
expiatory victim to the anger of the Lord, so dearly
did he love that sinful race.   On the other hand,
when Moses was obliged to punish, he knew how to
separate crime, from the perpetrators of it : he punished crime with death ; its perpetrators, he tried to
save, as far as he could.   At least he tried so to purify
his indignation, that no shadow of passion appeared
in it, and he so far followed the dictates of his meek
heart, as to make use of no other sword, save the
golden one of divine love.

17. Solomon, perceiving that God acted in so
mild a manner, expressed his joy at it in the Book of
Wisdom : "Great God !" he cries out, "what joy it
is for me to see Thee, the Mighty Lord of Hosts,
judging men so mildly and acting towards us so considerately, as though Thou didst fear to hurt us, or
cause us the least sorrow ! O, how happy are we,
that Thou canst do all Thou willest, and that Thou
willest not, what Thou canst do. By this Thy
gentle manner of treating us, Thou surely dost
wish to teach, that meekness is the bond of
union. Ah ! since Thou art so lenient to Thine

enemies, with what goodness and love wilt Thou
not guide Thy children, who are as the apple
of Thine eye." Solomon felt, strongly impressed by
this divine example ; he imitated it, and was called
the peace-making king — Rex pacificus. After he
had considered the Lord of Lords preferring to send
down manna from heaven for His sinful people, and
thus win their hearts by mildness, rather than pour
out His wrath upon them, he tried to govern so
moderately and so kindly as to deserve to be called
the joy of the Jewish people. Is not this example
sufficient to convince us ? Is man wiser than God ?
Does the creature know how to govern better than
the Creator ?

18. The whole of the New Testament is full of
the great examples of the humility and meekness of
Jesus Christ. All His precepts might be reduced to
the one precept of love and mercy. One day when
the Apostles felt themselves provoked, because the
inhabitants of a certain town would not allow them
to enter it, they asked of our Divine Saviour to make
fire come down upon them from heaven. But this
God of goodness and mildness blamed the Apostles
for this request, telling them that they spoke not as
Apostles ; that this severe spirit was not the spirit
which He had so often preached and sought to impart
to them. "Ye know not of what spirit ye are."
With what great patience and meekness did He not
for three years, bear with Judas, His betrayer, a
thief, without depriving him of the office of procurator, or deposing him from Apostleship. He

did not even so much, as reveal his crimes to any one.

19. With regard to St. Peter, we know that he wept more, than he commanded ; and, when there was question of entrusting to him the government of the Church, Jesus Christ required of him nothing but love.   Peter was asked if his love were greater than that of the other disciples — our Lord seeming as it were, to inculcate that love and meekness were the only means, by which to govern well.

20. "Now, we that are stronger," says St. Paul in his Epistle to the Christians, "ought to bear the infirmities of the weak, and not to please ourselves.   Let every one of you please his neighbor for his good, unto edification.   For Christ did not please Himself, but as it is written : The reproaches of them that reproached thee, fell upon Me."   And again he writes to the Thessalonians : "But we became little ones in the midst of you, as if a nurse should cherish her children.   So desirous of you, we would gladly have imparted to you, not only the Gospel of God, but also our own souls, because you were become most dear to us."[1]   And again he says: I have shown you all things : etc.[2]   I have shown you not only by my refusal of gifts, by my hardships, tears, affections, preaching, but also by my own manual labor, how you must receive and treat weak and pusillanimous souls.   .

How truly beautiful are the remarks of St. Gregory on this passage.   "If any one of us," says he,

[1] I. Thess. 2. C. 7.   [2] Acts. 20—25.

"had converted a very rich man to the service of God,
and should afterwards suffer from a want of the
necessaries of life, should he see that his rich convert
would not come to his aid, would he not at once despair of that rich man's salvation? Would he not
think that he had troubled himself in vain with him,
and that it was useless to interest himself any longer
in such a convert, seeing that he would not bestow
the first fruit of his conversion upon his teacher?
But Paul, being by his virtue of meekness, solidly
grounded on the summit of virtues, perseveres in
preaching, in loving, in order to accomplish the good
he had begun.

Thus, by this persevering meekness and farbear-
ance, he taught his disciples how they should always
endeavor, to exercise towards their neighbors, that
spirit of supernatural sweetness, which is, as it
were, the cream and flower of charity. He took the
greatest possible care, not to alienate in the least,
the hearts of the weak from Jesus Christ. If you see
the great Apostle represented with a sword in his
hand, you must not fancy that he used it in governing those whom he had gained over to Jesus Christ.
The sceptre of his authority and power, were his
tears. "Ever remember, that for three years, I
ceased not with tears, to admonish every one of you,
night and day."[1] Who could resist such tears?
Who is able not to weep, when he sees Paul weep?
"From what fountain," says St. John Chrysostom[2]
"have flowed so many streams of water, as flowed

[1] Acts. 20. 31.   [2] hom. 12. in epist. ad Coloss.

tears from the eyes of St. Paul? What fountain can you compare to his tears? Perhaps the one in Paradise which waters the whole earth? But even this is not equal to his tears. He carried all the faithful in his heart, in his memory, on his lips; as a mother or a nurse, carries her child on her bosom." "Were we allowed," says St. Chrysostom speaking in the person of St. Paul, "to cut open our heart, and show it to you, you would see in it yourselves: men, women, and children, every one occupying a large portion of it; for, so extensive is the power of charity, that it enlarges the heart, so as to surpass even the capacity of the heavens." This forbearing charity of St. Paul explains why he could write to the Galatians.[1] "You received me as an Angel of God, even as Jesus Christ, — — — and if it could have been done, you would have plucked out your own eyes, and would have given them to me." No wonder that the Christians would weep bitterly, and think they would have to die of grief, when they had to separate from so good a father, who spoke and effected more through his eyes, than by his lips.

In the same manner, every one whose duty it is to save souls, and to guide and lead others to perfection, must bear, nay, even make all efforts to cure the infirmities of those under his charge. "It is a sign that one is possessed of heroic virtue," says Cornelius a Lapide, "if he knows how to bear generously and patiently the weaknesses of his fellow-men." For this reason St. John Chrysostom,[2] says so beautifully:

[1] Chap. 4. 14.　　　　　　　　[2] hom. 52.

"Our tongue becomes, as it were, that of Christ Himself, if we imitate His meekness in speaking, in teaching, in reproving." And St. Dionysius[1] says, "that to govern the flock of Jesus Christ with great meekness and gentleness, is considered by the Divine Pastor, as a proof of the most excellent charity towards Himself."

21. All the great Saints who were founders of religious Orders, governed with great mildness. St. Macarius was called the "God of the Monks," because, although he directed so many thousands of men, he was never seen to be angry, nor did a severe word ever pass his lips.

22. One day, the holy Abbot Poppon was reproached for his great meekness; he was told that he would ruin the whole Community by his over great kindness, and that he was exposing himself to eternal damnation. He replied: "O, my brethren, how happy would I be, if I were damned because I had too much charity! Could I not justly answer Jesus Christ, my Master: Why didst Thou teach us to learn of Thee humility and meekness of heart, if Thou didst not wish us to practise them, and if Thou condemnest those who have imitated Thee in the exercise of these sublime virtues?"

23. In his second sermon on the Epistle to the Romans, St. Basil gives to patience and meekness, the preference over virginity, fasting, and all that is heroic in the exercise of the other virtues, and asserts, that the possession of this virtue, is sufficient reason

[1] Epist. 8 ad Demophilum.

to class a man among the Seraphim.   Saul, who was
inflamed with an implacable hatred for David, and
who sought on every occasion to sacrifice him to his
vengeance, was so greatly affected by David's meekness that he often called him his *son,* and could not
help publicly overwhelming him with praise.   A
sage of ancient times was accustomed to say, that
golden chains were better suited to fetter the heart,
than iron ones.   This truth was even admitted by the
heathen.

24.   On the words of the Holy Gospel, "Venite
ad me omnes qui laboratis—Come to me all ye who
labor," St. Augustine says: "Why do we all labor,
if not because we are weak, perishable mortals, carrying costly vessels, which cause us mutual anxiety?
But, if the flesh is straitened, then, let the bounds of
charity be enlarged."   And upon the words: "Tol-
lite jugum meum super vos et discite a me—Take My
yoke upon you, and learn of Me"—he says: "Our
Lord tells us, to learn of Him not to create the world,
not to make all visible and invisible things, not to
work wonders in the world—not to raise the dead to
life, and the like—but, learn of Me, that I am meek
and humble of heart—quoniam mites sum et humilis
corde."   What this great Doctor of the Church taught
in these words, he also practised, as he tells us in his
twenty-sixth homily: "Look upon me," he says,
"as the mother of your souls, which I desire to orna-
ment, as a mother, with her own hands, adorns her
daughter—in order that they may appear unblemished
before the tribunal of the Eternal Judge.   Desirous

of providing them, not only with ornaments, but also with remedies, I try to mend what is broken, to heal what is wounded, to cleanse what is stained, to restore what is lost, and, to adorn with spiritual pearls what is still pure."

25. St. Bernard acknowledges that when he was a young Abbot, he was too severe through injudicious zeal, and thereby rendered himself guilty before God and man. Every one was afraid of him, and some tried even to avoid him. Perceiving this, he begged pardon, changed his manner of acting, and, adopting and following principles which were directly contrary to those by which he had previously been influenced. He very soon won the hearts of his brethren, and governed seven hundred Monks with as much ease, as he could have guided a little lamb. Nothing could equal his gentleness. He was accustomed to tell his subjects, that he desired to be a kind mother to them : he called them, his eyes, his heart &c. From that time forward, everything that was done in the Convent, was performed through love. If he commanded anything, his brethren ran to fulfil the command, they felt no other pain in the execution of it, than the fear, that one might fulfil their Abbot's orders quicker than the other. His maxim was, that he who desires to guide others well, should direct them rather by entreaty than by command: "By praying and entreating, rather than by commanding. Entreat rather than command." In one of his sermons on St. Magdalene, he, the meek St. Bernard, expresses his surprise, that when God wished to punish His sin-

ful people, He asked permission of Moses to do so.
This astonishment at the great respect shown by God
to His faithful servant, let the holy Abbot to search
into the cause of it : the decision he gave, was, that
God had no other end in view, than to teach us that
meekness is the first quality of a good Master.   Has
God ever asked permission to do good to us? And
yet, when there is question of punishment, He delays
and begs leave for it.   Does He not plainly indicate
by this, that it is His will, that we should bind His
hands and wrest from Him the sword raised to strike
us ? Can any one think to please Him, by treating a
poor little sheep roughly — that sheep for which He
so diligently sought, and which, when He had found,
He carried, in the midst of such great difficulties,
upon His shoulders, and invited heaven and earth to
rejoice with Him upon its restoration? Ah! you who
govern severely, reflect that it is for this very sheep,
that Jesus Christ has worked so many miracles.   A
man like you, would have received Magdalene very
ungraciously on beholding her so loaded with crimes ;
but, Jesus Christ, Who knew better, acted towards
her, as one should always act towards sinners, receiving her kindly and affectionately.   Instead of being
her severe Judge, He became her kind defender ; and,
as St. Bernard says, received her with the greatest
affection.   He hid her in the bowels of His mercy.
He acted like the father of the Prodigal, who, as St.
Peter Chrysologus remarks in his sermon, upon that
subject, gave no other answer to his son's appeal for
pardon, than to fall upon his neck and kiss him.

"And he kissed him. No other reproach did his father make him, than a kiss. Thus does love revenge itself!" When a good father sees his son at his feet begging for pardon, he raises him up, presses him to his heart, and for his sole punishment, gives him the kiss of peace. The most excellent means to guide others, is to lavish benefits upon them, rather than to overload them with punishment and reproaches.

26. The letter written by St. Francis of Assissium to Peter of Catana, the Vicar-General of his Order, who had complained of the irregularity of some of the brothers, is worthy to be quoted here: "May our Lord," writes he, "protect you and preserve you in His holy love! I recommend to you, dear Brother, such great patience in all your difficulties, that, if any of your brethren, oppose you, or even scourge you, you may take it as a favor, and wish it to be thus, and not otherwise. Love those who treat you thus, and desire nothing more from them, than what God may send you. Love them so as to wish them to become better christians. By this, I will know whether you love God and me, His and your servant: namely, if no brother in the world, no matter how much he may have sinned, will ever be dismissed from your presence without having been pardoned. If he does not seek for pardon, ask him whether he would not like to be pardoned. Should he come to you a thousand times afterwards, love him more than you love me, so that you may lead him to the practice of virtue and be always merciful to such brethren. Communicate this advice to the

Guardians also, as much as possible, living up to it yourself at all times. Do not allow the Brothers who may be aware of some one's sins, to put him to the blush, or to think the less of him. Let them rather have pity on him and keep his fault secret, for, "They that are in health need not a physcian, but they that are sick."

27. St. Vincent de Paul says : "No better means can be used by Superiors to enforce obedience, than mildness." "Be careful," he wrote to a Superior, "not to be yourself a burden to any one. Treat all kindly and respectfully, and command rather by entreaty than with authority. Nothing more easily wins the heart than an affectionate and humble demeanor. This readily leads, to the fulfilment of wishes which tend to the honor of God, and to the salvation of souls."

28. St. Jane Frances de Chantal said : "I have made use of different modes of governing and have found none better than that based on patience and meekness." The more she increased in age and in perfection, the milder she became in the direction of her religious. In the latter years of her life she wrote as follows : "I have looked and turned to every side ; I have weighed and tried every method of governing and have at last found that, that which is mild, humble, sincere, and forbearing, is the best." Again, she wrote to a Superior : "My dear daughter, be firm in maintaining the rule, but be also careful to be more strict with yourself than with others. This I mean, not with regard to your corporal in-

firmities — for in this respect you ought to be charitable and lenient to yourself, otherwise you will be a source of anxiety to your daughters, — but I mean it with regard to spiritual weaknesses of your daughters. The longer I live the more clearly I see, how necessary mildness is to gain entrance into hearts, and exercise influence over them so as to lead them to the fulfilment of their duty towards God. Conduct then your subjects with a sweet charitable and cordial solicitude, free of anxiety and overgreat care. I know this is the best means to meet with success in the direction of souls. The more kindness, frankness, and charitable forbearance you manifest, the more you will gain upon the hearts of your subjects, which is the great means to advance them in the perfection of their vocation. Being in the complete possession of their hearts you will find it an easy task to guide them as you wish and to keep them united among themselves, to yourself, which is the blessing of blessings in Convents. Our poor nature always requires some relief and comfort ; if your subjects find it within the Convent walls, they will never be tempted to seek for it without ; which is certainly a great blessing for them." "Believe me, said St. Francis de Sales, "Superiors render great charity to their subjects by giving them ample time to say everything that troubles them without hurrying them, or showing themselves annoyed with them, for then they feel relieved and disposed to receive with profit the advice given them afterwards. Certain trifles often are to the weak-minded as troublesome, as great

pains are to generous souls. If your subjects have
not a special love for and confidence in you, they will
entertain particular friendships among themselves,
which are a true pest in Religion."

29. One day when St. Alphonsus was grossly
insulted, every one except the Saint himself felt indignant at the outrage. "See what it is to be a
Bishop" said he; "if a father does not bear with the
misdemeanor of his children, who will?"[1] When,
on another occasion, St. Alphonsus was insulted by
a Priest, the arch-deacon Rainone who was present
said to him: "My Lord, no one would dare to act
thus, if your condescension were not so great as to
encourage insolence." "Ah," answered the venerable Saint, "for forty years have I been trying to acquire a little patience, and would you have me lose
it in a minute?" On another similar occasion
Father Caputo, who was highly incensed, at an insult offered to the holy Bishop, wanted St. Alphonsus
to punish the offender. "Does not your Lordship see
that your kindness is abused?" asked Father Caputo.
The Saint answered with a pleasant smile: "Father
Monitor, I have had no little trouble to acquire a
slight degree of patience. God alone knows how
much it has cost me! It is the fruit of constant
struggles, and shall I now lose it in one minute?"
Father Caputo said that the Saint had acquired such
perfect mastery over himself, that he no longer appeared to be a man, but an angel in human form.
Father Don Sebastian de Jacobis, C. SS. R., relates,

[1] Life of him by Father Tannoja.

6

that the question, "which was the more useful in directing souls, mildness or severity?" being proposed in the presence of St. Alphonsus, the holy Bishop answered as follows : "Mildness is more in accordance with the spirit of God and of the Gospel. A severe Superior makes his subjects imperfect and deceitful ; because influenced by his severity, they will act only through servile fear. Learn of Me, that I am meek and humble of heart. God dealt gently with Adam ; Jesus Christ acted mildly towards Judas and the imperfect disciples. What good did the Jansenists do, by making a tyrant of our Lord?" As he always kept the example of our Lord before his eyes, in order to imitate Him; he let no opportunity pass of practising the virtue of meekness, of which Jesus Christ had set the example. "It seems," says Canon Robini, "as though I see the Saint now, ever master of himself, kind and amiable to every one, always with a sweet and cheerful smile upon his lips." "You cannot imagine," wrote the Saint to some one in Naples, "how hard it is for me, to treat certain persons harshly. It is my opinion, that more is accomplished by kindness, than by severity and force." If he remembered having made use of somewhat harsh language, he sought an excuse to recall the person, to whom he had thus spoken, and then gave him some proof of affection. Once he thought he had displeased the physician, so he sent for him to come and feel his pulse, although he was not at all sick. He did this only to show that he had no ill feeling against him. Severe towards himself only, he treated the greatest sinners with inexpressible meekness. Without excusing the sin, he showed the greatest compassion for the sincerely repentant sinner. It was his opinion, that the more deeply a soul was immersed in sin, the greater ought to be the compassion of the Confessor, in order to rescue it from the clutches of Satan, and cast it into the arm of Jesus Christ. In his old age, he said that he did not remember ever having sent away a sinner without having succeeded in reconciling him with God, much less with having treated any one harshly.

He was always most careful to anticipate the wants of the sinner with kindness, especially when he perceived that the sinner despaired of his conversion. He was so skilful in gaining hearts that he drew them almost irresistibly to Jesus Christ. The lower the condition was, of those who had recourse to him, the more friendly was their reception. The consequence was, that many who had been great sinners, led under his direction a holy life, and died in the odor of sanctity.[1] From this we may infer, how kind a father he must have been towards his own brethren in religion. We shall never be able fully to understand it. He said, and with truth, that he was ready to lay down his life for every one of them.

In the life of Catharine Mc'Auley, the Foundress of the Sisters of Mercy, we read, that she could never be induced to give vinegar applications a trial; she had read and heard quite enough about them; crossness she would not hear of at all: moroseness she

[1] Tannoja's Life of St. Alphonsus, Vol. I, chap. 12. 13.

deemed odious in a religious, especially so in a Superior, even seriousness, unless quite brief she regarded
as inadmissable. She practised the same unfailing
kindness to every one; she had never tried any method
of governing but one and that was the gentlest of the
gentle. When anything was to be done, she would
entreat in the humblest terms — a command never
issued from her lips. Her very manner of addressing
the Sisters won them. Whether in speaking or writing to them, she always prefaced her remarks by
some endearing epithet, as, "my dearest child."—
She loved to yield to them as much as possible and,
like St. Anselm, she took this method to prove that
she had become a little child for the kingdom of
heaven. She strove even to gratify their inclinations,
and when she could not do so, she was sure to make
up for the disappointment in some way or other.
Such then are the sentiments of charity with which
Superiors, in imitation of the Saints, ought to be
animated towards their subjects.

How just then, is not the remark of St. John
Chrysostom upon the words : "Ecce ego mitto vos
sicut oves in medio luporum — Behold, I send you as
sheep in the midst of wolves." "The Apostles," he
says, "certainly understood it to be a new kind of
warfare, an unusual mode of fighting, when Jesus
Christ sent them naked, having only one tunic, without shoes, staff, girdle, or purse ; and commanded
them to depend for food and raiment, upon those who
would receive them into their houses. He told them,
moreover, to go abroad with the meekness of sheep,

although they were to go in the very midst of wolves. Nay., He even commanded them to put on the simplicity of doves ; assuring them that He would manifest His power by causing sheep to abound where wolves had been superabundant ; that although in the midst of wolves, and lacerated by them, they would not only, not be devoured by them, but would change them into lambs." It is certainly a greater and more admirable work to change the hearts of enemies to the better, than to kill them.

"Let us blush for shame, since we act so differently towards our enemies, rushing upon them like wolves. As long as we act the part of sheep, we shall conquer ; even though a thousand wolves should surround us, we shall get the upper hand and come off victorious. On the contrary, when we act like wolves we shall be conquered ; the care of the divine Shepherd will be withdrawn from us ; for His duty is, to guard sheep, not wolves." The two following examples are striking proofs of this doctrine. In the speedy promotion of St. Anselm to the office of Prior, jealousy was excited, as he had only lately entered the Monastery. Various intrigues were formed against him. One monk particularly Osbere, a young man of fine mind and very skilful at all kinds of work, persecuted him continually in every manner which his ill-humor suggested. Feigning not to remark his behavior, the holy Prior undertook to gain by kindness, the heart of one, whose real worth he appreciated. He bore with his whims, praised his talents, excused his faults on account of his youth, and

granted him every lawful favor.   By this manner of
acting, he soon so softened and changed his rival,
that Osbere became not only submissive and docile,
but quite devoted to his Superior.   By degrees, Anselm withdrew the concessions he had before made on
account of his age, and by a gradual increase in
strictness of discipline, he finally led his young disciple to perfect observance of the severe rule of his
Order.   Osbere learned to bear with everything,
he became humble and docile, and proved himself
a worthy imitator of the example and lesson of his
master.   He loved him.   The gentle kindness of Anselm had triumphed.   Soon after, Osbere fell seriously ill, and died.   St. Anselm made a vow to say Mass
daily for the repose of the soul of the young Brother.
He was faithful to this vow as long as he lived ; for,
if he himself was unable to say Mass, he had the
Mass said by another Priest.[1]

St. Martin acted in the same manner.   He bore,
with wonderful meekness, the insults heaped upon
him, and finally gained the heart of one of his greatest enemies.   When Britius, one of his Priests and
his Secretary, was persecuting him with continual
calumnies and abuse, the rest of his household were
astonished that the holy Bishop did not punish so impious a man, and depose him from office.   On ex-
pressing their surprise, he replied : "Christ, our
Lord bore with Judas, His betrayer ; ought I not
then, to bear with Britius, my calumniator?"   By his
meekness he converted Britius, and so pleaded his

[1] Life of St. Anselm by Dr. C. Wurzbach.

cause with God, that he obtained for him the grace
of becoming a Saint, and his worthy successor in the
bishopric, as he had foretold.[1]

The Saints tell us that the Old Testament was
the law of rigor.   In it, everything was threatened
with thunderbolts, death, and instantaneous punishment.   God was pleased to be called the Lord of
Hosts.   What did He gain by all this?   Every one
fled from Him, scarcely any one served Him willingly, and all would rather speak with His servant,
Moses, than with Him.   In the New Testament, the
Word made Flesh took a different course.   He called
Himself the Lamb of God.   He avowed that He had
come for poor sinners.   He preached nothing but
meekness.   He repulsed no one.   Witness St. Magdalene, Zacheus, and the Publican.   His condescension was so great, that He did not even refuse the petition of the devils, when they begged Him to allow
them to take possession of the swine.   This amiability of His won all hearts, and converted more sinners,
than did His most zealous sermons.   The Jews saw
this plainly, and it was on this account they concluded to kill Him, believing that no one would
be able to resist so great kindness.   Mark the reasons
which they gave for desiring His death.   "Do you
not see," said they, "that every one is running after
Him ; and that if we take no measures to put a stop
to it, our Synagogues will be forsaken, and our Law
denounced?"   The people wished to make Him king
and waited only for His consent.   They followed Him

[1] Sulpitius Life of St. Martin.

in crowds into the wilderness.   Never had any one spoken like Him : all hearts, even the hardest were touched by His words.   See the difference between the two ways of acting.   God governed and guided His people with a stern and rigorous hand, and all fled from Him : He turned to the path of mildness and all worshipped Him.   Ah ! will man be senseless enough to believe that he can do what God could not, and that he knows how to govern his fellow-man better than God, the Creator and Sounder of hearts ?

Now, let me draw this chapter to an end by the following remarks : True virtue always keeps the right medium.   There are certain limits, which a virtuous man ought neither to fall short of, nor overstep.   The Superior ought to be affectionate, it is true ; he ought to show the love of a father, and the tenderness of a mother ; but at the same time, he should be careful not to be too free in manifesting by words or actions, the feelings of his heart, neither using himself, nor allowing from his subjects too tender caresses, such as might become a source of trouble to silly minds, and silly imaginations, nor yet too frequently, but only occasionally with innocence and cordial simplicity.

"The principal caresses which the Superior should show his subjects is the treating them cordially and mildly, with the heart of a mother and a nurse, and a readiness charitably to serve and assist them according to their wants and necessities, keeping secret whatever each one shall say to him, whilst the fondness of subjects for their Superior, should chiefly consist in the entire and perfect confidence which they place in him, in perfectly obeying him and faithfully following his direction."[1]

There is a medium in all things. St. Francis de Sales says, that an imprudent display of kind feelings, particularly in one who governs too mildly would produce the following consequences.

1. The subjects would become spoiled and unwilling to suffer anything.

2. The Superior would prejudice his own authority and render himself contemptible.

3. He would unconsciously draw the affections of his subjects to himself in such a manner, as to wean them from God; for they will then obey the man whom they love, rather than God whom they ought to obey and love in the creature. Consequently, although a Superior ought to be gentle, compassionate, and affectionate, yet his mildness should be so tempered with gravity and modesty, that his subjects may not only love, but esteem him. A love which is not accompanied with esteem easily degenerates. What the Bishop of Belley relates of his own love for St. Francis de Sales, may often be the case with many inferiors in respect to those Superiors, who, like the holy Bishop of Geneva, guide and direct with all meekness and love. "I must candidly acknowledge," says the Bishop of Belley, "that my pleasure was so great if I did anything which pleased him, that when he expressed his satisfaction I thought I was in heaven." "And," he adds, "if he had not

[1] St. Frances de Chantal.

taught me to refer everything to God, as to its last end, without thinking of him, many of my works would have been imperfect." Should a Superior notice a like disposition in any of his subjects, he ought to instil into his heart this doctrine of St. Francis de Sales, endeavoring to lead him by slow degrees to complete detachment and to the esteem of the happiness of a soul which is attached to, and depends on God alone. However in trying to accomplish this, he must not show himself cold, indifferent and repulsive in his manners, which might easily produce aversions and disquietude, and even a certain derangment, especially in the weak-minded.

Would to God, that in all Superiors, this virtue of sweetness would seem to clothe itself with the human form, so that they could be said to be gentleness itself, rather than men endowed with that quality. They would then possess such powerful influence over the minds of men, that all would give way to them; condescending to each one individually, and, making themselves, all things to all, they would see, on the other hand, how all would acquiesce in their desire which should be no other than to behold them all embarked in the service of God and the way of salvation. "My son, do thy works in meekness, and thou shalt be beloved above the glory of men."[1]

[1] Eccles. 3. 19.

CHAPTER V.

WHAT ARE THE MARKS OF A RIGOROUS GOVERNMENT?

T cannot be denied, that the greater part of men, even many of the wise, are in a deplorable state of blindness. There is so little self-knowledge, that even he who every one blames for his severity, thinks he is meekness itself. If he is told that his manner of acting renders his office of Superior insupportable and himself hateful, he taxes every one with impertinence and protests that no one knows him, that he always acts with the greatest mildness and the best intention. Now, this is an error, against which too much cannot be said. Never should we try to cover our faults with the cloak of a good intention. It is true, that we ought always to have a good intention in all our actions, but in this instance it is of no avail. We are judged by the exterior, not by the interior. Every one declares that he has a good intention. We are ready to believe this; but we desire to see the fruits. These are kind words and gentle dealings, the only tongues whose evidence is readily accepted. In order that there may be no mistake in the matter, we will here give some marks by which it may be known, that a Superior governs his subjects with severity.

1. When he is too decisive, hasty and cutting in his manner of speaking. When he abruptly gives a refusal ; as for instance, when he answers, on the spot by a "no" or some other such repulsive word.

2. When pride and displeasure gleam from his eyes, seeming to threaten all who do not accost him with extraordinary humility and trembling speech.

3. When he speaks in a haughty and magisterial tone, making use of peremptory language and playing the despot.

4. When the expression of his countenance is bold and arrogant. It must be acknowledged, however, that such a bearing may sometimes be natural ; still, it is scarcely ever blameless, and he who does not endeavor to correct it, will be the cause of many crosses for himself and others.

5. When he gives a refusal, without taking the trouble to listen to the petition, and when he contemptuously sends his inferiors away from him.

6. When he not only refuses a lawful request, but accompanies the refusal with sharp and unkind looks. Such treatment is capable of estranging the heart of a poor weak creature ! It is no matter of surprise that such a one would rather suffer want, than ask anything of so rude and unkind a person.

7. When he appears so unwilling, to grant what is asked of him, that the petitioner is sorry for having made the request. It is often more agreeable

to meet with a polite refusal, than to have a favor
uncourteously granted.

.   8.   When he decides roughly and hastily upon
the representations of his subjects, without taking
time for consideration or advice, condemning them
at the first word, and sending them away with their
reasons unheard.

9.   When he lightly makes use of harsh expressions, such as : I command you ; — It is my will that
it should be so : It suffices that it is my wish : — In
virtue of holy obedience, I command you to do this :—
Where is your obedience?—Am I not your Superior?—
Go, and let me hear no more of it ! If you do not willingly do, what you are told, we must find other
means to enforce obedience : — Your strange behavior
has long since been a subject of remark : — Mortify
yourself and do as you are directed. — All this is a
proof that a Superior exercises his charge with severity,
and, is so unmindful of the authority, with which he
is clothed, that he forgets to be a father, a brother,
and a servant. A man of weak mind, will make
more frequent use of such expressions in a month,
than a perfect Superior would in fifty years.

10.   When he easily listens to the false reports
of such as speak against their brethren and who frequently exaggerate matters ; when he credits their
representations, and upon the testimony of such witnesses, without further inquiry as to the truth of the
matter, gives vent to his zeal by imposing severe
penances and uttering bitter reproaches. This
hastiness is the cause of many faults. The first is,

judging a person without hearing him; the second is, that an innocent man often suffers unjustly; the third, the words escaping the lips on such an occasion are unworthy of a Superior, who seems to forget that he is a father, since he ignores that kindness which ought to accompany every action.

11. When at the commission of a slight fault, he flies into a passion, as if it had been a mortal sin, although, in all probability, the poor culprit has not even been guilty of a venial transgression. There is no surer mark of weakness than such hasty demeanor. A Superior ought not to be like one whose digestive organs are so disordered, that he is not able to retain anything upon his stomach. He should not let his tongue be moved by everything that falls under his eyes.

12. Other signs of severity in governing, is the want of charity and affection of a heart hardened against every kindly feeling; never to utter a cheerful or pleasant word; to seem to say by every glance of the eye, "you ought to mortify yourself: — you are too delicate: — you alone cause more trouble and annoyance, than all the rest: — you are too slothful in the practice of virtue, &c." Such are the genuine characteristics of a severe Superior, of one whose heart is made of stone or iron.

13. Those who enjoy good health, who have never been sick or undergone any hardship, and whose disposition is choleric and melancholy, are generally rude and unkind. Not knowing what sickness, sorrow, misfortune, or ill-health is, they judge others

lightly and think them over-tender of themselves.
Their hearts are too hard to be touched by compassion ;
and the most remarkable feature of their case is, that
they consider these faults as firmness of mind and the
true characteristics of a generous soul. They speak
of nothing but of their zeal, thinking there is no better way to exercise it, than by enforcing an inviolable
observance of the rule. They look upon it as mockery, if any one ventures to quote to them the proverb :
Summum jus, summa injuria. Justice is the rigor
of the law, mildness of expression reconciles us to its
necessity.

14. A severe Superior no sooner hears of some
single reprehensible act committed by one of his subjects than he believes him at once guilty of the corresponding vice ; he seems to forget that virtuous
habits are not extinguished by one contrary act ; he
seems not to know the distinction between sin and
vice. Break silence once, and you are in his opinion,
a great talker, a dissipated mind, a luke-warm religious. Make but once a remonstrance to him, and
he will consider you a disobedient, rebellious subject,
who has no respect for Superiors, his orders, or the
religious rules. Certainly, nothing shows better his
want of common sense and experience than this manner of acting.

15. When a severe Superior has once resolved
upon a thing, it must be done, nolens, volens : willingly or unwillingly. We would not infer that it is
advisable lightly to change one's purpose ; never,
however, should it be too firmly, stubbornly, and in-

exorably adhered to. The consolation of having his petitions at least, listened to and taken into consideration, should not be denied to a poor inferior. What harm can there be in this? It will only give him an opportunity to unburthen his heart, after which his trouble may disappear of itself.

16. It cannot be denied, that there are inferiors who are troublesome, forward, sullen, impudent, unmortified, obstinate, and even crafty. We readily admit that severity is called for by such characters; but it should be exercised so wisely, that those who have not shared in the misdemeanor, may not partake of the punishment. It is a great fault to wish to lead all dispositions by the same way,—a fault which ought to be carefully avoided.

Is it not ridiculous to see one who has been Superior for about two weeks, speak almost like the General or like one who has grown gray in governing others?—To show his superiority he pulls down what his predecessor built up, believing his reputation and authority to increase in proportion as he humbles his brethren. Does such a man not give evident signs of a weak mind and must we be astonished to see his subjects revolt against him, trying in every manner possible to cast off such a hard and insupportable yoke? Let such men become a little older before the direction of others is entrusted to them, in order to learn by experience how to treat their equals with respect and as persons possessing, generally speaking, more merit, virtue and holiness than they themselves. Let them listen to the Holy Ghost who says : "Be not as a lion in thy house, terrifying them out of thy household, and oppressing them that are under thee."[1]   Let the principal care of such Superiors, be to correct their own faulty character by following the foot-steps of those who govern with meekness, the marks of which government we shall, to their greater good, set forth in the following chapter.

[1] Eccl. 4, 35.

CHAPTER VI.

WHAT ARE THE MARKS OF A MILD GOVERNMENT?

T is, generally speaking, self-conceit in a man, to believe that he is as meek as he ought to be. This very presumption is a sign that he does not know how difficult it is to acquire a perfect degree of the virtue, which he imagines himself already to possess. There are but few who reach a high degree of meekness, because, generally speaking, the essence of this virtue is not properly understood. We will, therefore, give a few of its characteristics, drawn from the writings of great men.

1. Solomon says, in the Book of Wisdom, that when God commands His servants to do anything, He does so with great attention and respect: "Cum attentione et reverentia." When He determined to send the prophet Isaias to the Jews to announce His judgments, He might have addressed him in the following manner: I have chosen you as My prophet; I am with you, and I will always be with you, I therefore send you to My people. Go immediately. But such a manner of commanding is far from the Lord. All that He did, was simply to manifest to

the prophet, His wish, that he should go. "Whom shall I send,' said the Lord to him, "and who shall go for us ?"[1]

2. The holy Angels act in the same manner. Witness the words of the Archangel Raphael to young Tobias : — "Brother Tobias,—if it please thee, therefore, let us go before. . . ."[2] He could have said : "Quickly ; do this — God wills it — there is no time for reasoning &c." But this mode of address is unknown in heaven. The Angels do not speak in this way.

3. The Saints are also unacquainted with this manner of speaking. St. Paul, writing to Timothy, uses such expressions as the following : I conjure you by the love of Jesus Christ, or, by the love that you bear me ; or : I entreat you by the meekness of the Redeemer ; or : Do this, I beg of you, for the honor and glory of Jesus Christ. In a similar style does St. Gregory the Great write : "If it pleaseth your meekness : Your benignity will perhaps allow me to tell you. I promise and trust that your sincere charity will dictate to you the impropriety of such behavior. I believe it will be very agreeable to our Saviour, if your meekness will consider what has occured in this important matter." Thus, instead of making his subjects feel the whole weight of his authority, he addressed them in words of flowing honey. By this mild manner of government, he stilled, in the twinkling of an eye, the rising storms and brought back to the faith those who had wan-

[1] Isaias 6, 8. [2] Tob. xi. 2, 3.

dered the farthest, and whose influence might have
led to the greatest disorder.

4.   The manner in which St. John, the Disciple
of love, was accustomed to command others, may be
suitably adduced here. "My dear children," he
said, "if you love Jesus Christ, do what I tell you :
I entreat you, by the heart of Jesus, our Master, to
love one another sincerely and you will have done all
that I ask of you. Love is a good preceptor, it will
instruct you in every thing you have to do. Of myself, I have nothing to command you, but, Jesus
wishes this to be—more I need not say to you."

5.   The example presented by the Holy Family
is still more striking. How was it governed ? Who
commanded there ? Jesus Christ ? No : He was only
an obedient Child. "And He was subject to them
Erat subditus illis." He had come down from heaven,
for no other end than to obey. Did our dear Lady command ? No: she, who is always "Mother most amiable," was the humble servant of her God and of St.
Joseph. "Behold the handmaid of the Lord: ecce an-
cilla Domini."—Was it perhaps, St. Joseph who commanded? Far from it ! This great Saint surely was careful not to assume any authority over his God and the
Queen of Angels. Who then commanded in this holy
household? All three, or, rather, none of them. There
was such a mutual anticipation of each other's wants,
that command, became unnecessary. Thrice happy
family, in which no one commands and every one
obeys, or rather where every one commands, by doing
what duty requires ! Example is the most forcible

precept. Admire again the spectacle presented by
such a family. No one says a word, and yet, every
one does what he ought to do ; no one issues orders,
and every one punctually obeys ! What an admirable
household is that, where it costs more to command
than to act, where each one is rather a servant, than
lord and master, and where meekness and discretion
lead and direct.

6. The hermits were accustomed to call St.
Macarius, "the god of the monks," because his meekness and amiability had gained for him so great an
influence over the hearts of his brethren, that they
did more than he commanded. They, even envied
one another the pleasure of being able to obey him.
"My brethren," he used to say, "do what you see
me do. I will tell you to do nothing which I shall
not have first done myself. If you are not able to do
it, stay in your cells and rest. I will do it for you.
Do you only keep up your courage, and I will be your
surety with God."—Again, listen to his words to a
monk who had disobeyed him : "I know well, my
dear brother, that you would willingly have done it,
had you been able. You, have committed but one
slight fault ; but I am guilty of so many."—Again,
he said : "Brother, you and I must do this : you
choose which part you prefer, and I will do the rest."

7. A Superior like St. Francis of Assissi is not
easily found. He was the General of the Order and
yet scarcely ever gave a command ! This Saint used
to say : "My brethren, if you love Jesus Christ, do
this, I entreat you." The poor brothers almost killed

themselves in the effort to do all that their beloved Father had asked of them. It seemed to them, that he did not command them enough, that he spared them too much, and that all they did was, in reality, nothing.—When asked by the Guardians of his Order, how they ought to direct the religious, he answered : "Do as Jesus Christ did. If any one commits a fault, say to him : 'Sin no more.' Tell him that you forgive him most sincerely, admonish him to be more upon his guard for the future, and acknowledge that you commit many faults to his one ; nay, that were you not supported by the grace of God, you would be guilty of more and greater ones." If any one reproached him for having been too meek, St. Francis was accustomed to say, that he would rather be a father than a hangman, and that if he must hate something, he would hate sin, but not the sinner.

8. Moses, whom we must certainly allow to have been a perfect Superior, once complained to God in the following moving words : "Why wilt Thou have me carry this people in my bosom, as a little child or an innocent lamb? Dost Thou not remember that they number more than two millions of souls, that they are a rebellious nation, daily manifesting their faithlessness? How can I bear them all in my bosom?"—Still, this complaint did not induce God to change His will. He insisted, that Moses should speak to those passionate and indocile men precisely as he would to a child which had cast itself into his arms. Now would it not sound strange to hear any one receive a poor little child, flying to him

for protection, with terrible threats and hard blows?
"Moses," said God to the holy Lawgiver, "it is My
will that thou lead My people back to their duty and
maintain them therein in no other way, than by the
mildness of paternal affection." What confusion does
not this bring upon those Superiors, who, although
placed over only a handful of men, make more disturbance in a short time, than Moses did in forty
years!

9. When the pestilence broke out in Milan, the
holy Cardinal St. Charles Borromeo was for a time,
at a loss what to do to encourage his priests to assist
him in serving the pest-stricken people. To command them to do so, would have been a critical step;
to forsake his disconsolate flock and not trouble himself about them, would have been downright cruelty.
After long considering the matter, he hit upon the
following expedient. Addressing his clergy, he said:
"My children, let him who loves me, follow me."
He then immediately repaired to the dwellings of the
sufferers, where, without the least regard to his own
safety, he bade defiance to death itself. Do you think
it was hard to imitate one who thus courageously exposed his life for the good of others? All of his priests
so zealously and fervently followed the example set
them by their beloved Bishop, that there is little
doubt that their generosity in thus exposing their
lives, was one of the principal things which moved
God to stay His avenging arm.

10. It is stated in the Life of St. Peter of
Alcantara, that he never commanded his inferiors to

do anything which he had not himself first done. He wished to know by experience what that was, which he required of others. When he gave a command, he made use of so kind and gracious words, that he seemed rather to be begging a favor than giving an order. When forced to blame any one, he did it in the most soothing and affectionate manner. When the Fathers returned from collecting alms, he did not wait for them to come to ask his blessing ; but hastening to meet them, he would cast himself at their feet, and in this position, after he had blessed them, embrace them with the greatest affection. Then he would express his regret at their fatigue, thank them for their charity, and have something brought for their refreshment. Had they been on a long and tiresome round, he used to embrace them a second time. In the winter he would bring warm water and wash their feet so kindly and fervently, as to draw tears from the eyes of his brethren. He labored unceasingly to increase in humility and fraternal charity. He was so earnest in giving them marks of his love, that when he met them on their return from begging alms, he welcomed them as though he had not seen them for years.

A similar example is presented by St. Fidelis of Sigmaringa, who, whilst he hated himself, loved others with the devotedness of a mother's love. We may say with truth that the Saints, one and all, were distinguished for their exquisite refinement, charity and mildness, no matter, whether they earned heaven in a kitchen, like St. Tita, or graced a throne, like

St. Margaret of Scotland ; whether they sprang from the most degraded class, like St. Margaret, the penitent of Cortona, or ensanguined the baptismal robe with martyrs blood, like the gentle child St. Agnes; whether bred at the plough, like St. Vincent, or in a feudal Castle, like the sweet Saint of Geneva ; whether they passed their lives in a desert, like the first Hermit, or exchanged the sword of a Cavalier for the sword of the Spirit, like the brave soldier of Loyola ; whether they begged their bread, like the sainted Labré, or wielded a sceptre, like the last of the crusade kings ; whether, in fine, they offered fair children to martyrdom, like St. Felicitas, or served God in the cloister, like St. Teresa.

11.   Would you know the laws enacted by Jesus Christ for the establishment of His kingdom upon earth, you have but too consider how He instructed His representative.   He gave him one law only. "Simon," said He, "if thou lovest Me more than all the others love Me, be the shepherd of My sheep, and remember, that in order to make yourself worthy of the sublime office of My representative on earth, thou must love Me and love them for My sake."   What did St. Peter do after he had received this office ? He wept oftener than he commanded ; and his tears had a more powerful effect than all the threats of tyrants.

PRACTICAL CONCLUSIONS.

IT may be said that the Saints, in general, made use of the following maxims in order to govern their subjects with gentle firmness.—

1. Choose for yourself the more difficult task and leave the lighter one to others.

2. Never give a command over-hastily or abruptly.

3. Never command anything when excited, lest passion dictate the order.

4. Never defend obstinately your motives before inferiors; for bitter contention, not cheerful obedience, would be the result of such a proceeding.

5. Give to a heart oppressed with sorrow, an opportunity to manifest itself and prepare to receive with humility the orders which may be given it.

6. When obliged to refuse a request, do so in such a manner as to show the regret felt at not being able to grant it; declare to the petitioner, that you will profit by the earliest opportunity to oblige him; even offer to write to the Superior to obtain the desired permission, protesting, that it would be a thousand times more agreeable for you to grant, than

to deny the favor. If the person who proffers the request is not solidly grounded in virtue, give the refusal in a most amiable manner, alleging so satisfactory reasons for it, that he will go away better contented than if his desire had been gratified. Say with St. Vincent de Paul: "Since what you ask cannot now be well granted, I beg you to remind me of it at another time."

7. When a permission is to be given, grant it kindly, without, prefacing it with two or three refusals, or saying "yes" so ungraciously and with so many objections, as scarcely to leave the petitioner courage to say a word of thanks.

8. Act with the sincerity of a father's love. Then, nothing will be hard.

9. Act with the greatest politeness towards inferiors, saluting them first, and never using either in Conferences or conversation with them, a haughty tone, harsh, cutting words, or threatening gesticulations.

10. If any one looks as if he were suffering, call him and inquire how he feels.

11. Be not provoked by trifles. It often happens that things of little consequence are treated with a zeal called for only by matters of the greatest importance.

12. Treat your inferiors as persons, who are deserving more esteem than yourself, and not only rank higher in virtue and merit here on earth, but who may also possess in heaven a greater love of God, and a more elevated seat of glory.

13. If on some occasion, you were wanting in meekness, try at once to repair this fault ; ask pardon for it, and endeavor, by kind words, to soothe the heart estranged and wounded by it.

14. When severity becomes a necessity, protest like St. Francis Xavier, that you would like better to take the discipline, than to give it to another.

15. Often consider, that when a sheep has broken its leg, the shepherd does not beat it on that account, but, on the contrary, carefully tries to heal the broken limb, binds it up, takes the poor animal in his arms, and carries it to a safe place.

.16. Never reproach any one with the kindness shown him.[1]

17. Be kind to all ; let every one see, that he is always welcome no matter how often he calls, and that he may, with perfect confidence, have recourse to his Superior in all difficulties and necessities. At whatever hour Father L. Lallement, S. J., was applied to, however occupied he might be, he received every one that came with a smiling countenance and an open heart, and he seemed never to have anything else to do but listen to those who wished to speak to him, without ever betraying in his manner any signs of weariness.[2]

18. A prudential caution and reserve effect much ; but if excessive, they become injurious, and painfully wound and contract the heart, whilst, on the contrary, an unreserved confidential manner opens

[1] F. Binet, S. J.   [2] Life of Father L. Lallement.

and relieves it. Should you, notice any one to be wanting in confidence, you must be very careful not to manifest the least coldness or diffidence in him, but try to gain his heart by kindness and charitable services, always speaking to him with great frankness and holy cordiality. You must also be careful not to be prejudiced against any one, but show the same kindness to all, as otherwise you would do much harm to such a subject, who would no longer receive well the corrections of his Superior; for the assurance which a religious has of sharing in the cordial charity of his Superior, is for the latter the means by which he must make all his instructions and corrections, sweetly enter into the heart of the former to the great profit of his soul. If a subject discovers artifice and cunning in the prudence of his Superior, instead of sincere simplicity, he will keep his heart closed against him — such as the conduct of Superiors is, such will be that of their subjects — if the former are open hearted, candid and simple in their manner of acting, the latter will be so too. · Hence never manifest any resentment or utter any complaint against any one, no matter, how much he may have offended you either in word or action. Never show yourself astonished at being contradicted; receive everything from the hand of God, and keep your soul in peace and tranquility.

19. As a general rule, express your esteem for your inferiors, and manifest sometimes, satisfaction at their behaviour. This is a good means to inspire them with love for dependence and submission, and

to make them feel happy under the guidance of their Superiors.[1]

St. Alphonsus writes in one of his letters : "I entreat each of you, when he is far from me, to write to me in all his necessities. Do not yield to the fear, which the devil inspires, to disturb me and others, that it is not agreeable to me to speak or correspond with you. I wish you to know, once for all, that the more confidence you show me, the more you win my love and favor. Let each one be convinced, that all else shall be laid aside, when there is question of consoling one of my brethren ; for it is to me of more importance to assist one of them, than to do a good work for any one else. Since God has given me the office I hold, He requires this of me, more than the performance of any other act however laudable." In another letter, he writes, "As Superior, I am bound to listen to the least of my brethren and to read the letters he writes to me. This, my office demands of me. For the publication of books I am free to use that time only, which is left, after I have read, and answered the letters written to me. If any one wishes to speak or write to me concerning either his individual affairs or those which relate to the Congregation, I am ready to lay aside everything else. — Let all my brethren be convinced, that, next to God, each one of them is the only object of my love here upon earth, and that I am ready, at any moment to sacrifice my life for each one. They are still young and can, therefore, effect more for the glory of God than I, an old,

---

[1] B. Balthaz. Alvarez.

sick man, who is no longer good for anything, can.[1]
On page 208 of the same Letters, he writes: "I will,
however, serve you to the best of my power, and God
knows how much more dearly I love you all than I
do my own mother and brothers."

20. In order to gain the good will and affection
of inferiors, which are indispensably necessary for the
accomplishment of the good aimed at, a Superior
must manifest great love for them and express
pleasure at being in their company, guarding, nevertheless, against showing a particular inclination for
any individual; for this would be the ruin of the best
purposes.[2]

"Be firmly convinced," says St. Ignatius, "that
any show of preference to one, will excite envy and
make others think themselves despised. Consequently,
be exceedingly careful not to give cause for any to
believe that you esteem the learning, talents, or virtue of one more than another, except when it is absolutely necessary to do so."

21. When subjects belong to different nations
be still more careful not to excite the suspicion of being, in the least influenced by nationality in the
treatment of them. Treat all with charity and indulgence, without manifesting a particular affection
for any one, which might give rise to sadness or envy
in others.

22. When complained of, avoid showing surprise, sensibility, or displeasure. Express on the

---

[1] Letters of St. Alphonsus, Aug. 8, 1754, page 217.

[2] B. Balt. Alvarez.

contrary, pleasure at the candor of the com-
plainer; thus you will more easily appease his disquiet and obtain light for the better fulfilment of
duty.

"Be careful," St. Francis de Sales wrote one day
to a certain Superior, "not to show yourself discouraged for having been murmured at and complained of
by some of your subjects. Nothing is easier than to
blame, but it is not so easy to improve. No great
talents and skill are required to discover and speak of
the faults of those who have to direct others. If we
are reproached for faults in our direction, we must
bear it patiently, speak to God about them, and consult others also on the matter, and then do what
seems best, confidently hoping that God will direct all
to His greater glory."

One day, a woman who was angry with St.
Francis de Sales, went to him boldly and told him,
that she despised and disliked him from her heart.
"And I," said the Saint, without asking the cause
of her dissatisfaction, "love you so much the more."
"How can this be?" asked the woman in surprise.
"Because," was the answer, "you must be very sincere
to tell me your temptation, and that is a quality which
I highly prize and greatly love." "But," answered
she, "what I have asserted, was not a merely passing
feeling: at this moment this dislike is in my heart."
"And what I have said," replied the Saint, "is also
my present sentiment, which, with the grace of God,
I will ever preserve. . . . I am always glad when any
one tells me candidly what is weighing on the heart;

for when the wound is once discovered, the cure is easy."

24. Do not judge others by yourself, or condemn those who refuse to use those means which have made you advance in virtue. Make it a rule of conduct to avoid forcing personal experience upon others.

25. Guard against overtasking the spiritual strength of any one. Give to those who are well grounded in virtue, the more difficult duties, but to the weak, such work only as is proportionate to their strength, so that they may be encouraged to undertake greater things, instead of being disheartened.

26. As far as possible, give a favorable interpretation to everything, looking upon all with a father's eye.

27. Be slow in believing bad reports about inferiors ; and when reports are made in an evident state of excitement, require a written statement of the matter, for the pen is more cautious in what it writes, than the tongue is in what it speaks.

St. Francis of Assissium says, that a Superior ought to be very slow in listening to accusations against others, particularly when the accusers are great talkers, and not only ought he not to listen easily to such persons, but he should not believe them until a careful examination will have proved the truth of their assertions.

28. Be still more cautious in pronouncing judgement against the absent.

"Even though the accuser be a Saint," says St. Francis of Assissium, "let the Superior guard against

9

condemning the accused, until he shall have heard what the latter may have to say in his own justification."

"May God preserve us from Superiors," says St. Jane Frances de Chantal, "who give easy credit to every thing, for they will be guilty of many little acts of injustice : but still more may He preserve us from unjust inferiors. The Jews through a spirit of justice would have stoned the poor woman taken in adultery ; but Jesus delivered her through mercy."

29. Never allow an opportunity of gratifying inferiors to pass, and express by word and manner the paternal affection you bear them in your heart.

30. Although abstemious yourself, take care, that the young be well provided with good and palatable food, as far as the rule allows, and show pleasure at seeing any one eat with relish.

"Be neither miserly, stingy, too exacting, nor too liberal," wrote St. Jane Frances de Chantal to a Superioress. "Act in temporal matters generously and equally avoiding meanness and ostentation."

31. In case weak health requires better nourishment than is ordinarily served, take it as others do, not in secret, but openly, so as to encourage all to act in like manner when sick.[1]

32. Never treat any one with the least sign of pride or anger.

33. In order to lighten, the yoke of obedience, as well as to induce all to love it the more and act with greater perfection, never do give a stringent

St. F. of Assisi.

command, except in the most extraordinary cases ; but, even whilst imparting the simplest orders, kindly give the reasons of them, so that whilst obeying, the subjects may feel as if they were doing their own will.

34. Show confidence in the ability of inferiors. Thus you will win their affection.

35. Take an interest in the labors of subjects, assisting them in and forwarding their holy undertakings, employing them, whenever the opportunity offers, in works tending to the glory of God and salvation of souls, without wishing to do everything yourself, thus hindering by an excess of exterior business the performance of your duty of Superior. Such a manner of acting is very pleasing to inferiors ; and it encourages them to fulfil their duties properly when they are supported and encouraged by those who hold the place of God towards them.[1]

36. Do not interfere too much in the employment of your inferiors. By avoiding this, you will the more calmly and properly perform the duties of your office. Moreover, if the subjects should happen to commit a fault, you may correct them for it. But should you occupy yourself too anxiously with every little trifle, you will assuredly commit faults yourself, and thus expose yourself to the blame of your subjects, the danger of which blame you should avoid as much as possible.

37. When inferiors return from the accomplishment of any commission, welcome them heartily, in-

[1] Father Lallement, S. J.

quire about their success, and how things passed off.
If their efforts were successful, congratulate them, if
unsuccessful, comfort and encourage them kindly.

38.   When the fruits of the labor of inferiors
are spoken of, or when you yourself speak of them,
express great joy at them.   It would be even well to
have the letters containing these joyful tidings, read
aloud a second time, so as to encourage others and
awaken in their souls a holy emulation.

39.   When any one has accomplished a praiseworthy act, manifest in every possible manner, gratitude and satisfaction at it, and hold him up as an
example for others.   In order to please and reward
him, do everything that a dutiful son might reasonably expect from the most indulgent of fathers.

40.   Be extremely careful not to speak to any
one of the faults of an inferior.   The consequence of
this fault would be that the one to whom the imperfection of another is made known, would say : "If
the Superior speaks thus to me of one of my brethren,
he will not fail to do the same of me ; therefore I will
not open my heart to him or reveal my weakness."

St. Frances de Chantal wrote as follows to deposed Superiors: "My daughters, your kind hearts
will doubtless willingly hear of a light, which God
has vouchsafed to me.   It is this.   When a Superior
is elected, the deposed mother should, by no means,
under the plea of confidence, unless in a case of pressing necessity, speak to her of the past faults of the
Sisters.   This would only serve to excite distrust and
ill-feeling, which would be very wrong.   It is my

desire that the Sisters too, should be equally careful upon this point, and I myself will not speak to the newly elected Superior of the faults committed before her arrival amongst them. Act in this manner, and you will see that the practice of this common charity will draw down upon you the blessing of Heaven. Oh ! my dear daughters, the whole perfection of our little Institute depends upon the union of our hearts!''

41. A Superior must repress his aversions and other feelings of dislike, which may arise from ill humor, or otherwise in order not to be overhasty in his judgement and fall into a thousand faults.

42. If any one dislikes you, try to find out the cause of his ill-feeling and then abstain from all that might occasion it, and, if possible, even do exactly the contrary to what is displeasing to him and thus win him by mildness.

43. If you have to deal with characters, with whom it is very difficult to get along, try to gain them by condescension, and even when you would be justified in insisting upon certain things, yield for the time being, in order to win their souls for Jesus Christ.[1]

44. Be so kindly disposed towards all, that each one, after the commission of a fault, may fearlessly and unhesitatingly seek a place of refuge in your heart. Be sparing in imparting commands, pardon injuries readily, and be more willing to *bear* with sinners than to *overwhelm* them with reproaches.[2]

45. Do not give useless directions ; for this only

---

[1] St. Francis of Assissium.　　[2] St. Francis of Assissium.

serves to oppress inferiors and make the yoke of monastic life heavier, whereas you should endeavor to lighten it. Take care, rather, that the rules and costums already existing be well observed. St. Philip Neri often used to say : "No one can believe how difficult it is to keep rational beings endowed with free will in prompt subordination. It is best effected by kindness and by commanding as seldom as possible. Let him who wishes to be obeyed readily, command but seldom."

46. Consider, that a Superior is invested with authority in order that he may benefit and assist inferiors, but not that he may injure or oppress them. St. Bernard says: "In the dignity and office with which you are invested, value nothing so much as the power which it gives you, to promote the welfare and happiness of your neighbor. It is no particular happiness to be invested with the power of commanding, but it is a great misfortune not to make yourself useful to others, when you command."

47. Be not too prompt to promise this and that, or to satisfy fault-finding spirits, but take time enough to consider, if there be question about something of importance ; thus many annoyances will be avoided.

48. Do not wait until requested, before succoring the wants of any one, but inquire into and anticipate them. This manner of acting makes benefits and acts of charity twice as dear and valuable. There are certain bashful characters, who like better to suffer want than to have the appearance of being troublesome ; there are others who from a spirit of penance,

conceal even their most necessary wants ; others again
from a spirit of pride and self-conceitedness, will do
without the charity of their neighbor, or relieve their
wants by unlawful means rather than ask for it.   An
attentive and anticipating charity prevents all these
evils.   One day the Abbot Elias of Isauria asked of
St. Gregory the Great, in a letter, to send him some
Gospel-books and fifty dollars for the wants of his
convent ; but, believing that he had asked too much,
he asked in the course of his letter, for forty dollars
only ; and reflecting that perhaps even this sum might
be too great, on account of the many claims of charity which the Pope had to meet, he changed this
petition also, asking only for thirty dollars.   In
answer to this letter the Pope wrote as follows : —
"We send you herewith the Gospel-books ; and as to
the fifty dollars which you asked for the wants of your
convent, you thought, that this sum was too much,
and you took off ten dollars ; and believing that this
sum was still too much, you took off again ten dollars, asking only for thirty.   Now as *you* were so
generous, *we* must not be less so.   Therefore, we
send you herewith fifty dollars, and being afraid that
this sum might not be sufficient for your wants, we
send ten dollars more ; and being still apprehensive,
that even this sum might not meet your wants, we
have added twelve more.   We thank you for your
great affections for us, and your great confidence in
us."[1]

Father Tannoja relates, that St. Alphonsus con-

[1] Rohrbacher's Histoire Univer. de l'Eglise.

stantly sought to impress upon the minds of Superiors,
to be kind and affectionate to their inferiors, that
they should not advocate severity and penances, but
that they should rather prefer the method of gentle
and affectionate encouragement. The most affectionate father could not feel greater love for his children,
than St. Alphonsus did for his brethren.[1]

　　To two Fathers of the Society of Jesus, who had
just been promoted to important positions, St. Francis
Xavier wrote as follows: "Above all things I recommend to you mutual charity, first between yourselves
and then towards all the Fathers and Brothers. The
knowledge which I have of the members of our Order
gives me so great a confidence in them, that I do not
believe they need a Superior. Nevertheless, for the
sake of greater merit and so that all may go on with
order, Father A. Gomez will take charge of the College at Goa and you will be the Superior of the other
houses in the province. Once more does my sense of
duty compel me to recommend to you mutual love.
Do not meddle with each others duties. Cherish all
the Fathers and Brothers with particular affection,
assist them in their difficulties, as far as possible for
you, taking to heart all their troubles as if they were
your own. Try, therefore, when they ask anything
of you, either for themselves or for their converts,
whether for spiritual or temporal necessities, to comply with their request. The letters you write to those
who are far from you, ought to be exceedingly kind
and affectionate. Be particularly careful not to let a

---

[1] Life of St. Alphonsus. Vol. II., page 235.

word escape your pen, either through haste or negligence, which might grieve or discourage them. Think of the great sufferings they are obliged to undergo in the service of Jesus Christ, those especially who are in the Molucca Islands; for, they indeed, have to carry the cross. Towards those, who visit you occasionally, either when they come of themselves, or when they are sent by the Superiors for the good of their souls, act with great respect and make use of the proper means to restore or strengthen their zeal. I beg you to read this note once every week."

49. If a Superior thus proves himself a mild and affectionate Father, to his subjects, they, on their part, will always act towards him like obedient children, placing the fullest confidence in him, so that he may do with them whatever he wishes. If his love for them is such, that he is rather their servant than their Superior, they, in their turn, will never think of themselves or concern themselves about their health, but relying upon his fatherly care, will spare themselves no fatigue in labor, feeling sure that they will be amply relieved, when necessity calls for it. This entire confidence of the subjects in their Superior will give rise to a holy emulation; every one will do more than his strength sanctions, and show his respectful obedience in proportion to the love and solicitude of his Father.

CHAPTER VII.

ON CORRECTION.

IN the preceding chapters, several broad hints have been given as to the proper manner of correcting others. It will, however, not be amiss nor unprofitable, to devote a particular chapter to this important subject.

I. In governing and directing others, the manner of administering correction aright, is perhaps the most difficult point. It demands extraordinary prudence, experience, charity and firmness of will. This is a truth acknowledged by the greatest Saints. St. Frances de Chantal used to say: "One of the heaviest duties of a Superior, is his obligation to give admonitions and penances. Nevertheless, it is one of the most essential means to keep up regularity in a religious Order." This duty never appears more difficult than when imperfect, sensitive, unmortified, proud spirits are to be corrected, who have no zeal for their spiritual advancement, and but little love for Jesus crucified.

St. Alphonsus, speaking of the correction of such subjects, says: "I know well, that one may possess the patience of a saint, and yet not attain his end.

If reproof is necessary, particularly when there is question of certain faults which tend to scandal, it must be given without regard to the consequences. It will be only so much the worse for the offender if we do not chastise him; for then, God will take the punishment into His own hands." St. Gertrude having remarked that one of the nuns was not exact in some points of the rule, feared to displease God, if she did not try to bring about her amendment, at the same time she dreaded lest some of the other nuns, who were not so particular, might blame her, for troubling herself about the correction of such trifles. According to her custom, she offered up this trouble and difficulty for the greater glory of God. Our Lord expressed to her His joy at her manner of proceeding, in the following words : "Every time you accept anything of this kind for My love, I will make you stronger and more courageous, and surround you on all sides "as a city is surrounded by walls and moats ; so that no occupation may be able to distract you, or separate you from Me. To this favor, I will add another : viz : to your own merit will be joined that which each one of your Sisters would have gained, had she through love of Me, humbly and zealously received your charitable admonitions."

2. A Superior, then, in order not to become accountable for the faults of his subjects, must give correction. St. Gertrude understood from these words of Genesis : "Where is thy brother Abel ?" that God would call every religious to account, for the infringements of the rule, which he might have prevented, either by

acquainting the Superior of them, or by admonishing the guilty person. Our Lord said to her that those, who excuse themselves by saying that it is not their business to correct others, or, that they are themselves worse than the offenders are no more justified in the sight of God than Cain was, when he said, "Am I my brother's keeper?" Every one is bound to bring back his brother from his erring ways, so that he may advance in perfection. He who by disregarding the dictates of his conscience, neglects this duty, offends God : it is in vain for him to assert, that it is no affair of his, because, God by the voice of his conscience, admonishes him of the contrary. If he neglects to do it, an account will be demanded of his soul for it ; and this account will be much more severe, than that which will be demanded of the Superior, who was not present when the fault was committed, or who did not observe it, if he were present. For this reason does the Holy Scripture anathematize not only the evil doers, but with a two-fold curse, his accomplices also. Now you participate in the sin of your neighbor, when you consent to it, by appearing not to notice it, whilst, by revealing it, you promote God's honor and glory.[1]

One day in an apparition, Jesus Christ represented to St. Gertrude, the mystical body of the Church, under the form of His own natural body. His right side was clothed with a royal, god-like robe, whilst His left side appeared quite naked and covered with ulcers. She understood at once, that by the left

[1] Book 3, chap. 30.

side, sinners and imperfect souls were represented; and that by the right side, the elect of the Church were typified, and that whosoever did a service to any of these favorites of Christ, adorned His right side; she saw that there were many persons, who willingly rendered service to the just, but, few only who would blame and reprove the imperfect and sinners.

"There are some persons," said our Lord to St. Gertrude, "who care nothing at all for My wounds. They are those who, make so little account of the faults of their fellow-men, as not even to take the trouble of giving a gentle, charitable reproof. They fear bringing something unpleasant upon themselves, and using the vain excuse of Cain, they say: "Am I my brother's keeper?" They who act thus, spread a salve upon My wounds, which instead of healing, makes them worse and engenders worms; for it is on account of their silence that those faults increase, which, by a word of reproof, they might have prevented. There are others, who, when they do discover the faults of their neighbor to those in authority, become angry if the guilty ones be not at once reproved and punished. They resolve never more to render any one this act of charity; never to remonstrate with any person, no matter who it may be; imagining that their opinion is made little or no account of. Yet they will judge their neighbor harshly, and even speak of his faults to others, but they will not give him a word of admonition which might lead to his amendment. These also lay a plaster upon My wounds, which, indeed, covers them, but at the same time produces a smarting pain in them. Those who abstain from admonishing others of their faults more through negligence than through malice, tread upon My right foot.''

"I have, it is true,'' wrote St. Frances de Chantal to a Superior, "an indescribable partiality for these words of our holy Founder. 'We must bear with our neighbor, even to a degree of affectation.' Now since you wish to know how this is to be understood, I must necessarily tell you how I myself desire to practise it. It is to bear with those disagreeable whims and importunities; those little unseasonable and unreasonable remarks, certain foibles and thoughtless acts; because they proceed rather from a want of reflection than from real malice, in those who are guilty of them, producing no other evil consequences than some personal annoyance and inconvenience. But, my daughters, never did our holy Father teach toleration in cases where others were disedified; where the fault was wilful and where there was manifest malice and obstinacy. O truly, in those instances, it was his desire, that we should make use of every possible mild and energetic means to remedy the evil. For the greatest care is to be taken not to suffer souls to be habituated to negligence and to be hardened in evil; and though sweetness, cordiality, charity and discretion are to be employed, yet we must generously and fearlessly do our duty, in order to afford the sisters an opportunity of attaining perfection by denying their natural inclinations. I am, it is true, somewhat firm upon this point, for this house frequently sends members to other houses, and I would not have it said by them, that, our Mother at Annecy bears with everything, tolerates everything. This would be too injurious to our Institute. We, Superiors, ought to bear with our daughters in such a manner, as will not prevent us from bearing them to heaven."

"The difference between relaxed and observant Convents," says St. Bonaventure, "is not that in the latter there are no defects (for even there the religious are not angels but men) but that in the former transgressions are not reproved, while in the latter they are corrected and punished."

III. "To reprove any one," says St. Alphonsus, "is a kind act of charity, but if it is done unkindly, it rather injures than benefits.[1]

"The truth should always be spoken graciously," St. Francis de Sales used to say, "a bitter zeal is productive of no good. Reproof is a species of food, which is always difficult to digest. Fraternal charity should, therefore, so sweeten it, as to destroy its bitterness, else it will be like those fruits, which cause pain in the bowels. Charity does not seek its own advantage, but the honor of God. Bitterness and severity proceed only from passion, vanity and pride. An untimely use of a good remedy turns it into a deadly poison."

For this reason, our Lord said to St. Gertrude : "There are many who too severely blame and reprove the imperfect and sinners ; instead of remedying the evil, they rather increase it by their impatience ; and

[1] Life, Vol. II., page 216.

by blindly following the impulse of their own will
without caring whether they scandalize My elect or
not ; these pierce My hands with red-hot awls. May
some at least learn from My example, how to remedy
the faults of their fellow-men ; let them by mild and
kind remonstrances try to induce them to forsake their
imperfect habits, before they have recourse to more
energitic means."   St. Dionysius relates of St. Carpos
how Jesus Christ one day appeared to this Saint, reproving him for his severity and rude behavior towards some of the gentiles who had induced some of
the Christians to apostatise.   "Strike Me," said
Christ to him, "for I am ready to suffer again for the
salvation of mankind.   This I would do with pleasure,
provided other men did not sin."

Hence St. Augustine says :   "Never correct any
one, unless your conscience tells you in truth, that
you are induced by the pure motive of charity to give
the admonition ;"   and St. Basil[1] says : "Superiors
and others must act like good physcians, who never
become angry with their patients, but work only
against their diseases."

We read in several chapters of the lives of the
Fathers of the Desert, that if the elder ones reprimanded with too much severity those of their disciples, who were laboring under temptations, they
soon after fell themselves into the same temptations.
The Lord permitted this, that they might learn how
to have compassion on the tempted. *"Considerans
te ipsum, ne et tu tenteris."*[2] Not to show compassion

[1] Reg. 51.   [2] Galat. 6, 1.

for the infirmities of our neighbor, but to judge and condemn him unmercifully when he has committed a fault, is a sign of some hidden vice and imperfection. "An evident proof," says Cassian, "that you are not yet purified of the filth of sin is, if you have no compassion on those who have committed faults, but pronounce a rigid sentence of condemnation upon them; for how could perfection have entered your heart which has not as yet acquired what the Apostle considers to constitute the perfection of the law, saying: "Bear ye one anothers burdens and so you shall fulfil the law of Christ."[1] Nay, you have not as yet reached even that degree of charity of which the same Apostle says: "Charity is not provoked to anger, is not puffed up, thinketh no evil, it beareth all things, endureth all things, believeth all things."[2] "For the just regardeth the lives of his beasts, but the bowels of the wicked are cruel."[3] Hence it is an evident proof, that you are guilty of the same fault for which you censure your neighbor without indulgent charity and with inhuman severity.[4]

But how shall we be able to recognize whether the correction we give proceeds from charity? The reply to this question is given by St. Francis de Sales. "Truth proceeds from charity," says he, "when we speak it only from the love of God and for the good of him whom we reprove. It is better to be silent than to speak a truth ungraciously; for this would be to present a good dish badly cooked, or to ad-

---

[1] Galat. 6, 2.
[2] I Corinth.
[3] Prov. 12, 10.
[4] Col. 11, c. 11.

minister medicine unseasonably. But is this not to detain truth a prisoner unjustly? Certainly not; to act otherwise would be to bring it forth unjustly, because the real justice of truth and the truth of justice, reside in charity. That truth which is not charitable, proceeds from a charity which is not true. A judicious silence is always preferable to an uncharitable truth."

IV. We are told, that St. Vincent de Paul so gently, yet so firmly pulled up the weeds he observed in the hearts of his disciples, that the roots came up with the stalks, and not a fibre was left to engender evil. Upon the subject of correction he expressed himself thus :

1. "Good example must precede it, otherwise it may justly be said : "Physician, heal thyself."

2. Patience must defer it, because, being a disagreeable remedy, it should be used, generally speaking, only when every other means has proved useless.

3. It must be applied with charity, lest while healing one wound, others might be inflicted.

4. Humility must accompany it, accusing ourselves and thus assuming a part of the disgrace of him whose weakness we have discovered.

5. But we ought to be particularly careful, to administer reproof in so mild a manner, as to lessen the bitterness of this remedy to which nature is radically averse, thus rendering it so efficacious as to make it strike at the very root of the evil.

6. According to St. Ignatius, in the punishment

to be given, attention must be paid to the nature of the fault, its consequences, and to the progress of the delinquent in virtue. St. Ignatius, for example, was accustomed to reprove and punish severely the slightest faults of those who were deeply grounded in virtue. His design in doing so was to edify others by the humility with which these holy men received correction, and also to give them an opportunity of advancing in perfection.

7. It is sometimes good and advisable, before reproving or punishing a person, to point out to him the nature and magnitude of his fault, and then propose to him to impose for it, a penance upon himself. If he takes upon himself a very severe penance, it would be well to lessen it. Father Laynez had been nominated by St. Ignatius, to the provincialship of Italy. It was not long before he complained to his Superior that his most distinguished and gifted members, were taken from him and sent to Rome, where, he thought, they were less needed than in his own province. To this complaint the holy Founder replied: "The house at Rome is the centre and very home of the society. It is from the Pontifical City that nearly all our Fathers have been sent forth to spread themselves in every part of the world; it is, therefore, at Rome, that our brightest lights must shine." To Laynez these motives were far from proving satisfactory, and he rejoined, adding other remarks, in which he endeavored to point out the necessity of retaining in his province learned professors and preachers, capable of combating victori-

ously the enemies of the Church. St. Ignatius, after
reiterating the explanations he had already given,
censured the persistence of Laynez, and concluded
thus : "Reflect thereupon, and inform me, if you
feel that you have been in fault, and if you consider
yourself guilty, tell me what penance you are disposed to undergo for your fault."   Father Laynez
was one of the first disciples of St. Ignatius, his
bosom friend, and one of the most energetic and able
members of the society, a shining light of the Church ;
but, for all this, he was the more humble. The
letter of his beloved General reached him at Florence.
The effect that it produced upon him, and the profit
he derived from it, will be better understood from
his own words.   Here is his answer :
    "Father !
    "When the letter of your Reverence reached
me, I turned to God ; and after offering up a prayer,
with eyes overflowing with tears — a rare occurrence
with me — this is the decission I have come to, and
which I now confirm, with tears in my eyes : I desire, that your Reverence, in whose hands I place
myself, unreservedly, I desire, I say, and I ask it
for the love of Jesus, that, as a punishment for my
sins, and to subdue my unruly passions, which
occasioned them, you would withdraw me from the
government of the province, from preaching and
study, so as to divest me of every thing but my
breviary ; that you would make me beg my way to
Rome, and that there you would employ me until my
death in the lowest occupation of the house, or,

should I be unfit for that, that you will order me to
spend the remainder of my life in teaching the
elements of Grammar, having no consideration for
me, and never looking upon me but as the dust of
the earth. This is what I choose, first of all for my
penance.''

Thus he wrote, and thus he condemned himself
he who had attracted the admiration of the entire
Council of Trent; he whom the Sacred College had
solicited the Sovereign Pontiff to clothe with the Roman purple, in order that they might be enlightened
by his brilliant talents and Superior knowledge.

Thus is verified what, St. Jane Frances de
Chantal says, ''the penance of a contrite heart is
great when it sees itself kindly dealt with. Let us
blame the offence, but spare the offender.'' St.
Francis of Assissium says the same.

8. When any one has corrected a fault, embrace
him over and over again as your child, forget the
past and treat him as if nothing had happened. In
this way you will heal wounds, without leaving the
vestige of a scar. St. Alphonsus' firmness towards
those who persevered in their faults, was changed
into mercy, when he saw them contrite. He loved
with an exceedingly great love, those in whom his
admonitions were followed by proofs of amendment.
He pressed them to his bosom, forgot their faults and
never again alluded to the pain they had caused him.[1]

''I am informed,'' writes the Saint in his book
''Preparation for Death'' ''that the celebrated Sig-

[1] Life Vol. III, chap. 36.

nore Peter Metastasio has published a little book in
prose, in which he expresses his detestation of his
writings on profane love and declares that, were it
in his power, he would retract them and make them
disappear from the world, even at the cost of his
blood. I am told, that he lives retired in his own
house, leading a life of prayer. This infirmation
has given me unspeakable consolation ; because his
public declaration and his most laudable example,
will help to undeceive many young persons, who seek
to acquire a great name by similar compositions on
profane love. It is certain, that by his retractation,
Signore Metastasio has deserved more enconiums,
than he would by the publication of a thousand poetic
works : for these he might be praised by men, but
now he is praised by God. Hence, as I formerly
detested his vanity in prizing himself for such compositions, (I do not speak of his sacred pieces, which
are excellent and deserving of all praise) *so now I
shall never cease to praise him ; and were I permitted,
I would kiss his feet,* seeing that he has voluntarily
become the censor of his own works, and that he now
desires to see them banished from the whole world,
at the expense, as he says, even of his own blood.''
Would to God, that all Superiors acted in the same
spirit on similar occasions !

9. In the infliction of chastisement, great regard should be paid to the dispositions of subjects.
Sometimes a courteous little admonition, such as the
reproving glance of our Lord at St. Peter, will be
sufficient. Very often it will be very useful to give

the reproof in such a manner that it will appear rather as praise than blame.

If a word chastises, cast the rod away. If a look suffices, have no word to say.

10. If the fault was not public, the punishment may sometimes be entirely omitted. Should, however, the magnitude of the offence, or the necessity of example demand chastisement, it would be well, first, to lay before the Culprit the quality and consequences of his fault, in order to move him to repentance. Should he love his Superior much, it might be a sufficient punishment, merely to dismiss him with a serious countenance saying : "Go !" For one who is much attached to his Superior, this chastisement would be more efficacious than any other.

11. In reproving or punishing any one for a fault, there should not be the least sign of excitement. "A physician who is suffering under delirium or any other violent disorder," says Father Crasset, S. J., "should be first healed himself before he attempts to prescribe remedies for others. A father who corrects a child when he is under the effects of passion, deserves greater chastisement than the Culprit whom he punishes."

12. Neither affection for the guilty person, nor respect for his high position, nor consideration for the services he may have rendered to the Order, should induce a Superior to be less severe in his admonition. St. Ignatius warns Superiors to watch carefully over those, whom every one esteems on account of their high birth or learning ; for such persons

may be either very useful or very injurious to an
Order.

13.   The same Saint says that, if any one commits a rather serious fault, kindly remonstrate with
him the first time, if the fault is repeated, add a
little vinegar to the oil of gentle reproof, and do it
in such a manner, that the delinquent may feel his
guilt and blush at it, but if the fault is committed a
third time, give the offender a public penance.

"The Superior," says St. Alphonsus, "ought to
punish faults committed against the rule, but this
punishment should always be preceded by repeated
admonitions, which must always be most kindly
given."   Hence, he laid down the following rule of
correction for Superiors.

14.   "In the punishment and correction of faults,
the Superior must practise the greatest prudence and
discretion, never using words which would detract
from his dignity, and which might justly offend or
even scandalize his subjects.   Let him always have
the honey of kindness in his mouth and a pruning
knife in his hand, so that he may be rather loved
than feared.   Let him punish publicly, faults committed in public, and secret faults secretly ; but in
such a manner, that having always in view the
greater glory of God, the good of his subjects, and
the preventing of scandal the punishment may be
not only a salutary warning, but also an act of re-
paration to the Community."   i

In general unless prudence requires it otherwise,
the Superior should first kindly and affectionately

admonish the delinquent; then in a friendly manner endeavor to inspire him with confusion for his fault; in a word, the Superior should act so that fear of chastisement may not drive love and confidence from the heart of the offender; otherwise he will cause the fault rather to increase than to be remedied. "I wish," writes St. Frances de Chantal to a Superior, "that you could see me in our recreations, even when I speak in private to our Sisters. I try to be as *sweet and cordial* as possible. I correct *them in this same manner*; because every day experience teaches me better, that we must rarely make serious corrections; they do more good when made with a cordial and animating sweetness; for this manner dilates the heart of the one who speaks and of the one who listens, and sends her away full of courage to do good, and of the sweetness, which she finds in her whom God has appointed to serve her."

With the obstinate and those who relapse into the same faults, the Superior should deal more severely, and where his own authority is of no avail, he should have recourse to that of a Superior of a higher rank. "Extraordinary punishments," says St. Frances de Chantal, should be inflicted only on the obstinate and incorrigible and on those who scandalize a whole Community and do much harm to it; they should be inflicted only after all patient and charitable remonstrances and exhortations have had no effect. But to those who are brought back to a sense of their duty by kind and charitable treatment, I would not give any other penance, unless it be

11

absolutely necessary for the benefit of the Community."

15. If a fault be committed in the presence of the Superior and others, he should not correct the offender on the spot, unless the offence is of such a nature as to call for immediate reproof for the sake of example.

16. If any one should show contempt for his authority, especially in public, he must not fail to punish him, but in doing so let him not confound severity with prudence, and prudence with humility and fraternal charity ; for, his authority, not himself, must be defended.

St. Alphonsus, as we read in his life, was accustomed to give his first reproof mildly and humbly ; if it effected no amendment, he would give a second admonition mildly but sternly ; if this proved useless, then he had recourse to punishment.[1] "The guilty must be punished, it is true," said the Saint, "but they ought to be dismissed so kindly that their amendment will soon follow."[2]

One day St. Gertrude was praying for a person, whose conscience was disturbed, because he feared he was guilty in the sight of God of not bearing patiently enough the negligence of certain individuals, whose bad example might probably lead to the ruin of monastic discipline. Our Lord deigned to instruct St. Gertrude upon this point and spoke to her as follows:

"If any one desires to make of his zeal, an offering acceptable in My eyes and beneficial to his own soul, he must pay attention to three things : *a.* When necessity or charity requires him to give an admonition, let him, by his cheerful and mild countenance, as well as by his words and works, manifest his affection for the guilty person. *b.* Let him not reprove the delinquent at a time and under circumstances that would preclude a hope of amendment. *c.* If his conscience dictates to him the duty of admonishing any one for a fault, let him not be moved by human respect to pass it over in silence, but with a pure intention of increasing the honor of God, and of advancing the salvation of souls, let him consider by what means the fault may be remedied, and then charitably make use of them. If he acts thus, his reward will be proportioned to his endeavors to correct the fault, and not to the success of his endeavors. Should his efforts prove fruitless, it will not be laid to his account, but will rather add to the guilt of him who is not willing to listen to his admonitions."[1]

17. The faults of those, who sin more through weakness and ignorance, than from any other reason, ought to move the Superior to pity rather, than induce him to exercise severity. He should kindly and earnestly encourage them to amend their faults and to avoid relapsing into them.

18. Whether the Superior corrects faults in public or in private, he ought never to make use of opprobrious epithets, such as fool, simpleton and the like. He should speak and act mildly, seeming rather to advise than to reprove, saying, for example : "Does

[1] Life of St. Gertrude, Book III, C. 80.

it not appear to you, that such and such a thing is an abuse? That whoever acts so and so, exposes himself to censure?" This manner of acting is more convincing and effective than any other. Prudence, then, demands that it should be preferred to a more arbitrary course."[1]

19. "In no case ought the Superior to give a reproof when he is excited. His first duty is, to try to restore peace to his own heart, for after that is effected, and not before, will he be in a fit disposition to admonish others. The reason of this is, that all the commandments of God have in view charity and renovation of heart. This twofold aim is lost sight of whenever the Superior exercises his authority with impatience and unkindness. He ought therefore carefully to avoid manifesting his uncharitable feelings."[2]

20. "If a Superior," says B'd B. Alvarez, "is too severe in things of little moment, or too frequently finds fault with his subjects, he will make the yoke of obedience a burden, and his admonitions even in weighty matters, will prove fruitless; for as a corporal remedy proves useless when applied too often, so does the spiritual remedy of correction."

21. If any one is troubled at a reproof or takes it badly, the Superior should not be astonished at this, but ought to have command over himself out of compassion for the offender; considering that it is the devil who disturbs his soul and excites him to discontent. "The Superior should also remember, that those, who have charge of souls, cannot always

[1] Blessed Alvarez.   [2] Blessed Alvarez.

say with St. Paul: "I am innocent of your blood;" that is to say, of the faults this people committed; but we, on the contrary, are frequently guilty both of our own faults, and those of others, either for having corrected too severely, or for having tolerated too much; for having neglected correction, or for not having mingled with it the sugar of holy charity."[1] If the Superior does not succeed in gaining the mastery over himself so far as to bear with the delinquent under the circumstances, he may ruin this soul. In such a case, it is his duty to draw a lesson from his own weakness, and act with meekness and kindness towards the guilty person. It is written, that, as we treat others, so shall we be treated; that God will forgive us, if we forgive those who have injured us. The Apostle gives us the following important lesson: *"Noli vinci a malo, sed vince in bono malum.* Be not overcome by evil, but overcome evil by good."[2]

"Never show yourself astonished," wrote St. Frances de Chantal to a Sister, "at any contradiction or at any occurrence whatever, or at the different states of mind of your daughters. If your daughters should be wanting in submission and humility, you must not, on that account, be wanting in charity for them. Do not be uneasy on account of the faults of your daughters. The Lord has not confided them to your care in order to render them perfect; you have but to teach them in what their perfection consists; if they believe you and profit by their instructions, they will be happy, if they do not, you cannot help

[1] St. Frances de Chantal's Letters.   [2] Rom. XII. 21.

it, it is your duty to plant and to water; the rest must be left to God. Teach every one her duty according to her capacity; you must have patience and advance slowly and be satisfied with the little fruit you get from each one, and be not annoyed at those who may give you none. Proceed with meekness in everything you do, supplicating, remonstrating, and correcting whenever it be necessary and then leave all to God; for He takes more interest in those souls than you yourself. You must never show yourself disgusted with their conduct or despair of their amendment; no, never, this would make them lose all courage and give up altogether; you must encourage and strengthen them by your sweet manners, showing how much hope you entertain of them and how you are pleased in their company and how happy you feel to serve them. This manner of acting increases their courage and spurs them on to serve the Lord with cheerfulness and perseverance. Their conduct will furnish you with occasions to practise thousands of little interior and exterior virtues.

Never permit aversions and ill-feelings to take root in your heart for the faulty; hate only their faults, but bear great compassion and charity to the faulty. Nothing keeps hearts more disunited than mutual diffidence, and nothing keeps them more closely united than mutual confidence. Let them enjoy great and holy liberty among themselves and also with the Superior, for nothing is more detrimental to the minds than keeping them under restraint. In the spirit of cordial charity lead them to see and acknowledge their faults, to make them profit by them. After they have become members of the Order, the shortest way is to bear with them in all charity, for it is easy to talk; there will be such spirits in all Communities, even the smallest; God permits it for the trial of the Superior and the Sisters."

22. After giving a reproof, it is sometimes use_ful to add the following assurance of St. Alphonsus. "As Jesus Christ forgets our faults as soon as we have humbled ourselves for them, so do I forget yours; because, as I hope, you have humbled yourself for them. Let each one be convinced that, if unfortunately he commits a fault, but immediately humbles himself for it from his heart, I also pardon him from my heart, nay more, by this very act of humility he becomes dearer to me than ever. I say this in order that no one may be discouraged at his faults."

23. In order that corrections may be well received and be made with more freedom, a Superior will do well, now and then to show his subjects how difficult and disagreeable it is to correct others; and how on this account good religious, in order to diminish this unpleasantness for the Superiors, would ask of him never to be afraid to tell them seasonably and unseasonably, anything that he might judge necessary and profitable for their spiritual advancement. Moreover, it will be well for the Superior to propose occasionally the following question in a spiritual Conference, namely: How may one know whether he advances in virtue? In the opinion of St. Francis de Sales, one of the best signs and proofs for

this is, if one takes corrections and reprimands well.
To digest hard food easily, is a sign of a good healthy
stomach ; likewise to digest the bitter food of corrections well, is a sign of good spiritual health. To
lend a ready and humble ear to corrections which
make us seriously reflect upon our manner of living,
is an evident proof of our hatred of vice and a sign
that the faults we commit proceed from surprise,
from a want of reflection and from human frailty,
rather than from malice and an obstinate will.

He who loves correction, loves the virtue contrary to the fault for which he is corrected. He resembles a sick person who earnestly wishes to recover
his health ; no medicine is too loathsome, too bitter
for him to take. He who is in earnest about acquiring
virtue which is the fullness of health and the true
soundness of the soul, finds nothing difficult, not
even corrections and severe reproofs in order to attain
to his end.

Reflections like these will easily induce subjects
who have still something of a good spirit, to open the
way of themselves to correction, by asking of their
Superior freely to correct them at any time. "Well,
my dear brother, a Superior may then say, "You
have asked me to correct you whenever I should deem
it necessary—this is the true religious spirit; we
may always remain easy as long as we like correction. I will be then so free as to make the following
observation."

24. If a correction is to be given to persons
whose dignity must be particularly respected, to

priests, for example, it is well to include one's self in the correction, speaking in the first person, of the plural number; according to the manner of St. Gregory when addressing his clergy: "How much do we offend God, my beloved brethren, if we ourselves commit sin, who should prevent others from doing so. We do not seek the salvation of souls, we seek only our own comforts, the praises and honors of men; we give up the cause of God for the sake of earthly occupations; we live in the sanctuary of the Lord, and love but what is transitory."[1]

25. If exterior faults, which are more or less unbecoming and disedifying, are to be corrected in a person who, on account of his age, education, or other circumstances might feel the mortification rather keenly; to spare him this pain, a Superior would do well to tell another religious to commit in the presence of such a person, the very fault which is habitual with him, in order to have the occasion to reprove him for it. If this be noticed by the one who is really guilty, it will cause him to reflect and say to himself: 'It is I who deserve that reproof and penance, more than he; because that fault is habitual with me.' I will take care not to commit it again.

We read of St. Francis of Assissium, that the burning zeal which led him to watch so carefully over the perfection of his brethren, was united to the greatest affection. He always spoke to them kindly and mildly. When he was obliged to censure any-

[1] Hom. 17, in Luca 10.

thing, he acted rather as a father than a judge. He spoke without anger or excitement ; nay, even without raising the tone of his voice, thus manifesting his magnanimity of soul, and peace of heart. The Apostolical power and the paternal kindness with which he was endowed, so won the love and reverence of his children, that they always obeyed him punctually and even anticipated his wishes. He gave the following beautiful maxims to the Guardians of his Order, for their guidance in the correction of others.

26. "Be surgeons, but not torturers. Correct the faults of your subjects with the mildness of a father ; and let not your admonitions be given with the harshness of an enemy.

27. Perfection in the direction of others consists in these five words : watch, love, bear with, and nourish them with the sweet doctrine of Jesus Christ, Whom the Holy Scripture represents under the figure of a lamb.

28. A perfect Superior is an enemy to all transgressions, but a physician, to the transgressors ; he watches over them and seeks means to restore their souls to vigorous health.

29. Guard against listening willingly to those great talkers, who are so quick in observing and reporting the faults of others. They themselves are generally the most guilty, and it is one of their secret artifices to direct the eyes of the Superior to the faults of their neighbor, in order to turn them away from their own.

30. A good Superior never pronounces sentence against any one without giving him a hearing, even though his accuser be a saint. If he acts otherwise, he will expose himself to the danger of committing irremediable faults. "Some Superiors believe what they hear," says St. Alphonsus, "without further inquiry, and instantly reprove and punish the accused; such conduct leads to a thousand evils and disturbances, because the accusation which has been made may be without foundation."

31. I have resigned the office of General, because I desire to correct my children by no other means, than that of my example, and the efficacious mildness of my exhortations. I have no desire to torment them, like the people in the world, who take pleasure in punishing others with severity.

32. A perfect Superior detests the faults of his brethren, but as far as possible, he loves those who are guilty of them. He will at least, by his kindness, try to win and convert them.

33. When any one commits a fault, it is my desire that the Guardian, if he loves God sincerely and as a true son aspires to imitate Him, be satisfied with saying: "My child, you have done wrong : do not act so again."

St. Vincent de Paul made use of the following rules of prudence, in administering reproof.

34. He reproved no one on the spot for his faults : he was accustomed to say, that medicine should not be given to the sick when their fever is high, except in extraordinary cases. He, there-

fore, took time to consider the affair before God, and
to decide upon the best and most useful manner of
making the correction, particularly so, when the fault
was of a serious nature, and the offender of a hasty
temperament. Then, when a favorable moment presented itself, he would, with all humility and confidence, ask the guilty person if he, although
himself full of faults and imperfections, might not
take the liberty of giving him a friendly admonition.

35. In order to gain the affection of the offender,
he first modestly praised his good qualities ; then,
with the greatest delicacy, he placed before his eyes
his fault, reminded him of its unhappy consequences,
and proposed the proper remedy for it. To this he
not unfrequently added, that the remedy was one
which he himself was obliged to make use of to correct his own faults.

36. He never revealed the person who had reported the fault to him. Nay, when he had reason
to fear that the guilty person might easily suspect
the informer and conceive a dislike for him, he made
no reproof at all, because he believed, that peace and
union in a Community ought to be preferred to everything else.

37. He always concluded a reproof with some
encouraging words, saying, that God allowed such
faults in order to humble us, and to increase our
diligence in acquiring virtue.

38. Now and then he used to feign not having
observed the fault at all.

39. At other times he would merely slightly refer to it, as he did on one occasion to a Superior who had repeatedly neglected his orders : 'Your delay,' said he, 'has almost the shade of disobedience.'

40. We must be particular, said he, to watch for a favorable time to admonish the delinquent ; then we must give the admonition kindly and courteously. The second time we may display a little severity and seriousness, but even this should be softened by meekness, and a proper remedy should at once be proposed. The third time the most zealous and energetic language should be used ; and the offender should be informed, that the most severe remedy will be applied if the fault be not corrected.

41. Under certain circumstances, he gave the admonition publicly without naming the guilty person. "This should be done," he said,

a, when the evil is deeply rooted, and it would consequently not be advisable to admonish individuals in particular ;

b, when the offender has a good heart, but is too weak to take the reproof well ;

c, when it is to be feared, that others might commit the same fault, if the warning is not given in public. Excepting these cases, fraternal correction ought ever to be given in private."

"I also recommend to Superiors," writes St. Alphonsus, in his letters, "to give their admonitions in private, because when imparted in public, they are of little avail. I except cases, however, where the fault was public; for then a public reproof would be serviceable to others; nevertheless, it must be admitted, that even then, it is more useful to the offender to admonish him first in private, and then afterwards in public, yet with kind words."

42.   "If necessity obliges us to correct our neighbor," says St. Augustine,[1] we should carefully examine,

a) whether it be for such a fault as we have never committed ourselves.   In this case we should be mindful that we are men and might have committed the same.

b) If we ever committed the same fault, but have succeeded in ridding ourselves of it, we should remember our common weakness, in order that our correction may not be preceded by passion, but by charity.

c) If we are guilty of the same fault, for which we want to reprove our neighbor, we should let the correction alone; we should be very sorry for our fault, and try not to commit it again and induce our neighbor to imitate our example."

43.   "In correcting the aged," says St. Alphonsus, "you must have recourse to entreaties and sweetness, saying : My brother, you know, how much I esteem you ; I entreat you not to violate such a rule ; we are advanced in years, we must give good example to the younger ones."

"The aged," says St. Francis de Sales, "cannot be so easily managed ; they are not so flexible ; for the sinews of the soul as well as of the body have

---

[1] lib. 2 de serm. Domini in monte. C. 20.

grown stiff." Hence to reprove them by way of entreaty is the best for them.

44. "Sometimes it is necessary to feign not having noticed a certain fault;" says St. Alphonsus, "this may be done when the fault is a small one, confined to the person who commits it, and is not easily committed by others. We must leave many things to God, and implore of Him to apply a remedy."

"Do you wish to see a brother corrected? Weep, exhort, embrace his feet, be not ashamed to caress him like a brother, if necessary, if you wish to see him soon amended."[1]

45. "May God preserve you," says St. Alphonsus, "from ever seeking revenge against a brother who has opposed or contradicted you, or who has spoken disrespectfully of you during the time you are in office; guard, I say, against giving him any pain or humiliation on that account; this would cause very great scandal. You should rather, whenever it can be done without scruple endeavor to treat, with particular respect and attention any brother, who may have opposed you. Thus you will please God and give great edification to the Community."

46. Finally, before giving a reprimand, always recommend yourself to our Lord, humbling yourself in his presence by acknowledging, that you are more faulty, and consequently, more blamable and deserving of punishment, than your brother. This lesson was given by our Lord, to St. Magdalene de Pazzi.

---

[1] St. John Chrysostom. Homil. 4 ad pop. Ant.

St. Vincent de Paul says, that those who are spiritually sick, ought to be more tenderly treated, than those who are corporally sick. "I beg you," he wrote to a Superior who had notified him of the desire of a lay-brother to leave the Congregation, "to assist and encourage him to resist the temptation, but do it mildly and affectionately, seeming rather to advise than to reprove him, as is our custom." He also tells us, that although during his whole life, he gave a sharp reproof three times only, yet each time he was forced to regret it, because notwithstanding the apparent just reason for reproving sharply, the correction proved fruitless, while on the contrary, those reproofs which he had given mildly, were always effective.

St. Juliana Veronica occupied the post of Mistress of Novices for several years. During this time she had two novices who were of a head-strong disposition. One of them received her charitable admonitions in such ill part, that they produced not the least amendment. She was therefore expelled by the Chapter. However, St. Veronica obtained for her, from the Blessed Virgin, the grace of being received into another Convent, where she corrected her faults. The other novice forgot herself so far, as to strike her Mistress in the face, and with such violence as to bruise her lips. The holy woman, grieved at the scandal, and at the excommunication which the novice drew upon herself by this act, implored of God so earnestly her amendment, that she shed tears of blood. For a time, the rebellious Sister did better, but her amendment was not permanent. One day, when she was again kindly reproved by St. Veronica for not fulfilling her duty, she felt so terribly provoked, and pushed the Saint so roughly, that she would have fallen, had not those standing near her come to her assistance. The prudent Superior said nothing about the affair at the time, as she knew that a reproof, at the time would be useless, nay, even injurious, because the offender was under the influence of passion. She merely remarked to those who insisted upon the punishment of the novice, that it was necessary to have patience, and that her only grief was, that God had been offended. At the next Chapter, however, she calmly reproved and punished the fault. The fruit of this moderation was, that the delinquent entered into herself, and blushing with confusion at the sin she had committed, performed the penance imposed upon her. From that time forward, she watched so carefully over herself, that she lived and died a true religious.

On another occasion, when St. Veronica was Superior, a Sister had not arranged something in the Church properly. The Saint kindly pointed out her neglect, upon which the Sister answered : "Pay attention to yourself, you do nothing but worry me." "Veronica replied in a gentle, yet dignified tone : "It is your duty to obey and think of nothing else." The Sister continued, however, to murmur. The Superior paid no further attention to her just then, because she saw, it was not a proper time for admonition; but at the next Chap-

12

ter she reproved the offender in a most kind manner.[1]

A short time after Father Lallemant had been appointed Rector of the College of Bourges, the brother baker came to him one day, and rather rudely complained of having too much to do ; he told the Rector to see to the matter and put some one else in his place. The Father calmly listened to him, and promised to relieve him. He then went himself quietly into the bake-house and began kneading the dough with the greatest diligence. After the brother had become calm again, he returned to the bakehouse, and found, to his great surprise, the Father Rector doing his work for him. He immediately threw himself at his feet and begged his pardon, being filled with confusion at his fault, and moved by the meekness and humility of so compassionate a Superior.

Father Lallemant acted thus on all similar occasions, so prudently using lenity that every one readily conceded to him whatsoever he desired. He used to say, that experience daily taught him more and more, that discipline should be kept up in the Company with extreme mildness ; that the Superiors ought to study to make themselves obeyed rather from love than from fear ; that the way to maintain regularity is not by rigor and penances, but by the paternal kindness of the Superiors, and their diligence in attending to the wants of inferiors ; and in preserving and increasing in them the spirit of piety and prayer.

[1] Life of St. Veronica Juliana.

EXAMPLES IN ILLUSTRATION OF WHAT HAS BEEN SAID.

1. One day St. Vincent de Paul heard that one of his priests was too inactive during the missions, and that severity towards the people prevailed over charity in his sermons ; he wrote to him as follows : "I write to you, dear Sir, to inquire your news and to communicate to you ours. How do you feel after your great fatigue ? How many missions have you given ? Do the people seem disposed to profit by your labors ? Do these labors produce the desired fruit ? It would be a great consolation for me to be informed in detail of all you have done. From other houses of the Congregation I have received good accounts, thanks be to God ! Their labors are to their great content blessed with happy results. The strength which God has given to Mr. N. is truly wonderful. For nine months he has been laboring in the country, and his missions, according to the testimony of the Vicar-General, the religious of the place, and others have done incalculable good. This result is ascribed solely, to the mildness and charity with which this gentleman seeks to win the hearts of these poor people. This induces me to recommend more earnestly than ever the practice of these virtues. If God deigned to bless our first missions, it was evidently on account of the kindness, humility and sincerity with which we treated every one. Yes, if God deigned to make use of the most miserable among us, that is of myself to convert sinners and heretics, it was, as they themselves unanimously ad-

mitted, in consequence of the patience and benevolence with which I constantly acted towards them. Even the galley-slaves were won in this manner. When I dealt severely with them, all my efforts were vain, whilst, on the contrary, when I pitied them, praised their resignation, kissed their chains, sympathized with them in their misfortune, or told them, that their sufferings were their purgatory in this life, they listened to me and took the necessary means to save their souls. I beg you, therefore, my dear Sir, to help me to thank God earnestly for these favors and to beg of Him to bestow the grace upon all our Missioners, to act towards every one, privately and publicly, even towards the most hardened sinners, with meekness, charity and humility and never to make use of wounding words, or bitter reproaches, or preach severe sermons. I doubt not, Sir, that as far as you are concerned, you will carefully avoid a manner of acting, which is so exceedingly unbecoming a Physician of souls, and which instead of winning hearts and leading them to God, only estranges and embitters them. Christ, our Lord, is the eternal delight of both Angels and men : we must also try to be the delight of our fellow-creatures, so as to lead them to their eternal happiness.

Thus St. Vincent knew how to draw the attention of his priests to their faults and imperfections, without wounding their feelings. He excused them as far as he could, manifested his love and esteem for them, and reproved so modestly and humbly, that none ever felt abashed or discouraged, but, on the contrary, all were edified and encouraged by his very reproofs.

2. To the Superior of one of his houses, who greatly exaggerated the difficulties of his office, Vincent gave the following answer: "What you write to me is both true and not true. It is true in respect to those who do not like to be contradicted by any one ; who wish every thing to be conducted according to their opinion and will ; who desire to be obeyed by all without opposition or delay, and who would like to see their every command approved of. What you write is not true, however, in regard to those who consider themselves as the servants of others, and who, whilst they perform the duties of Superior, keep constantly in mind their model, Jesus Christ, Who bore with the rudeness, jealousy, want of faith, and other faults of His disciples, and Who said that He had come into the world not to be served, but to serve. You used formerly to go through your duties patiently, humbly, and cheerfully, and I know well that your only design now in using these exaggerated expressions is, to explain your difficulties better and to induce me to remove you from your post of Superior."

3. It was, however, by no means the opinion of St. Vincent, that Superiors should connive at every thing in their subjects. He wished that the guilty should always be reprimanded and even punished, insisting, nevertheless, upon the reproof being given in the spirit of meekness and in accordance with the above quoted principles.

He was once told, that one of his priests, a very zealous man, who at that time was the Superior of a Seminary, treated the Seminarians too harshly. In a letter to this priest, he reproves him in the following manner : "I believe all that you have written, quite as readily as if I had seen it with my own eyes, and I have too many proofs of your zeal for the good of the Seminary, to doubt your words. For this very reason, I have withheld my judgment in regard to the complaints which have reached me of your severe government, until I should have learned from yourself the true state of things. In the meanwhile, I beg of you to reflect seriously upon the manner in which you act, and to resolve to correct, with the help of God's grace, whatever may be displeasing to Him in your conduct. Although your intention may be good, yet the Divine Majesty is offended, and the following are a few of the evil consequences of such conduct.

First, the Seminarians leave the house dissatisfied ; virtue becomes distasteful to them ; the consequence of which is, that they may fall into sin and ruin their souls ; and this, merely because they were, by your severity too soon forced out of the school of piety. Secondly, they talk against the Seminary and are the cause of others not going, who otherwise would have come to receive the instructions and graces necessary for their vocation. Thirdly, the bad reputation of one house easily reflects upon all the others of the Society, paralyzing the members thereof in their ministry, so much so, that the good which the Lord, until now, has deigned to perform by their instrumentality, immediately commences diminishing more and more. To say that heretofore you have not noticed these faults in your own person, betrays, no doubt, a want of humility on your part. For were you possessed of that degree of humility which Jesus Christ requires of Missionary Priests, you would not hesitate for a moment to believe, that you were the most imperfect of all and guilty of all these things. You would attribute to a hidden blindness your not noticing in yourself those defects which are so easily discovered by others, and for which you have already been reprimanded. I have learned, that you do not like correction. Should this be so, Oh! how much should you fear for yourself! How far does your virtue fall short of that of the Saints who annihilated themselves before the world and were rejoiced at seeing their little failings made known to others. Are we not to imitate Jesus Christ, Who notwithstanding His innocence, suffered the bitterest and most unjust reproaches, without even opening His mouth to avert the disgrace from His sacred Person? My dear Sir, let us learn from Him to be meek and humble of heart. These are virtues of which you and I must continually ask of Him, and to which we must always attend, in order not to be drawn away by the opposite passions, which make us destroy with one hand what we have built up with the other. May God enlighten us with His Holy Spirit to discover our blindness and to submit to those Whom He has given us for Guides.''

To the Superior of a mission-house, he wrote as follows: God be praised that you went yourself to do

what Mr. N. refused to do. It was very good that
you preferred doing this, rather than insisting any
longer upon obedience to your command. There are
some people who, although devout and pious, and
having a great horror for sin, will still from time to
time commit some faults through human frailty ; we
must bear with them, and not excite them still
more. As God otherwise blesses this gentleman in
the Confessional, I think we ought to connive a little
at his caprices, so much the more as they are of no
serious nature. With regard to the other priest of
whom you write, I hope that this word has escaped
him from want of reflection, rather than from real
malice. Even the most discreet when surprised by
passion, may say something of which they soon after
repent. Finally, there are men who show aversion
to persons as well as to offices, but who still do much
good. Alas! it cannot be otherwise; live with whom
you please, you will still have something to suffer,
as well as something to merit. I hope, that he, of
whom I speak, will still be gained, if we use towards
him, charitable forbearance and kind corrections. Do
pray for him, as I unceasingly do for your whole
Community.''

To another Superior he wrote: "The priest of
whom you make this report, is a pious man ; he practises virtue, and before he entered our Congregation,
he enjoyed a great reputation in the world. If he
now manifests a restless spirit, meddling with temporal affairs, and those of his family, and thus becomes
a subject of annoyance to his brethren in religion, he

must be borne with in meekness. If he had not this
fault, he would have another ; and if you had nothing
to suffer, you would have no occasion to practise
charity. Your Superiorship would moreover bear
little resemblance to that of our Divine Redeemer
Who chose, for Himself, imperfect and uneducated
disciples, both to manifest His charity and patience,
and to give an example to those who have to direct
others. I beseech you, my dear Sir, to imitate this
Divine Model. From Him you will learn not only
how to bear with your brethren, but also how to treat
them, in order to free them more and more from their
defects. Certainly, on the one hand, we must not
allow, through human interest, evils to increase or
to take deeper root, but on the other hand we must
try to remedy them by degrees and in a charitable
manner."

To a priest who was in company with another on
a distant mission, he wrote thus : "I hope, that the
goodness of God will bless your efforts, especially if
charity and patience reign between you and your
assistant. I beseech you in the name of the Lord, to
see that this be your principal care, because you are
the elder and consequently the Superior; bear, therefore, in patience whatever you may have to suffer on
the part of your companion. Bear all, I say, so as
interiorly to renounce your authority, and to be guided
only by the spirit of charity. By this means Jesus
Christ gained His Apostles and corrected them of
their faults. You also will gain this good Priest by
this means only. Have then a little regard for his

13

character ; do not contradict him at the first moment, though you believe, you have reason for so doing, but wait awhile and then give him a charitable remonstrance. Above all, take great care not to let any one perceive the least difficulty between you and him, for you are exposed to the observation of all, and one single unkind look on your part, if noticed by the people, would make so bad an impression upon them as to paralyze all your labors. I hope you will follow my advice."

If all these admonitions and reproofs were, or seemed to be, of no avail, still, Vincent did not lose courage, but continued to bear patiently, to pray, and to hope, that God would, in the end, show mercy to these strayed sheep. This perseverance he also recommended to others. When Superiors of the different houses requested him to send such and such a priest to another house, he recommended patience to them, reminding them of the common lot of all men, to have faults. If any of his subjects acted otherwise than he had told him, he would say only : "Sir, had you followed my advice, you would have succeeded better in your undertaking." Sometimes he would not say anything at all.

St. Francis de Sales was one evening visited by a nobleman. His servant forgot to put lights in the house, and in the room of the Prelate, so that the Bishop was obliged to accompany the stranger to the gate, in the dark. The only reproof which the Saint made to the servant, consisted in this : "Do you know, my dear friend, that two little pieces of candle would have been of greater value to us to-day than ten dollars?'' Once one of the servants of St. Francis de Sales returned home rather late at night being quite intoxicated. He knocked at the door, but no one answered, all having gone to sleep. The Saint, who alone was still awake, went to open the door, and seeing that his servant was intoxicated to such a degree as not to be able to walk, he took him by the arm and conducted him to his bed-room ; there after having undressed him and taken off his shoes and stockings, he laid him on his bed, covered him well and retired. The Saint on meeting him alone next morning, said to him : "Oh ! my dear friend, you were no doubt, very sick last night." On hearing this the servant fell on his knees, and bathed in tears, begged the Prelate's pardon. The holy Bishop touched by his sorrow, gave him, though a severe, yet a paternal reproof ; he reminded him of the danger to which he exposed himself of losing his soul, and imposed upon him the penance of mixing a certain quantity of water with his wine at table. The Culprit accepted the penance, and was, from that time, so faithful, that he never again committed a similar fault.

"One day," says the Bishop of Belley,—"I was to preach at the Church of the Visitation. Being aware that our Saint would be present, and that a large concourse of people was expected, I felt a little personal anxiety on the occasion, and I prepared in good earnest. When we had retired to his house, and were alone together, "Well," he said, 'you

have given general satisfaction to-day ; people went
away exclaiming, mirabilia ! at your fine and elegant
panegyric.   I only met with one individual who was
not satisfied.'   'What can I have said,' I replied, to
displease this person? Well I have no desire to know
his name.'   'But I, for my part,' said the Saint,
'have a great desire to tell it to you.'   'Who is he
then, that I may endeavor to give him satisfaction?'
'If I had not great confidence in you, I should not
name him ; but as I know you well, I willingly do
so.   Do you see him here?' I looked around, and
saw no one but himself. 'It is you, then,' I said.
'Myself,' he replied. 'Certainly,' I rejoined ; 'I
should have valued your approbation alone more
than that of the whole congregation.'   Thank God,
I have fallen into the hands of one who wounds only
that he may heal! What, then, did you find fault
with ? For I know that your indulgence will not excuse anything in me! 'I love you too much,' he re-
sumed, to flatter you ; and if you had loved our Sisters
after this fashion, you would not have amused yourself in puffing up their minds, instead of edifying
them ; in praising their state of life, instead of teaching them some humiliating and more salutary doctrine.   It is with the food of the mind as with that of
the body.   Flattery is windy ; and windy food, like
vegetables, is not nutritious.   We ought, in preaching, to provide, not empty food, the memory of which
perishes with its utterance, but meat which will endure to life everlasting.   We must never, indeed,
ascend the pulpit, without the special object of build-

ing up some corner or other of the walls of Jerusalem,
by teaching the practice of a certain virtue, or the
means of avoiding a certain vice; for the whole fruit
of preaching consists in making the people do away
with sin and practise virtue. O Lord, exclaimed
David, I will teach the unjust Thy ways, and the
wicked shall be converted unto Thee.' 'What sort of
conversion,' I retorted, could I preach to souls delivered from the hands of their enemies, the devil, the
flesh, and the world, and serving God in holiness of
life?' 'You should have taught them,' he said, 'to
take heed, since they stand, not to fall; to work out
their salvation, according to the Counsel of the Holy
Spirit, with fear and trembling; and not to be without fear, even with respect to sin forgiven. You
described them to us as so many Saints; it costs you
nothing to canonize the living. You must not place
pillows under elbows in this way, nor give milk to
those who need bitter herbs and wormwood.' 'My
object,' I said, 'was to encourage and fortify them in
their holy undertaking.' 'We must encourage,' he
replied, 'without running the risk of exciting presumption and vanity. It is always safer to humble
our hearers, than to exalt them to high and admirable things above their reach. I feel persuaded,
that another time you will be cautious in this
respect.' " "The next day he made me preach at a
Convent of the Nuns of St. Clare. He was present;
and the Congregation was not less numerous than on
the preceding day. I took care to avoid the pit-fall
he had pointed out to me: my discourse was very

simple, both in words and ideas, aiming at nothing except edification. I proceeded with much method, and pressed home my subject. Our Saint, on our return, came to see me in my apartment, which, in fact, was his own; for when I was on a visit to him, he always gave me his room. After tenderly embracing me, he said, 'Truly, I loved you dearly yesterday, but much more to-day.' You are, indeed, quite after my own heart; and if I am not much mistaken, you are also according to God's heart, Who, I believe, has been pleased with your sacrifice. I could not have believed, you would have been so yielding and condescending. It is a true saying, that the 'obedient man shall speak of victory.' You have conquered yourself to-day. Do you know that most of your hearers said, "To-day is very unlike yesterday," and they were not as much pleased this time as the last; but the individual who was not satisfied yesterday, is wonderfully pleased to-day. I grant you hereupon a plenary indulgence for all your past faults. You have fulfilled all my wishes to-day; and if you persevere, you will do much service for the Lord of the vineyard. Preaching must not seek its strength in the words and the notions of human wisdom, but in the demonstration of the Spirit and of power. If you faithfully adhere to this method, God will give to your labors a full and honorable increase; you will become prudent in the words of mystical wisdom, and will possess the science of the Saints, the science that makes Saints. What, after all, do we desire to know, save Jesus, and Jesus crucified."

One day Cardinal Cheverus learned that a parish priest was at open warfare with his parish. He went to the place with the view of re-establishing peace. The pastor in question, was a man of irreproachable life and ardent zeal, but of an excitable disposition which sometimes hurried him beyond all bounds. It was from this defect, that the dispute originated. A child had been brought to him for baptism whose god-mother had neglected to make her Easter communion. Adhering rigidly to ancient regulations, he would not permit her to stand Sponsor, which so exasperated the parents, that they refused to seek a substitute, preferring to leave their infant unbaptized. On his arrival, M. de Cheverus begged the pastor to withdraw his opposition ; but in vain. The Cardinal then directed one of the priests who accompanied him to perform the ceremony, in order that the poor child might no longer remain the victim of a quarrel. Irritated at this beyond all self-control, the pastor gave the most insulting language to his Arch-bishop. The meek Prelate opposed nothing but silence and calmness to the storm. He repaired to the Church, where, he ascended the pulpit and invited all the parishioners to peace and union with their parish-priest, on whom he pronounced an elaborate eulogium, detailing all the good qualities of which he was possessed. 'You have,' he said, "but one complaint to make of him; he has, you say, a hasty and violent temper; alas! my friends, who is without defects? If I were to remain twenty-four hours in your midst, you would perhaps discover so many faults in me,

that you would not be able to tolerate me: you see
but one in your pastor; forgive then that single fault
in consideration of so many virtues." Having finished his discourse the Cardinal went to the Sacristy,
where he found the priest abashed and ashamed, and
embracing him with the utmost kindness, he said:
"My dear friend, I love you with my whole heart;
how shall we begin the service?" seeking by this
means to do away with the recollection of the offence
which had been committed and prove his condescension in regard to everything which was not inimical
to his duty. The service over, the Cardinal called
upon those of the parishioners who were the most embittered against the pastor, and spoke to them so im-
pressively, that they declared themselves ready to do
whatever he wished. The reconciliation was forthwith accomplished; the kiss of peace was given, all
sat down to the same table, and every heart was
united in that of the Arch-bishop. Thus did he
everywhere spread the dominion of charity, and illustrate by his example the words of the Apostle:
"Charity is sweet and patient, not hasty to anger,
but pardoneth and suffereth much.".

St. Alphonsus' manner of correcting may be seen
from the following letter, which he addressed to a
Superior, of his Congregation. "To speak with all
freedom, I remark above all, that I do not believe,
that your Reverence wishes me to treat you with too
much consideration, in regard to obedience and as a
subject, weak in virtue, to whom nothing can be said
for fear of giving offence. I have a better opinion of

your Reverence, and I believe that you desire what is best and most pleasing to God. Now let me tell what I desire to see in you. Your Reverence knows how much I have always esteemed you ; I have given you proofs of this on several occasions. It would pain me very much were I to be told, as sometime ago — that your Rev. is a holy man indeed, but unfit for the Rectorship for the following reasons : — first, because when Superior, you would be seldom at home ; — secondly, that you would at the same time busy yourself with too many affairs, write too many letters, trouble yourself about so many things that would not concern you, and introduce so many devotions to which you seem to be attached, that the regular observance of the rule, would soon suffer. I know of course, and every one acknowledges, that your Reverence does not go out for the sake of pleasure, or for some other similar reason, but from the motive of pleasing God in everything but *ne quid nimis!* Now that you are in the Congregation, and especially now that you have been made Rector, you must be convinced, that you can do nothing more conducive to the glory of God, than to take good care of the wellbeing and regular observance of your Community which is one of the most fervent, nay, even the most fervent of all we have. The number of your subjects being small at present, this regularity cannot be so perfect as yet ; however, you must endeavor to make it as perfect as circumstances will allow. As regards going out, your Reverence knows from your own experience, that if the head be wanting, all the rest is in disorder. Nevertheless, I do not forbid you to go out on an important affair for the good of the house, or the Congregation, or if the greater glory of God is in question ; · but should your Reverence wish to take part in all that contributes to the glory of God in your diocese, you could never be at home. The greatest glory you can render to God is, the accomplishment of His holy Will. I repeat it therefore, henceforth, your Reverence must mind only the good of the house, and the Church, Mater Domini ; and the regular observance of the rule, that none of the things may come true which some have predicted of your Reverence. I speak with all charity, because I esteem you, and esteem you very much, and because I have a good opinion of you, trusting that you belong to the number of those who endeavor to sanctify themselves in the Congregation like Fathers Cafaro, Villani, Mazzini and others, who have renounced their own will ; and that you do not resemble those who wish to be treated too delicately, and whom I will treat thus, but of whom I foresee that they will never sanctify themselves, because they do not obey blindly."

CHAPTER VIII.

ST. FRANCIS DE SALES, A TRUE MODEL OF A SUPERIOR.

T would be difficult to find a better model and one easier to imitate than St. Francis de Sales. It seemed to him, as he said on one occasion, that God only truly loved poor sinners and knew how to compassionate and forbear with them in all their infirmities. To him may be fitly applied what St. John tells us in the Apocalypse, viz: that he saw an immense multitude of men having a lamb sitting in their midst, which guided them with such great ease, that there appeared something divine in it. Now, the holy Bishop of Geneva was so meek and amiable, that every one obeyed him with that ready obedience which would be given to a Seraph. It may be said, that, as he neither refused nor commanded anything, his people tried to anticipate his wishes, and never asked a favor of him which he could not conscientiously grant. The government of his diocese was no burden to him. He had time to write books, to found a religious Order, to reform others, to keep up a correspondence with thousands, to preach twice a day, to speak with every one: yet all this he did so quietly, that it seemed as if he had nothing to do: So true it is, that meekness can accomplish all things!

1. He used to say pleasantly, that all things were possible to him, that he could do whatever he wanted; because, he wished nothing but what God willed, he expected nothing from men but what their weakness allowed them to do. If they could not comply with his desires in a day, they would be able to do so in a month, or, at least, in a year, and he must wait for them.

2. If a religious was praised in his presence, for being very mild and virtuous, he asked whether he had ever held an office or was, at the time, burdened with one; "for," said he "many practise virtue, as long as they have nothing to do and have no burden but their own to carry. To speak in strict accordance with truth, this in many, is not so much a virtue, as a desire to avoid detection and ridicule. But, if a religious is put to the trial, if he has an office which obliges him to guide and endure others; then it will be seen, whether he possesses virtue,—true charity to bear the weakness of his inferiors, real humility to suffer contempt, — prudence to wait for a favorable time to do what duty requires, and to suppress that false and perverse zeal which is nothing else than masked impatience. This is the test of true virtue, otherwise, I have very little confidence in it, for I often perceive, that an inert disposition is looked upon as virtue. I am amused at those who are always ready to give advice, but who do not know how to follow it.

3. One day, he was accused of having yielded to anger. He answered : "I am, it is true, a miserable creature and subject to passion ; but, by the grace of God, since I was consecrated Bishop, never have I said an angry word to my people."

The meekness of St. Francis de Sales was not, however, that false meekness practised by worldlings through politeness, which consists in a few gracious words and actions. It was that genuine meekness that proceeds from the heart and is, as it were, the flower of love, which fills the soul with tenderness, condescension, and compassion, and manifests itself exteriorly by a graciousness of manner and wisely-tempered demeanor, — the fruit of a holy affection. Nor was his meekness, that bashful and awkward reserve, which sometimes passes for virtue. Much less did it partake of the nature of that apathetic indifference, which is disturbed at nothing, because it feels nothing, which hates nothing, because it loves nothing, and which always yields, because everything is alike to it. His meekness was full of life, but, at the same time, serious and discreet. It seldom descended to caressing marks of affection ; "for," said he, "we must not be lavish of such things, or make use of sweet words on every occasion, bestowing them in profusion upon the first one we meet." In a word, his meekness was characterized by nobleness, dignity, and majesty, producing, upon those who were brought in communication with him an effect in which piety, love and reverence were equally blended. This virtue was exteriorly manifested by the serenity of his

countenance, the affability of his manners, the graciousness and mildness of his words, which made everything he said agreeable.

4. "My Lord," said some one to him, "you go
too often to Geneva, to see that old fool of a Beza, who
is so ill-disposed to listen to your Conferences. Indeed, to speak plainly, your condescending and friendly manner towards him, scandalizes us. Why do you
not use this time for other business of the diocese,
of which you are now the Provost and will some
of these days be the Bishop? Why do you not rather
spend your leisure in conversing with so many good
souls to whom you would certainly do more good?"

"Ah!" was the answer, "do you not remember,
that Jesus Christ, our Master, said, he had come into
the world not so much for the just, as for the sinners?
If, therefore, in imitation of our Saviour, we ought to
seek after those who are the most deeply immersed in
error, why should I not do for Beza and all like him,
everything that a Minister of the Gospel can do in
this world? He is a wandering sheep: ought I not to
snatch him from the jaws of the wolf and bring him
back to the fold? I would rather renounce every other
dignity, though a thousand were offered me, than
give up the care of the salvation of sinners and the
honor of bearing with their weakness and imperfection."

5. "But, my Lord, you are entirely too kind
and forbearing: the wicked abuse your goodness and,
in all probability ridicule it. The very worst seem to
be the most welcome with you. You embrace them

as if they were your dearest children ; and, yet, you very well know how bad they are." "Ah!" exclaimed he, "how agreeable it is to be blamed for being too meek! Why does God the Father allow Himself to be called .the God of Mercy? Why did the Word made Flesh assume the name of a meek lamb, and why did the Holy Ghost appear in the shape of a dove, the symbol of meekness? Had there been anything better than this divine virtue, surely Jesus Christ would have taught it; and, yet, He recommends only two points to us. "Learn of Me that I am meek and humble of heart." Would you, then, hinder me from imitating in the most perfect manner, a virtue so highly esteemed and taught by God Himself? Do you think, that we are wiser than God?"

6. "It seems to me," said he, "that I love nothing but God and the souls of men, for God's sake. All that is not God or for God, is nothing to me. O, when will we see our fellow-creatures in our Saviour's heart? He who considers them in any other light, runs the risk of not loving with a pure, constant and unvarying love. But in this divine heart, who could not love his neighbor? Who would not be willing to bear with him, to put up with his imperfections? Who would become tired of him or find him a burden?" To help and serve his fellow-men, was the holy Bishop's constant occupation. "It has pleased God" he used to say, "to mould my heart in this manner. Oh! yes: I desire to love my dear neighbor so very, very much! O, when will our hearts be overflowing with meekness and love for our fellow-men? To them

I have devoted my body and every pulsation of my
heart, so that they may make use of them according
to their wants."

7.   "I feel so great a joy in loving my enemies,"
he once said, "that were God to forbid my doing so,
it would be hard for me to obey Him."   As the
greater number of the persons who claimed his kindness and attention, were of the female sex, his former
preceptor, the Abbé Déage, warned him that such
frequent visits from women, would prove injurious to
him, that it would give room for malicious tongues to
talk, &c.   To this, the holy Bishop answered: "God,
Who is Charity itself, has given me an office which
calls for the practice of this virtue.   In it, I am the
debtor of all, but particularly of the weak and infirm.
My Saviour knows that His love alone influences my
every action.   So long as I keep close to Him, His
Almighty hand will uphold me.   A reed in God's
hand becomes a pillar of the temple."

On another occasion, Mr. Déage remarked to
him, that he could not understand why the women
ran after him so, since he did not say much to them.
"Ah!" replied the holy Bishop with a smile, "do
you think it nothing, then, to let them talk.   Ears
to listen to them, are needed more than a mouth to
speak to them."

"We ought," said he, "to listen quite as willingly to persons of low condition, and be as ready to
help them in their difficulties, as in the case of the
rich.   If a soul is troubled only about a trifle, we
ought, nevertheless, to try to comfort it.   The little

troubles of poor people are great troubles to them :
and, besides, it is no insignificant matter to console a
soul redeemed by the precious blood of Jesus Christ.''

. 8. From the following example we shall learn
how he dealt with hasty and choleric dispositions.
A young nobleman became enraged at some supposed
offence offered him by St. Francis. After giving
vent to his anger by creating a great noise and disturbance in front of the holy Prelate's house, he went,
at last, to his room. There, he reviled the saintly
Bishop by every disgraceful expression that rage could
suggest. Looking mildly at his abuser, (who stood
before him foaming with anger) St. Francis answered
not a single word. The young nobleman considered
this silence as a mark of contempt, became still more
enraged, and gave full vent to his passion. The
Bishop continued calm and silent. When the bold
intruder had withdrawn, a witness of the scene asked
the holy man how he had been able to keep silence on
such a provoking occasion. ''My friend,'' was the
answer, ''my tongue and I have made an inviolable
contract with each other, agreeing that whilst I am
under the influence of excited feelings, it will never
utter a word. The excitement over, it is free to say
what it pleases. How could I have better taught
this young nobleman to speak kindly and properly,
than by being silent? And by what means could I
have sooner and more easily subdued his anger, than
by silence? After the lapse of a few hours, he will regret his behavior and come to beg my pardon.
Should he not do so, I will beg his, and this from my

14

heart. Ought we not to be merciful to a poor fellow-creature, who is such a slave to passion? If God were to strike us with death when we are in the heat of passion, what would we think of it? It is an acknowledged fact, that no one ever regretted being silent, whilst many often feel remorse for having spoken."

9. "One day," says St. Frances de Chantal, speaking of St. Francis de Sales, "I represented to him, that he had spent too much time, in talking with a person possessed of very little judgment or consideration. He replied: "I am the debtor of all, of the wise and of the foolish."

On another occasion, she reproached him for having held a long conversation with a poor man, about a trifling matter, which she termed nonsense. He answered: "What appears a piece of nonsense to you, is for these poor people of great importance."

When it was remarked to him, that it seemed like money and time lost, to bestow alms and kindness on persons who would not go to confession and amend their lives, he replied: "Human misery is so great, that we should always have compassion upon it and never despair of any one's conversion."

"Men," said he, "ought to be patient with one another. Those are the most courageous, who can best bear with the foibles of their fellow-creatures. This mutual endurance of imperfections, constitutes in a great measure perfection and is one of the best means to practise fraternal charity. It is easy to love persons of an amiable and attractive disposition: but to bestow affection upon those who are obstinate, ill-humored, and irritable, is the touchstone of charity. We ought also to be kind and gentle towards our neighbor, when he proves burdensome and disagreeable to us, for then we are sure that there is nothing in him to excite our love. Consequently, loving him only for the love of God, our charity is more sublime and meritorious, because it is pure and free from human respect.''

In his writings, as well as in his Conferences, the holy Bishop insisted particularly upon certain virtues, which, he said, were not well enough known and valued. These were sincerity, patience, courteousness, kindness, and forbearance with the faults of others. He considered it an error for any one to imagine that he was capable of doing great things for his neighbor, when he could not patiently bear with the untimely intrusion of ill-mannered, cross-grained, rude, and particularly, tiresome people. Influenced by these principles, he bore with everything from all indiscriminately, never causing pain to any one; and he recommended every one to act in like manner. For this reason, he would never tolerate detraction, from any person whatever. When the faults of others were mentioned in his presence, he was accustomed to excuse them, saying: ''Had a fault a hundred sides, we ought to look only at the least displeasing one.'' When he could not excuse the fault, he would exclaim: ''O, how great is human misery! 'Sciant gentes quoniam homines sunt.' Let the nations understand, seeing they are men! How violent, too, are temptations!

Through how many critical moments has not the heart
of man to pass!'' Again, he would say: ''Without
the protecting grace of God, we might have done
worse, — perhaps, we would already have been in hell!
They may yet be converted and become great Saints.
St. Augustine and holy David are proofs of this.''
Again: It is strange that so many have the love of
chastity and yet so few possess the chastity of love;
that is, true, genuine, pure love, which is the queen,
mother, and soul of all the other virtues.''

He did not wish any one to be disturbed at improper conversations, that might arise in company,
without his concurrence. ''In company with others,
be not disturbed,'' he says, ''at what is said or done.
If it is anything good, thank God for it: if it is bad,
then you have an opportunity to serve God by turning
your heart from it, without showing either surprise or
displeasure at it. You cannot remedy the evil, neither
have you the authority to put a stop to it. Therefore
an effort to do so, might induce the offenders to say or
do still worse. By acting in this manner you will remain uninjured by the hissing of the serpent.'' He
would not even have us think those damned, who had
led bad lives. ''Final perseverance does not depend
upon our merits. God has reserved for Himself the
knowledge of those on whom it is bestowed.''

10. Sometimes it happened that Apostates
would fly to the holy Bishop of Geneva for refuge,
and cast themselves into his arms. He received them
with open heart, as his lost children. ''Come, come,
my children,'' said he, ''come to my arms! God will

yield to despair: with our Lord's help, everything
will be right again." Some were scandalized at his
acting in this manner. They said, that he thus
eulogized wickedness and suffered it to go unpunished,
which would be followed by bad consequences. "Ah!"
was his answer, "are they not my sheep? My Saviour
gave them all of His blood: how could I refuse them
my tears? They, whom you now look upon as wolves,
will, by degrees, become lambs: nay, the day will
come, when they will be greater Saints than any of
us. Had Saul been rejected, we never would have had
Paul. Have a little patience and charity. For my
part, I would rather send them to purgatory, than to
hell. Tell me, I pray you, to whom ought we to be
merciful, if not to sinners? God sends them to me, so
that I may heal them and draw them from the abyss
of perdition. Would you have me thwart the designs
of God? Ah! my heart is not hard enough to harbor
so little love and pity. I will be lost with them, or
try to save them. They are my dearest children. As
their Bishop, I know it is my duty to admonish them
somewhat severely; but I prefer to treat them with
the tenderness of paternal love. He who is in favor
of severity, need not expect a hearing from me: I will
not enlist in his party, for it is my firm resolution,
not to be severe."

11. One day he was asked whether it might be
allowed to wish for a faultless Superior, one who would
be an unspotted mirror for all. The Saint gave the
following clear and simple answer: Such an impos-

sibility ought not to be desired, or else the wish should be accompanied by a prayer, that Almighty God would send down from heaven such a one.   It is rank heresy, to consider a man in this world faultless : and even supposing that God would deign to send to us from heaven such a so-called guiltless creature, voices would be raised against him, and justly could it be said with the olden sage : 'In hoc errat quod nunquam errat— He errs because he never errs.' What confidence would be placed in such a man? Would it not be said of him, that he knows nothing of human weakness? St. Peter committed a great fault, nevertheless, he was chosen to be the head of the Church.   Cast, then, your eyes rather on the virtues of Superiors, than on their faults.   The weaker and more miserable thep are, the more meritorious will be your obedience.''

12.   ''My Lord,'' was it said to him, ''you have often declared that a Superior ought to have a tender, affectionate heart ; that you consider this absolutely necessary, to render him capable of directing and governing souls properly and of winning their love.''   He replied : ''One must have a father's or a mother's heart, or rather, the two united, in order to understand what a tender heart is.   That agonized mother, whose every feeling of love asserted its power, when Solomon decided that her child should be cut in two, and divided between her and the pretended mother, could better explain this, than I.   It is learned, not from rule and principle, not from the golden words of eloquence, but from the exercise of sincere and heartfelt affection, which love awakens in our innermost

soul. The father of the Prodigal Son could also tell you what it is. He received his child with open arms, with tearful eyes, and a swelling heart, which was overflowing with love and joy at the Wanderer's return.

"Therefore the tender love of a good Superior consists in this:

First: His heart ought to be so very affectionate, as to be always ready to pardon and excuse the faults and imperfections of his subjects.

Secondly: This love of the heart should be manifested by kind and gentle words, which will impart such a charm to everything he says or does, as to satisfy and please each and all.

Thirdly: He should never utter a harsh or imperious word. On the contrary, he ought to assume and preserve a kind and amiable countenance, beaming with mildness and love, so as to cheer and encourage his brethren. He ought, above all things, to guard against those fierce and sullen looks, which of themselves repel and refuse a petition, as in the case of those who grant a favor so unwillingly, that the recipient does not even thank them for it.

Fourthly: His manner of conversation should always be mild, calm, sincere, simple and unaffected; for where there is constraint, there is no affection, as we learn from the teachings of the Holy Ghost and the grace of Jesus Christ."

13. Our Saint possessed all this in the most perfect degree. Many flattered him, others showed him the greatest marks of respect, whilst some, on

the contrary, threatened his life and heaped injuries upon him. But sincerity, love, and serenity constantly shone upon his countenance. His kind and innocent eyes, his moderation in speech, his personal consideration, in fine, his whole exterior, produced so powerful an effect, that but few words were necessary to transform these wolves into lambs. "Gentlemen," was he accustomed to say to the flatterers, "I know myself better than you know me. Francis de Sales is a miserable creature ; of this God and my Confessor are aware. Our Lord and His angels rejoice at the return of a sinner, and should not I be glad when a poor, unfortunate man throws himself into my arms, after having caused me so great care and trouble? We might almost say, that Jesus Christ showed more love, to sinners than to the good, since in His mortal life He was pleased to welcome them, eat with them, and work miracles for them, so that He might have an opportunity to pardon them. Thence we must conclude, that if we desire to gain the hearts of others, we should guide and govern them mildly and affectionately."

14. "My Lord," asked some one of him, one day, "how are those to be governed who are constantly falling into the same faults, after repeated admonitions? "How must we act in such circumstances?" replied he. "We must do as Jesus Christ has taught, namely, we should forgive, not only seven times, but seventy times seven times, and in case of necessity, seven hundred thousand times, and seven million times, and even as long as eternity lasts.

If God bears with them, why should not man? Will it not suffice, if they be at last converted? And, even should this not occur, are we excused from making use of every means in our power, to lead them back to the right path? Am I not Bishop rather for sinners than for Saints, who do not need my assistance? Is not the shepherd placed over the fold for the sake of the wandering sheep? For whom is the physician for the sick or for the healthy? Did Jesus Christ, come for the just or for sinners? Charity is not to be extended so much to the good, who stand in no need of our help, as to the wicked. Nor is humility as necessary in the praise and honor bestowed upon us by the good, as in the revilings of the bad. Few understand how to guide men according to the Spirit of God."

15. One day he saw a shepherd, running over mountain and valley in pursuit of one of his flock, which was fleeing from him, springing over the precipices in its way. The poor shepherd ran over the ice and through the snow, and at last fell into a deep chasm. Another shepherd sprang after him, to try to save his life; but his efforts were vain. The poor man was already dead and stiff with the cold. The holy Prelate heaved a deep sigh, saying: "My God, what a beautiful lesson for a Bishop or Superior! This poor shepherd has sacrificed his life, to save a stray sheep, and I, alas! have so little zeal for the salvation of souls! The least obstacle suffices to deter me and make me calculate my every step and trouble. Great God! give me true zeal and the

15

genuine spirit of a good shepherd! Ah! how many shepherds of souls will not this herdsman judge!"

16. One day, he was told, that a certain Prelate never tired reading his books and speaking well of him. "Sir," was the answer, "this Prelate would please me much better, were he to read me, as I am. I know Francis de Sales better than any one in the world does. My heart and my Confessor are the two witnesses of my misery. It is my opinion, that a good Bishop or Superior ought not to pay the least attention to what is said of him. Neither should he take pleasure in the good opinion which others have of him, or in the reputation won by the little good he may have done. This dazzles him and obscures self-knowledge. The best resolution he can take, is to meditate upon his faults in all sincerity of heart. A man who believes everything he does, to be well done, and who thinks that he commits no faults, or very slight ones, is a shepherd who feeds himself, and not his sheep, a person who gives himself much trouble and gains nothing. Consequently, since he his faithless to his trust, the blessing of God will not rest upon him and his labor. The greatest treasure of a Superior, is that deeply rooted humility, which ascribes to God all the good that is done, and to itself all the faults that are committed by self or others. Those who boast of always being in the right, are very suspicious characters. They are like those persons who look steadily at the sun in broad mid-day. They believe everything they see to be a sun; but the by-standers know that they are

looking at nothing but thorns, filth, and worthless objects. So it is with the would-be-impeccable. Their eyes are overflowing with light; but it is the blinding light of self-love."

17. Whilst he was in Paris, invitations to preach, poured in upon him. His mornings and evenings were equally engaged. A priest remarked to him: "My Lord, you are absolutely killing yourself. Excuse me for saying that you are over-burdened with sermons." Smiling, he took the hand of the kind remonstrator, and said: "Father, I assure you, it is easier for me to deliver a sermon, than to say no. Since God has made me a Bishop and preacher of His word, is it not but just that I should work at my trade? But I am really astonished at Paris making so much of me; since my tongue is so heavy, my ideas so simple, and my preaching so common-place. You yourself are aware of this. You know that I speak the truth: and tell me, are you not yourself surprised, at seeing so many of the good Parisians at my sermons?" "Do you think, my Lord, that all these people can hear your beautiful discourses? It is enough for them to see you in the pulpit. Your heart speaks through your countenance and eyes, and were you to say only four words, they would be satisfied with the sight of a man like you. Your seemingly heavy tongue makes so much the deeper impression; your simple, home-spun expressions burning with the fire of love, penetrate into the heart and soften it; and there is an extraordinary something in your words, which cannot be defined.

Each one of them has its own weight, each forces its
way into the soul, each one makes a strong impression. You say nothing, and yet everything is said.
Another might talk four times as much as you, and
yet produce no effect. It would be useless, because
no one would attend to it. You are master of a certain Savoyard or heavenly rhetoric, which brings
forth the most wonderful fruit." Here, St. Francis
de Sales embraced the good Priest Father Binet,
S. J., and smilingly enforced silence upon him in
this point. When he could not help refusing, the
manner in which the refusal was given, made it
doubtful whether the petitioner had met with a disappointment or received a favor.

18. One of his maxims deserves to be held as
an oracle from Heaven. "As sugar seldom spoils
anything," said he, "so it is with meekness: and
even should a fault happen to be committed in the exercise of this virtue, it will be free of blame in the eyes
of God, or it will lead to such good, that what the
Church sings of the sin of Adam, may be applied to
it. "O happy fault, which brought down from
heaven the Redeemer of the world, and with Him a
superabundance of happiness !" On the contrary, a
harsh and repulsive manner produces little good and
much evil. It closes the heart, excites hatred, spoils
and even destroys the good that is already done. It
makes a man so disagreeable, that no one thanks
him for a favor, or even feels an obligation of acknowledging a service." He tells us the surprising
fact, that for three whole years he studied the virtues

of the Heart of Jesus, humility and meekness, and, yet at the end of that time, was not satisfied with the practical knowledge which he had acquired. If he, who was amiability and kindness itself, spent entire years in such an exercise and yet believed that he made so little progress in the practice of these virtues, what will they do, whose hearts are full of thorns, whose actions are rude and repulsive, who have none but bitter words in their mouths, whose countenance inspires fear, and whose whole demeanor is arrogant and magisterial? How can such persons imagine themselves to be capable of governing others, when they cannot even master a miserable little passion? This holy Bishop will judge many a Superior and servant of God.

He was accustomed to receive everybody with unparalleled kindness, even priests of bad reputation. Many blamed him for this and took scandal at it. Our Saint only smiled and said. "Is it not better to lead them gently to the purgatory of a good penance, than roughly to cast them into the hell of black despair and final impenitence? Think you that severity would lead those to purgatory, who would scarcely be willing to purchase heaven by submission to such rough dealing, which must, indeed be quite intolerable to a heart already tortured by a thousand fears? I find no better remedy against the impatient swellings of the heart, which pass under the name of zeal, than a gentle, unreproachful silence. For, however little we may say, there is in it too great a mixture of self-love, and so many thoughtless words escape us, that for twenty four hours afterwards, the heart is embittered by them. If we say nothing, but let the evil wind blow over, then be assured, anger and impudence will stand amazed, and the heart will ere long overflow with joy.

"Another thing which must naturally be unpleasant and burdensome to Bishops and Superiors, is when a thousand persons and things appear together, or come in quick succession one after the other, each demanding a prompt hearing and settlement, without leaving one time to breathe. But I have made a covenant with my heart and tongue, and I do as Job did, when one servant after another came to him, bringing bad news. He spoke to each of them; and when two talked together, he answered both at once. This trial is presented to us by our Lord, in order to see whether we are prepared to meet any attack. There are some children who are always running after their mother. A hen is never angry when its young ones run all together under its wings. On the contrary, she spreads them out as wide as she can and covers the little chickens as far as she is able. It seems to me, that my heart enlarges in proportion as these good people increase, and I have so accustomed myself to look upon them all as my children, that one is as dear to me as another."

19. The Bishop of Belley having one day remarked to St. Francis de Sales, that too great familiarity with such people ought to be avoided, since, according to the old proverb, familiarity breeds contempt, the holy man answered: "It is true, that

gross familiarity is to be blamed, but not that which
is polite, kind, chaste, and virtuous; for, since it
proceeds from charity, it produces true love, which
is never devoid of esteem, and consequently, never
wanting in reverence. There is no one for whom we
feel greater reverence, or whom we would more fear
to displease, than a person whom we love with our
whole heart. We ought always to be mindful, that
our servants are our brethren and our poor fellow-
creatures. Charity obliges us to love them as ourselves. Let us then love these dear brethren who
are so closely connected with us, dwelling under
the same roof, and let us treat them as we
would wish to be treated, if we were in their
place."

He was accessible to all, we are told by his
biographers, to the bold and importunate, as well as
to his best friends. He received the crowds who
visited him, with a holy joy and admirable cheerfulness. Never did he suffer the clouds of lassitude or
aversion to darken his countenance. If unimportant
matters were spoken of, he listened with as much
earnestness, as if he were incapable of discussing
weightier subjects. If important things were the
subject of conversation, he gave that attention to
them, that seemed to deny the fact of his ever having
taken part in the discussion of trifles. He listened
with pleasure, and preferred every one to himself.
He gave full scope to the talents of others, without
ever attempting to bring his own superior endowments to light.

20. Whoever wishes to see the spirit of this great Saint, as it were, in a mirror, need only read the rules he wrote for the Order of the Visitation. In them, there is nothing but sincere affection, child-like simplicity, maternal love, incredible forbearance and condescension, the most extreme meekness and charity, compassionate indulgence for the weakness of others: in a word, they breathe the fervor of divine love and invincible patience. It is easily seen, that in the same ecstacy in which he was told that he was to be the founder of a religious Order, he was inspired with this divine manner of making the direction of souls a less burdensome charge, than it had hitherto been. His tears were his weapons. His commands assumed the form of gentle and amiable petitions, so that no heart could withstand him. His great principle was, to ask for nothing and to refuse nothing. But this maxim may truthfully be divided into two parts. We may say that he, indeed, never asked for anything, but that, at the same time, nothing was ever refused to him, when it was known that he liked it. His servants loved him as their father. He never spoke harshly to them, and they, in their turn, strove day and night to serve him with filial love. He was also wont to say, that pure and genuine charity is more readily recognized in services done to the imperfect, than to others, that it is better to exceed in kindness and charity, than in that false and perverse zeal, which is often nothing but impatience.

21. One who has not a generous heart, will never make a good Superior. Narrow hearts are

drowned in a glass of water; whereas, generous ones sport in the deepest oceans. As soon as an inferior has committed a blame worthy fault, a narrow-minded Superior tries to get rid of him. He finds a thousand reasons to send him elsewhere. Now, this is sheer weakness and betrays a cowardly heart and little virtue. A generous-hearted Superior is surprised at nothing. He never wishes to get rid of any one. His heart is large enough to receive all. He believes that, since God has given these imperfect subjects to him, it is precisely in this point, he ought to prove his fidelity to his charge. Would it not be strange, to see a physician run off at the sight of a sick man, or a shepherd take to flight on the approach of a wolf? Some may say, that they are willing to direct those who perform their duty, but that they cannot burden themselves with the care of the troublesome. Such persons will never make good Superiors; for he who cannot steer a ship in stormy, as well as in calm weather, is not a good pilot.

O how many there are, who, under the pretence of humility and amiability, prove faithless to God and rob themselves of merit in His eyes!

22. St. Francis, however, did not wish that under the pretext of kindness and mildness, faults should be allowed to slip into religious communities or suffered to go unpunished, without any effort to restrain the boldness of the prevaricator. He desired meekness and severity to be prudently blended, according to necessity. He says: "Towards effeminate and selfish souls, we ought to act with determination,

always opposing such false delicacy of feeling where-
ever it may appear and ever guarding against its
appearance. However, this is not to be confounded
with corporal infirmity. Where it is evident, that
the weakness is natural, the greatest compassion
should be felt, particularly for such as commit faults
through surprise or mere human frailty, without
malice. Too great tenderness towards self, either
with regard to soul or body, is a fault, which is quite
as detrimental to steadfast piety, as precipitation.
Both are marks of great self-love: consequently, we
ought ever to be on our guard against them." St.
Gregory says: "Be affectionate, but not weak; strict,
but not repulsive, compassionate, but not to such a
degree as to lose your authority."

Whilst St. Francis de Sales was one day deliver-
ing a sermon, he noticed in the Church a young
man, who was behaving very badly, and, among
other acts of boldness, constantly peering into the
face of a young woman. Such demeanor was so painful to the holy preacher, that giving free vent to his
zeal, he cried out: "What! would you make of the
house of God a robber's den? If you do not cease
your improper conduct, I will point to you with my
finger, and thus draw the attention of all present,
upon you. Were I alone concerned, you might pass
unnoticed; but there is question of the honor of
God, a thing too dear to my heart, to suffer me to
leave anything undone, to keep every one within the
limits of duty." According to necessity, he could
be as zealous as Elias, and as courageous as a lion.

In his communication with the Pope, the King of France, or the Duke of Savoy, he spoke freely and uninfluenced by human respect. He would have God honored as God, and he was ever ready to give up life, honor and property for His service. This made him so great a mirror and model for Bishops and Superiors.

23. Having, one day, taken for his text the following words: "But if any man strike thee on thy right cheek, turn to him the other also"[1] on leaving the Church, he was publicly accosted by a Calvinist in a very rude manner. "Since you tell us, that when one cheek is struck, the other should be presented, that is, doubtless, the cause of both of yours being red. But, tell me, if I were now to give you a box, would you really practise what you have just been teaching? It is more probable that you are of the number of those who—say and do not.[2] "My friend," answered Francis, "I know very well what I ought to do, but I do not know what I might do, for I am a miserable creature. I put my trust in the grace of God, Who can turn a frail reed into a firm pillar. But if proving unfaithful to grace, I should not happen to bear the insult in a christian manner, the Gospel teaches, in the very place just quoted by you, where it blames the preacher for not practising what he preaches, that my words and not my works are to be followed." "But," objected the Calvinist, "our Saviour did not offer His other cheek to the servant of the high-priest, when he was struck by him."

[1] Matth. 5, 39.   [2] Matth. xxiii. 3.

"Would you, then, reckon our Saviour among those who do not observe what they teach?" asked Francis. "God preserve us from thinking thus of Him Who is the model of all perfection ! All His works are perfect, and we have no right to blame any of them or demand an account of them. Nevertheless it is easy to imagine the reason why our Lord did not offer His other cheek. Burning with zeal for the salvation of that impious man, he wished to move him to repentance, by drawing his attention to his fault. Later in His Passion, He practised most perfectly the counsel which He had given ; for He presented not only His cheek, but His whole face, to the blows and spittle of the rabble, and His entire body to the scourgers." The Calvinist was satisfied with this answer, but the Catholics present, were not so, by any means. They would have rather heard the holy Apostle sharply rebuke this bold young man for his insolence : but the Saint was far from being of their opinion. The words of the Calvinist would have been still bolder, had Francis de Sales been less mild in his answers. He avoided everything that could, in the least, wound heretics, never making use of an injurious or degrading word to them. Never, in the pulpit or elsewhere, did he speak of them in an angry or contemptuous manner. Instead of alienating their hearts, by throwing ridicule on them in the refutation of their errors, he tried rather to win them by laying before them, first, the truth, and then the beauty of Catholicity ; and this he did so mildly and politely, that they could not help seeing how much he loved them.

24. He treated controversial points so delicately, that it was difficult to perceive that they were such. His manner of proceeding was as follows.— He represented the truth in its genuine simplicity, and he so naturally extolled the grace and beauty peculiar to it, that all hearts were irresistibly won. And yet, it seemed all the while, as if he were only proving and elucidating his subject. The objections which he raised, he solved so easily and with so clear and simple an explanation ; that all difficulties disappeared, without even the semblance of opposition. Then, he passed on to such pious reflections and thoughts as the subject naturally suggested, and it was in this principally his hopes rested : "for," said he, "my experience of thirty-three years' preaching has taught me, that man is converted only when his heart is touched. When we present moral propositions with piety and zeal, they are like so many burning coals thrown into the faces of our hearers, who are edified by this manner of preaching, become more tractable, and are more easily induced to receive private instruction upon points in which they differ from us." When such sermons did not complete their conversion, the holy Prelate was accustomed to finish the work by private conferences, in which he mildly and kindly listened to all that the heretics or infidels had to object. When it was his turn to speak, instead of wasting time in disputation, he began clearly and simply to explain the controverted points, without, however, allowing a word to fall from his lips that would have seemed like

controversy. On the one side, he would represent the beauty of the Catholic faith, when well understood, in its clearest light, and on the other side, he would depict the impiety of those preachers, who had defamed it. This, as experience had taught him, was the best way to convert dissenters.

25. In vain did heretics attack him with embittered hearts, in vain did they treat him disrespectfully and insolently. He always answered them calmly and mildly, without the least appearance of contention, in accordance with the doctrine of the Apostle : "But if any man seem to be contentious, we have no such custom, nor hath the Church of God."[1] He called them all "brother," according to the custom of the early Fathers of the Church, who gave this name to the heretics of their time. He gave the following reason for this : "Protestants are our brethren, as Christians and as men, because by baptism we are all children of the same God, and by birth we descend from the same father, Adam.—"Moreover," added he, "those to whom I speak, are my country-men and fellow-citizens : consequently, there exists between them and me a kind of fraternity."

This manner of acting was not pleasing to some of his fellow-laborers in the vineyard of the Lord. It was their opinion that heretics ought to be treated as men of uncircumcised hearts, as rebels against God, as stiff-necked and obdurate creatures, as a brood of vipers, in fine, as the children of Satan. They thought themselves justified by the Holy Scriptures, in using

[1] I. Cor. 11, 16.

such language. The Saint tried to undeceive them, by representing that mildness had more influence over men, than severity, just as with a spoon-ful of honey more flies are caught, than with a barrel of vinegar; that pride, which is so natural to the human race, and particularly to religious sectarians, should be treated with indulgence and forbearance. Having no infallible authority for their doctrine, the spirit of pride becomes characteristic of them. Consequently, every severe and harsh word embitters and excites, instead of instructing them. He gave his own experience in proof of this. "Every time I have made use of cutting language, of reproachful or fault-finding words, I have had cause to regret it. If it has been my good fortune to win over some heretics, it must be ascribed to the power of gentleness. Charity and sincere affection have more influence over the heart, I will not say, than severity, but even more than the force and solidity of argument." In further support of his principle, he pointed to the example of Jesus Christ, Who, although He might most justly have thought severity necessary towards the stiff-necked Jews, nevertheless, taught His divine doctrine with unparalleled amiability and affection.

26. He thought that those who allow their zeal to get the better of their temper, when conversing with heretics, make their cause suspicious; that the light of truth, even when presented by a cautious hand, often injures the weak eyes of dissenters, but when it is rashly, regardlessly of feelings or dispositions, thrust full into the face, it entirely blinds them.

"Never," said he, "will truth make its way forward, without charity." It is quite different with regard to impiety; for if we abstract from the works of Luther, Calvin, Zwingle, and Beza, all the calumnies, abusive language, invectives, and mockery against the Pope and Catholics, there will be little left to engage the attention."

27. When he was in conversation with persons of distinction, he showed them the greatest honor, addressing them by that title which he thought the most pleasing to them : "for," said he, "as there is no one who cares less about receiving honor, than I do, there is no one more willing to show honor to others." On an occasion in which he had treated a nobleman's servant with great distinction, a remark was made to him about it. He answered: "I scarcely know how to discriminate between persons : one thing alone is ever before my eyes,—which is, that they are all Christians."

In his conversations, he contradicted no one, as long as conscience allowed him to be silent. Was he obliged to meet falsehood with truth, he did it mildly and modestly, without the appearance of contesting with his opponent; "for," said he, "nothing is gained in a cause which is conducted with bitterness."

28. Such reasoning was of no avail with his fellow-laborers. They held to their own opinion in the matter. They went farther. Thinking that Francis de Sales was wrong, they held a meeting, in which it was determined to rebuke the Saint in so earnest a manner, that his eyes would be opened to his fault.

They did so. They represented to him, that, thinking to do good, he was ruining everything ; that his
mildness would lead the heretics to imagine the
Catholics were afraid of them, and would have no
other effect than to strengthen their pride ; that it is
the duty of a preacher of the Gospel to admonish his
hearers, and not to flatter them ; that heretics are
sooner converted when boldly dealt with in the
beginning, than when treated with too much indulgence. The holy Apostle received these admonitions most respectfully, kindly, and gratefully. He
said not a word to justify himself. He knew that
any effort to undeceive them would be vain, because,
as he said later, they were like persons looking through
colored glass. Everything around seemed to be of
the same color as the glass. His conscience, however, did not allow him to embrace their opinion, and
he continued in his usual mild style of preaching.
Observing no improvement in him, his zealous co-
laborers resolved to lodge their complaints against
him with the Bishop of Geneva. They begged his
Lordship to recall Francis to Annecy. They asserted
that he undid in one day, a month's labor of theirs.
They said he preached more like a protestant Minister, than like a Catholic Priest, even forgetting
himself so far, as to call heretics his brethren, a
scandal which rejoiced the Protestants ; for they
promised themselves an easy victory over him, hoping
to draw him by degrees over to their party. Consequently, they ran in crowds, to listen to his musical
and flattering words, they lent a willing ear to his
16

fraternal language, as if there could be anything in common between light and darkness, the children of Jesus Christ and those of Belial. The Bishop of Geneva knew the holy Apostle too well, to pay any attention to such complaints and petitions. He limited himself to giving them a kind answer, and recommending to them—for he knew their intentions were good—charity, union, and mutual support. On his part, Francis de Sales continued to treat them with his usual affability, applauding the success of their labors, praising them on every occasion, and ascribing to them the fruits of the Mission.

29. "My Lord," said a convert to Francis de Sales, "I was born a Calvinist and I have only lately joined the Catholic Church. The objections which I have just laid before you, were still troubling me, and had you not so clearly and mildly removed them, to-morrow would have seen me again a Calvinist."

30. On an occasion, in which St. Francis de Sales had borne with a gross insult without uttering a word in self-defence, his brother asked him whether he had felt no movement of anger. "Certainly I did," answered the Saint; "the blood was boiling in my veins, like water in a vessel on the fire, but by dint of careful examination of conscience, which I have constantly practised for twenty-two years, and with the help of unwearying watchfulness, constant struggles, and repeated victories gained over myself, I have, if I may be allowed the expression, so collared my anger, that it is entirely in my power."

31. The following directions were given by St.
Francis de Sales to all Superiors of the Visitation.

"He laid down as a primary principle, that the
Superiors should distinguish themselves by their
meekness and humility, because these were the virtues
which our Lord required in the Apostles, whom He
had destined to be the spiritual rulers of the whole
world. Dive deep into the abyss of your own nothingness, seeing that God has vouchsafed to make use
of so insignificant a person for the important task of
guiding the souls of others. In order to perform this
duty well, be neither haughty nor obsequious, but
gentle, amiable and kind. Love all with a sincerely
maternal, a protecting love. Be everything to each
one, a mother to each, a help to each, and a joy to
all. If you act in this manner, everything will go
on well: if you proceed in a contrary way, nothing
will succeed."

His second principle was, that a Superior should
put her trust in God, which is much more efficacious
than self-distrust. The consciousness of His assistance, should fill her with humble energy and
strength, with the strength of Him Who manifested
His omnipotence in the humility of the cross.

"Since your divine Master has imposed this duty
upon you," said he, "He is obliged to lend you His
helping hand. Do you believe, that so kind a
Father would appoint you to be the nurse of His
children, without supplying you with an abundant
store of milk, butter, and honey? God has laid these
souls on your bosom, so that you may make them

worthy of Him: be assured then, that He will stretch
forth His Almighty arm in proportion to the work
imposed upon you."

After the Saint had given the above principles as
a guide for the Superiors of his Order, he spoke
of the duties of their office in the following manner:
"Strive most carefully to acquire a holy equanimity of
mind and body. Never appear sad or sullen, whatever may have happened. Let there be no trace of
frivolity in your countenance or demeanor, which
should always be serious, but, at the same time, mild
and humble. Let your laugh be moderate and your
eyes generally downcast. Be courteous and kind,
but not to such a degree as to detach from the reverence and respect due to you. Follow the Community
simply in everything, without doing more or less
than the other Sisters. Each one looks up to you for
good example; and all expect this example to be accompanied by great affability. As the lamp is fed by
oil, so does the effect of good example depend upon
this virtue. Nothing is so edifying as that meekness
of heart, which remains undisturbed by time or circumstances."

With respect to direction, he did not wish, that
Superiors should be too strict with the sisters, nor
yet to allow them too great freedom. He cautioned
them against showing any mistrust of their inferiors.
Whilst he wished them to yield nothing of their
authority as Superiors, he taught them to bear with
the sisters, meekly and with kind-service to treat all
alike, avoiding the least indication of partiality or

aversion for any individual. He bade them remember, that the Superior was not so much for the strong, as for the weak, although it was her duty to take care of all, so that the more advanced might not fall back, and the most imperfect might find that support in her tender affection, which would lead to amendment. He warned them not to show displeasure at whatever might be communicated to them, encouraging them to resolve firmly, to do all for God. Acting thus, he said, they would not feel hurt at being blamed for their manner of governing, they would listen calmly to everything, lay all before God, and, after having conferred with their counsellors, would do what was considered best, with the pious confidence that Divine Providence would turn everything to their honor and advantage. All this, they should do with so great peace and meekness, that their subjects would have no pretext to show less respect and reverence due to the Superior, nor would the Counsellors have any reason to imagine, that the Superior stood in need of their assistance in the direction of the Community. "Be firm in the strict observance of the rule," said he. "Be discreet in your own deportment and try to preserve your house in good repute. Teach your sisters to love, praise and serve God with one heart. Tell them that He has brought them together so that they may assist one another to serve Him in an extraordinarily excellent, generous, heroical and steadfast manner. Encourage them to strive after the great and perfect virtues of firm, unvarying and noble hearted piety, self-denial, love of objection and contempt, mortification of the senses and sincere charity. Instruct them to do whatever is prescribed by the Superior, neither more nor less, and without any other intention, than to please the Divine Majesty. It is hard, he added, to deny, and, as it were, to annihilate one's self at every moment; but the skill of a gentle and affectionate Mother knows how to lessen the bitterness of these disagreeable potions, by mixing them with the milk of holy friendship, being always ready to receive her children cheerfully and kindly, so that they will run to her with joy and allow themselves to be moulded, like sealing-wax, in the fire of her burning love.''

32. At the close of a mission, where he had been day and night hearing confessions, he wrote to St. Jane Frances de Chantal as follows : "These have been golden days for me. Oh! what joy I feel, at the conversion of so many souls! I have been reaping in smiles and in tears of love, amongst my dear penitents, O, Saviour of my soul, what joy was mine to see, among others, a young man of twenty, brave and stout as a giant, return to the Catholic faith, and confess his sins in so holy a manner, that it was easy to recognize the wonderful workings of divine grace, leading him back to the way of salvation. I was quite beside myself with joy and gave him many a kiss of peace.''

CHAPTER IX.

ON THE ZEAL OF A SUPERIOR TO PROMOTE THE SPIRITUAL
ADVANCEMENT OF HIS SUBJECTS AND TO PRESERVE
THE PRIMITIVE FERVÓR OF THE ORDER.

> "Feed the flock of God which is among you,
> taking care of it not by constraint, but willing-
> ly, according to God, and when the Prince of Pástors
> shall appear, you shall receive a never-fading crown
> of glory." I Peter.

OUR Lord Jesus Christ asked St. Peter three
times in succession: "Simon, son of John, lovest
thou Me more than these?"[1] and St. Peter
answered each time: "Yea, Lord, Thou knowest
that I love Thee." To each of these answers our
Lord replied: "Feed My lambs," thereby giving
clearly to understand, that He required as a sure
pledge and proof of Peter's love for Him, the faithful
feeding, or direction of His flock to a life of holiness
and perfection. Hence the principal duty of a
Superior is to feed his, or rather Christ's flock, by
his prayers, example and exhortations, directing
them to lead a life of sanctity. "The faithful discharge of this duty," says St. Alphonsus, "is a work
extremely pleasing to God; for the Lord values a

[1] John 21, 15.

perfect soul far more highly, than a thousand imperfect ones." The reason for this is, because there is nothing more like unto God, than a man most holy. Among a thousand likenesses of himself an emperor will value that one most highly, which represents his person most perfectly. God, in the same manner, values a soul, in which His Image and Likeness shine forth most perfectly, a thousand times more, than a thousand other souls, which resemble Him less perfectly. Hence it is, that all holy and truly enlightened Superiors apply themselves to the spiritual progress of their subjects, in such a manner as if they were not accountable to God for anything else.

It is related of Blessed Balthazar Alvarez, S. J., that holiness of life was everything with him ; talents and noble extraction if compared to virtue, were of no account. "We need Saints," he used to say, "not learned or wealthy men, destitute of the splendor of virtue." If he met, among his subjects, with one particularly qualified for the spiritual life, though possessing but moderate talents, he would take particular pains with him, often calling him to his room to give him proper instructions for his progress in the spiritual life. He would make greater account of the smallest spiritual good, than of the most important temporal affairs. For the sake of the latter, he would not permit his subjects to neglect any of their spiritual exercises. "The Superior," he would say, "must keep far from his mind all such thoughts and plans as would prevent him from complying with the duties of his office. The Lord has charged him with but one thing, viz: with the management of his Community; every other occupation is for him but a work of supererogation; should it prevent him from fulfilling his duties, it would be a real illusion.   Hence he must take care not to have too frequent intercourse with outsiders; to these he will render better services by educating for them holy religious, than by charging himself with their affairs."[1]   A Superior who does not act in accordance with these sentiments, will draw upon himself God's chastisement.   We read in the life and revelations of St. Gertrude,[2] that the Lord one day sent tribulations upon a certain religious for having preferred, from human motives, a temporal good to her spiritual progress.   "For I have declared in the Gospel," said our Lord to her, "that you should *seek* first the kingdom of God, and its Justice, and then, not that you should *seek* the temporal goods, but that they would be *added* unto you." What great pleasure, on the other hand, does not that Superior give Jesus Christ, who zealously endeavors to promote the spiritual welfare of his subjects, especially of those, whom he notices to be endowed with the gifts of nature and grace.   "The Lord does not work miracles every day," says St. Frances de Chantal, "if He grants these gifts to certain souls, it is a sign that, if they co-operate with them, He wishes to be served by them in a special manner, in matters of the greatest importance; souls endowed with a sound jugdment, great humility, and love for the regular observance are more precious than gold."

[1] Life of Balth. Alvarez.   [2] Lib. iii. 91.

17

As many souls as he has advanced in the road of perfection, so many never-fading crowns shall he receive in heaven in reward for his trouble. It is related of St. Aldegundis, that one day she saw, in a vision, St. Amandus surrounded by a multitude of holy souls, who had been converted by him; he was in their midst like a giant surpassing them in stature and heavenly glory; all looked up to him as to their spiritual director and father, offering to him the crowns they had received.[1] With the great Apostle St. Paul such a Superior can exclaim: "What is our hope, our joy, or crown of glory? Are not you in the presence of our Lord Jesus Christ at His coming? For you are our glory and joy."[2]

As a religious pleases God and renders himself perfect only in proportion as he lives in accordance with the spirit of his rules, a Superior should understand thoroughly the spirit, the obligations and all the advantages of his Institute, in order to be able to point out most clearly to his subjects, the road upon which they must walk. "All the perfection and sanctity of a religious," says St. Alphonsus in one of his letters, "depend on the faithful observance of his rules. The rule is his true guide; if he goes by it, he will sanctify himself." "You cannot please Me better," said our Lord to B. Margaret Alacoque, "than by walking, with constant faithfulness on the road pointed out by the rules of your Institute. The least wilful faults against them are great before Me; a religious person labors under the greatest illusion,

[1] Her life.   [2] 1 Thessal. ii, 19—20.

and withdraws from Me, if she believes that she will
find Me on another road than that of the punctual
observance of her rules.''[1]

But as experience teaches, that only such religious will, with constant faithfulness, comply with
their religious duties as are thoroughly embued with
a clear knowledge of the sublimity of their state, and
with great esteem and love for their vocation, one of
the most powerful means a Superior can adopt to inspire his subjects with zeal and fervor for their spiritual progress, is to make them understand as far as
possible, and often hold out to them, the sublimity
of the grace of their religious vocation.

We read of B. Balthazar Alvarez, that in order
to make his subjects conceive a high idea of their
vocation and fill them with unusual esteem and love
for the same, he would often point out to them the
principal advantages and prerogatives, which they
were enjoying in the Society of Jesus ; he marked out
fourteen, as we read in his life, and he was never
weary of placing them before their minds.

Among all the methods St. Alphonsus made use
of, to encourage his sons to put off the old man, the
most efficacious was that of inspiring them with a
high idea of their vocation. "In calling us to this
state," he said, "God has not conferred on us a
merely ordinary degree of grace, but a grace as great
as it is uncommon. We must therefore pray, that
Almighty God will cause us to understand the value
of this grace, for if we do not correspond to so holy a

[1] Life.

vocation, we shall run the risk of eternal ruin."
The high idea which he had conceived of the religious
calling, caused his affliction to be extreme, when he
saw one of his subjects overcome by temptation and
ready to fall back.[1]

According to St. Francis de Sales a Superior
should, moreover, inculcate, upon the minds of his
subjects, three principles of the spiritual life, which,
if put in practice, procure an unspeakable peace and
consolation for the soul, proceeding as they do from
love. viz:

1.   To do everything for God and nothing for
themselves, not only in temporal but also in spiritual
matters concerning their progress in the interior life.
"Oh, how happy should we be," St. Francis de Sales
would exclaim, "were we to do every thing for the
love of God! for His love is infinite for a soul that
rests in Him."

2.   Not to be one iota less punctual and faithful
in the compliance with their respective duties on account of the privation of spiritual consolations, dryness of soul and other crosses, which the Lord sends
upon them. "One act performed in the state of
spiritual aridity, is far more pleasing to God, than
many other acts performed with great tenderness of
devotion; because their is in it a stronger, though
less tender love for God.

3.   To bless the Lord just as much in adversity
as in prosperity, according to the example of Job,
whose song of praise and mourning was the same.

"The Lord gave, and the Lord hath taken away: Blessed be the name of the Lord."[1]

To these general principles a Superior should add particular ones concerning those virtues especially, by the practice of which religious Orders are maintained in their primitive fervor of spirit. Now in reading the lives of the holy Founders of Religious Orders, we find, that besides the *Spirit of Prayer* upon which I have spoken at length in my little book lately published on this subject, and *discretion in the election of Superiors*, of which I believe I have said enough in my preface to this book, they recommended and insisted most energetically upon the promotion of the spirit of fraternal Union, and charity, obedience and discretion in admitting subjects to membership, as so many efficacious means to preserve their Orders in their primitive fervor.

[1] Job 1, 21.

CHAPTER X.

ON CHARITY.

"THE soul of our neighbor," says St. Francis de Sales, "is the tree of knowledge of good and evil, which we are forbidden to touch under pain of chastisement, because God has reserved the judgement thereof to Himself."

There is an inconsistency very common amongst men, who are, by nature, inclined to judge in a matter, wherein they are ignorant, namely, the *interior* of others, while they are averse to judging that which they do know, viz: their *own* interior. The former is forbidden, the latter commanded. To avoid this vice, St. Francis de Sales gave the following excellent rule. If an act might be viewed in a hundred different lights, always look at it in the most favorable. If we cannot excuse an action, we may lessen its magnitude, by excusing the intention; should that not be possible, we must lay it to the force of temptation, or ignorance, surprise, or human weakness, so as at least to endeavor to diminish the scandal. In short, he said, those who keep a watch over their conscience, seldom commit the fault of rash judgment. It is the act of an idle soul, which has no occupation within itself to restrain it from scrutinising the actions of other persons.

1. "A Superior then," says St. Ignatius Loyola, "should direct all to avoid, as far as possible, diversity of opinion, knowing that the wills of men are very often drawn into the disputes in which the intellect is engaged.

2. He should forbid every one, unless he be in authority, or have received a special commission, to reprove his brother religious, or to interfere with his business.

3. He should require all to strip from their hearts, all national predilection, and love of country, or fellow-country-men, so that each may bear a stronger affection, as it were, to men of another nationality than his own. "Do not love one person more than another," says St. John of the Cross ; "if you do, you will err greatly, because as he is most worthy of your love whom God loves the most ; so you cannot tell whom He loves the most ; love every one therefore equally.

"Be most careful not to think, and much less to speak of anything that happens in the Community, whether it relates to a certain religious, or to his character, disposition, or discourse. Do not even speak of important things, under the pretext of zeal, or for the amendment of his life, except to mention the matter to the proper person, at the proper time.

"Whatever you may see, or hear, never be scandalised or astonished ; but endeavor to efface

everything from your mind, because though you may
live amongst angels, yet if you wish to see and know
everything, you will see some things which may
appear to you not to be good, on account of your not
properly understanding them. Consider the example
of Lot's wife, who because she looked back upon the
destruction of Sodom was changed "into a statue of
salt." Thus we see, that though we should live
amongst demons, we must not turn our head to examine their actions through curiosity, but leave them
altogether, without giving ourselves any trouble
about them. Rather should you endeavor to occupy
your soul entirely with God, than trouble yourself
with this or that person. Be assured, that in all
Communities you will always find something that
may scandalize you, because the wicked spirits never
cease tempting the religious. This God permits, in
order to prove them and exercise them in virtue.
But if you do not observe this advice, you will never
become a good religious, nor attain holy detachment
and recollection ; the devil will know how to deceive
you in one way or the other. Remember what the
Apostle St. James says : "And if a man think himself to be religious, not bridling his tongue, but de-
ceiving his own heart, this man's religion is vain."[1]
Wish others to be preferred before you in all things ;
do this with all the sincerity of your heart. Thus
you will conquer evil with good ; you will drive
the devil away from you, and fill your soul with
joy.

Chapt. I, 26.

"Endeavor also to practise these virtues towards those who do not esteem you, rather than in behalf of those who love you. If you do not act in this manner, you will never acquire perfect charity, nor advance in perfection. In order to free yourself from all anxiety and trouble, which may arise from the conduct or disposition of other religious, and that you may derive advantage and profit from every event you will do well to remember that you have entered the Convent as one over whom your brethren are to watch, and whom they desire to perfect, some by their works, and some by their actions, and more by their opinions and sentiments unfavorable to you. All these strokes, as it were, you must patiently receive. If you do not observe these rules, you will not be able to live happy with your brethren in the Convent, nor will you acquire holy peace of soul, but you will expose yourself to great evils."

4. A Superior should keep far from his Community, the so-called domestic enemy, that is to say, the spirit of murmuring, censuring, or criticising the manners and ways of acting of Superiors, other officials, or equals. In the opinion of St. Vincent de Paul, this spirit is one of the principal enemies of mutual charity, and as this vice too often obtains admittance into religious Communities, he persecuted it sword in hand, as it were, and left nothing untried to caution his subjects against it. He compared it to a wolf which no sooner enters the sheep-fold, than it commences to kill and devour the sheep. "There is scarcely anything," said he, "which does greater

harm to a religious Community, than this vice, when
it has once affected its members.   Men who have become accustomed to murmur at,   and criticise everything, are never at peace, always finding something
to contradict or to censure." In order to inspire all
his subjects with a wholesome fear of this abominable,
satanic spirit,   he ordered,   that,   on seven Sundays
successively,   a Conference,   on this subject,   should
be delivered in order that every one might have an
opportunity to declare himself a deadly enemy of this
vice.   He believed that thus his Society would remain
free of the evil spirit,   after all had solemnly spoken
and protested against it.

St. Frances de Chantal says, in one of her letters
that she knew a religious Order of the strictest reform
and observances,   into which this evil had obtained
admittance, but that the Superiors had no sooner per ·
ceived it, than they made it a reserved case, in order thus
to apply to it, at once, a speedy and efficacious remedy.

"If you believe me," she wrote to a sister, "you
will put a stop at once to all those little accounts concerning faults of the past ; they serve only to diminish
charity.   From the very beginning give your sisters
to understand plainly,   that you consider that one
among them most virtuous who is most charitable in
every respect and most cordially united with the
sisters,   and that we are respected and esteemed by
others in proportion as we respect and esteem them.
Finally,   tell them that we should think of nothing
but of walking with simplicity and faithfulness in the
ways of God."

How much our Lord is averse to this vice, we may gather from what we read in the life and revelations of St. Gertrude. A religious of her Community who had listened to murmurs and detractions, appeared after her death, to the Saint, in her living form, having, in punishment for her fault, her ears closed with a hard substance, which she could remove only with great difficulty and by slow degrees; her mouth also was covered with a kind of bridle, for having uttered some detractions, so that she could not taste the Divine sweetness. It was revealed to St. Gertrude, that this person had sinned through inadvertence and ignorance, and had repented of her fault; but that those who persisted habitually in this sin, would be punished far more severely, and their sufferings would be so intense and horrible, as to make them objects of aversion to the citizens of heaven.

5. An enemy not less hurtful to mutual charity, are particular friendships. These must never be suffered to creep in. "They are," said St. Vincent de Paul, "like a cancer, constantly gnawing at and undermining fraternal union and charity, and proving ruinous to the common religious discipline." They are a great obstacle to perfection, keep mind and heart captivated, chase the love of God from the heart, and prevent the soul from being united to God."

"Be particularly careful not to permit any particular friendships," says St. Alphonsus, in his advice to an Abbess, "either among your subjects or with externs. And should you be unable to prevent them, you should have recourse to the Superior of a higher rank. In endeavoring to prevent such an abuse, you may incur the displeasure of some, but there is no alternative. There are certain evils, such as particular friendships, feelings of aversion and dislike, which must not be allowed to strike root, but must be opposed at once, for fear of their becoming too difficult to be extirpated.''

6. "One of the worst dispositions, which a mind can have," says St. Francis de Sales, "is to be easily inclined to throw ridicule on others. God hates this vice exceedingly, and punishes it in remarkable ways." When this Saint heard any one ridicule another, his countenance testified his dislike of the conversation; he would introduce another topic to create a diversion; and when he could not succeed by this method, he would rise and say: "This is trampling too much on the good man, and passes all reasonable bounds. Who gives us the right to amuse ourselves this way at the expense of others. Would we like to be treated thus, and have all our foibles dissected with the razor of the tongue? To bear with his and our imperfections, is a great perfection, and it is a great imperfection to cut him up, in this way by ridicule.''

7. A Superior should also endeavor constantly, to effect, that every one may recognize, in his brother, the image of Jesus Christ, so that the love of the object represented, may overcome any feeling of aversion, to which his defects may give rise. If every one ought to show great respect for a Crucifix, the dead

image of Jesus Christ, though poorly executed, how much greater should not be his respect for the living image of God, executed by the most skillful hand? Moreover, is not every one a tabernacle for Jesus Christ in Holy Communion? And shall any one have so little faith as to show irreverence to this tabernacle?

8.   According to St. Francis de Sales, the greatest effect of charity is, to make us love our enemies. Another effect of charity not less important is, to make us patiently forbear with our neighbor in spite of all his faults. "Bear ye one another's burdens, and so you shall fullfil the law of Christ."[1] To do this well, is to be another St. Christopher, who made himself a bridge for all kinds of persons, carrying them for the love of Jesus Christ, over a dangerous stream.   It is quite an easy matter to love those who are amiable in all their manners and dispositions, but to love those who are fretful, morose, stubborn, quarrelsome, meddlesome, and the like, is not less disagreeable than taking bitter pills.   But, this very thing is the touchstone of true Charity.   "I know," says St. Francis de Sales, "that little vexations, on account of their frequency and annoyance, are often more disagreeable than great ones, and that it often seems harder to bear the inmates of the house than strangers ; but I know also, that our victory, in these trifles, is often more pleasing to God, than many apparently brilliant victories, which are more glorious in the eyes of worldlings.   For this reason, I admire

---

[1] Gal. 6, 2.

the meekness with which the great St. Charles Borromeo suffered, a long time, the reprehensions which
a great preacher of a strictly reformed Order uttered
against him in the pulpit, more than all his patience
under the assaults which he received from others. O,
Lord, when shall we be so far advanced in perfection,
as to bear with our fellow-men, with a truly strong
love and affection !

In the lives of the Fathers of the Desert,[i] we
read the following little incident. One day, a religious
saw one of his brethren carrying a corpse. "Are you
carrying the dead," said he to him, "go and carry
the living." Such as do this shall be called the children of God. No faults should be censured with
more force, than those which tend to disunion, or to
impair, in the slightest degree, the divine virtue of
charity, which must ever be deemed the Queen of all
virtues, and the foundation of religious perfection.

A Sister of a certain Convent, wrote to St. Frances
de Chantal, that she wished for a change of place, as
she was unable to endure the company of certain persons, who were incessantly thwarting her, and afford-
ing her subjects of humiliation. To this communication, the Saint returned the following answer: "Lord
Jesus ! my dear Sister, in what school have you been
trained, not to have learned forbearance towards your
neighbor? with whom did our Redeemer Himself as-
sociate? was it not with a thief, who murmured at
the attention shown His divine person, and injuriously
asserted in full company, that what was expended

---

[i] Book 5, chapt. 16, by Herbert, S. J.

on that sacred object was absolutely lost? Was it not with a traitor, who sold Him for a contemptible sum? O my daughter, remain no longer ignorant of that lesson which prescribes forbearance to your neighbor. Alas! under the pretext of avoiding contempt and contradiction, are we to persist in showing our want of charity? Believe me, employ a consideration, which I have suggested with effect in a similar case. Where do you hope to dwell for an Eternity? Unquestionably, you look forward to the attainment of immortal happiness. The dear souls, with whom you are at variance, are advancing to the same term with rapid strides. Now tell me, how can you expect, that God should unite you eternally in the same abode, if you cannot, for the love of Him, live together for the short space of your mortal existence? Think not, therefore, of separating from your neighbor from a want of forbearance ; for such an event would be a separation from God.''

Another Sister assured St. Frances de Chantal, that it was impossible to live with a certain person, whom indeed she professed to love, but whom she could not be induced to see, and with whom she wished to have no intercourse. The holy and charitable Mother made the following reply : ''Unless you adopt the plan of a charitable forbearance towards your neighbor, our Redeemer will say to you at the hour of your death : 'I have loved you with an eternal charity ; I still love you, because you are my work ; but I can neither see nor speak to you ; a separation must take place—depart from Me.'' This forcible consideration produced the desired effect. Another Sister, informed her, that a daughter, consecrated to God, showed her such a degree of coldness, as to chill her very soul ; to which the holy Mother replied : "My dear daughter, it is not a principle of Christian charity to suffer ourselves to be overcome by evil : accustom yourself, I entreat you, to follow, with exactness, the maxims of the Son of God, that the ardor of your cordial charity may melt that coldness which exists in the heart of your Sister."

A Sister once reported, that her defects had been a subject of reproach by one in the Community; "and," replied the holy Mother, "what resolution did you form on hearing such censorious remarks upon yourself?" "I endeavored," said the Sister, "from the pure love of Christ, to excuse and palliate, to the best of my power, the faults of her who had treated me so unkindly." "Truly," rejoined the holy Mother, "you restore to me the vigor of youth by your Christian conduct." Then with the utmost tenderness of manner towards the charitable Sister, she uttered this memorable exclamation : "God grant that this resolution may never be erased from your mind ; I would forfeit my life to see it engraven on the heart of every daughter of the Visitation."

CHAPTER XI.

ON CHARITY TOWARDS THOSE WHO LABOR UNDER TEMPTATIONS.

"BRETHREN, if a man be overtaken in any fault, you who are spiritual instruct such a one in the spirit of meekness, considering thyself, lest thou also be tempted. Bear ye one another's burdens and so ye shall fulfil the law of Christ."[1] If there be any time when a Superior ought to exercise charity, meekness and patience, it is undoubtedly when any of his subjects is laboring under great temptations, such as those against faith, hope, purity, or against his Superior, or his vocation. Let us see what two great Saints have said on this subject. We read in the life of St. Vincent de Paul, that some of the Society would now and then, so far forget themselves, as not to show due respect to their Superiors. The Superiors then would begin to doubt, whether they should reprove their subjects for such behavior or not; or whether they ought to be silent on the matter, fearing on the one hand that their silence might prove hurtful to their authority, and on the other, that the correction might not be well re-

Gal. vi, 12.

18

ceived. In this case, St. Vincent de Paul required
the Superiors to evince an unwavering patience, and
an exceedingly great compassion for the weak, and to
allow them time to enter into themselves. To a
Superior who complained of having been treated contemptuously by one of his subjects, he said : "I sympathize with you ; the Lord permitted this insult to
try your patience, and to render you still more fit for
the government of your subjects. From this treatment you will also learn how great must have been
the kindness of Jesus Christ in forbearing with His
disciples and Apostles, and how much He must have
suffered, not only from the wicked but even from the
good. You will learn, moreover, how the Superiorship, as well as any other state of life has its thorns ;
and how Superiors endeavoring by word and example
to fulfil their duties, will always have a good deal to
suffer. Let us, then, offer up ourselves to God to
serve Him in this office, without expecting gratitude
from men. Let us entertain the firm hope, that His
Divine Majesty will not fail to bestow upon us an exceedingly great reward, if we are most zealous and
punctual in keeping all our rules, and endeavoring to
acquire humility and mortification, virtues so essential to a Missionary priest. My dear Sir, how great
is the wretchednessof human nature, and how indispensably necessary to Superiors is patience."

St. Ignatius speaks in the same manner. "Towards those who are grievously tempted, we must
show ourselves extremely kind, affectionate and compassionate ; we must often speak to them words of

consolation, and pray, and perform works of penance for them. Should we notice one to be melancholy and cast down, we must be exceedingly affable to him, exhibiting to him great exterior and interior joy and sweetness. For the greater edification and consolation of those in temptation, we must incline to the disposition contrary to their own." It is related in the life of St. Francis of Assisium, that the tenderness of his heart was particularly evinced towards those who were laboring under temptations. He deeply sympathized with them in their troubles and afflictions.

One day Brother Ricer, the Father Provincial of Ancona, a holy man, was suffering extremely from the temptation that he was a reprobate, and for this reason, an object of hatred to his Saintly Patriarch. In order to find out whether this harrassing thought was a temptation or not, he resolved to go and see his Father Francis. "A kind reception on the part of my Father," said he to himself, "will be a sign for me that may affliction is but a mere temptation." St. Francis, to whom our Lord had revealed the temptation of Brother Ricer, sent his brethren, Masser and Leo to meet Brother Ricer, bidding them embrace and kiss him in his name; and to tell him, that among all his brethren there was no one whom he loved more tenderly than him. They did so, and Brother Ricer was at once delivered from his temptation experiencing a great interior joy, and thanking God for having blessed his journey. Having arrived at the Convent, Francis, weak and feeble though he was, went out to embrace him, and said to him:

"Brother Ricer, my son, among all my brethren you
are the one whom I love most affectionately," and
having made the sign of the cross upon his forehead,
which he kissed several times, he added: "This
temptation, my son, is most salutary for you, from
this time forward it will not harrass you any more."
Francis loved his brethren so much, that he could
not bear the least cloud of sadness to be cast over any
one's mind, fearing lest it might destroy the spiritual
joy of the heart. "My dear Brethren," he would
say, "preserve your interior and exterior joy in the
Lord ; if a servant of God endeavors to keep up this
joy which is the fruit of purity of heart, of fervor in
prayer, and of other exercises of piety, the evil
spirits will not be able to hurt him.' We cannot,
they say, do any harm to this man, we have no ac-
cess to him, because he rejoices in adversity as well as
in prosperity." The infernal spirits are glad if they
succeed in diminishing this spiritual joy in the
smallest degree ; for, if they can communicate to a
servant of the Lord ever so little of their own dispositions, they at once begin to make a beam out of a
mote, by trying constantly to add something more,
unless the soul endeavor to destroy their work by the
power of prayer, by acts of sorrow, by confession,
and works of penance. Spiritual joy, then, my
brethren, being the fruit of purity of heart, and of
frequent meditations, and fervor in prayer, you must
endeavor to acquire these two goods, in order to be
rendered worthy of this exterior and interior joy for
the edification of your neighbor, and for the confusion

of your arch-enemy, the devil. This is my most ardent wish for you. Satan and his servants only, have reason to be sad, but we on the contrary, must always rejoice in the Lord." "A Superior," said this Saint, "must be full of compassion for the tempted and afflicted ; he must be their solace, because he is their last refuge, should he not apply remedies to their sufferings, their weakness might throw them into despair." We read of St. Peter of Alcantara that, when he saw one of his brethren in religion cast down and melancholy, he at once called him with a more than fraternal affection, inducing him by his irresistible tenderness, to communicate to him the cause of his sadness and uneasiness, and he would not dismiss him before he had rendered him happy and easy again.

If a Superior must show great compassion, tender affection, and true christian meekness to the tempted, in general, he ought to do so more particularly towards those who are grievously tempted in regard to their vocation ; for this sort of temptation may grow very dangerous, as the devil endeavors to make those who are thus tempted, see things in an entirely false light. In order to be moved to great compassion for one tempted against his vocation, let a Superior consider well, that no religious, by having embraced the religious life, has rendered himself impeccable ; that the devil envies him for nothing so much, as for his religious vocation, and that he uses all means in his power to make him lose this unspeakable grace. Let the rules of a religious Order, and the means to preserve their faithful observance be ever so wise, yet, human misery will make its appearance everywhere, by grievous temptations, heavy falls, great scandals and apostasies. A Superior must be no more astonished at this, than at seeing water run down hill. What is more natural to man, than to commit faults? Hence, St. Augustine replied so beautifully to those who reproached him with a scandal which one of his people had given : "How much soever the good order and regular discipline of my house may be attended to," he said, "I am a man, and I live amongst men ; neither am I so presumptuous as to believe my house better than the Ark of Noah, in which one of eight was a reprobate ; nor is my house better than that of Abraham where it was said ; 'Cast out this bondswoman and her son ;'[1] nor is it better than the house of Isaac, who had to hear it said, in reference to his sons, 'I have loved Jacob, but have hated Esau ;'[2] Nor is it better than the house of Jacob and David, in which incest was committed ; nor better than that in which Jesus Christ Himself lived, in which the eleven faithful Apostles bore with the perfidious Judas, nor better than heaven itself, in which the Angels apostatised."

What is to be done under such circumstances? Shall no mercy or compassion be shown towards the delinquents, who perhaps, in the violence of temptation, were near losing their mind? Are they to be dispensed from their vows and dismissed at once? What would be the consequences? Among several,

[1] Gen. 21, 10.   [2] Malach i. 3.

I will mention but one, namely : 'Little esteem and regard for the vows. If dispensations and dismissions should be too easily granted ; their binding power will be considered to be nothing more than something conventional. As people cease to look upon too frequent oaths, as upon sacred acts binding in conscience, so in the same manner will they begin to lose respect and veneration for religious vows, if their dispensation be too frequently and too easily granted. Jesus Christ says : "I will have mercy,"[1] and St. Paul writes : "Brethren, if any man be overtaken in any fault, you who are spiritual, instruct such a one in the spirit of mildness, considering thyself, lest thou also be tempted." Let Superiors practise this lesson of our Lord and of St. Paul. We read in the life of St. Vincent de Paul, that this Saint could not easily resolve to dismiss subjects from his Society, if he could discover in them marks of a true vocation. If they were strongly tempted against their vocation, he would represent to them the great danger, to which they would expose themselves, were they to leave. He called their attention to the source of their dissatisfaction, and furnished them with the proper means to overcome their temptation. If all proved of no avail, he at last advised them to leave by the door through which they had entered, viz : by going through a spiritual retreat. To a Superioress of the Sisters of Charity, he wrote as follows : "Know my dear Sister, that a Sister is but seldom dismissed, and if dismissed, it is only for grievous faults, if they

[1] Math. ix, 13.

are not frequent and causing scandal to others; and even in this case, we must be slow to dismiss and think of doing so, only after all means have been exhausted in vain to bring her back to a sense of duty. This charity and patience is shown especially towards those who have already grown old in religion, so that should some leave, they do so on their own responsibility, either from a spirit of levity, or because God Himself, in Whose service they became lukewarm, rejected them, before the Superiors thought of their dismissal.''

There were several of his Society who had relaxed in their primitive fervor and become a real burden to their brethren by their constant murmurs and complaints. Vincent, however, wished to try every means before dismissing them. If some represented to him, that it was just and equitable to dismiss such brethren, the common good of the Society requiring it, he would say: "Be it so: but every virtue has its time, let us still persevere in bearing them patiently and charitably, hoping that they may do better. Meanwhile, let us try every means to help them, by entreaties, exhortations, works of penance, and by prayers, beseeching the Almighty to enlighten and encourage them by His grace to lead a better life. Jesus Christ did not reject Peter, although this Apostle denied Him three times; nay, He did not expel Judas, although He knew, that he would become His betrayer, and would die in his sins. Hence I believe, that God will be pleased, if we extend our charity towards the degenerate, leaving nothing untried to win them over again to the Lord." Vincent adhered to the opinion of St. Gregory, namely, "that the faults of our neighbor should excite our compassion rather than our indignation, and that true zeal always inclines and tends more towards forgiveness than revenge."

When a Superioress complained to St. Francis de Sales, that the faults and imperfections of some of the nuns were frequent and always the same, so that she was no longer able to correct or tolerate them, and that on this account, she begged to be relieved from the Superiorship, he would answer her with a sweet smile : "But, my dear Mother, do you commit no faults yourself, or will you never be guilty of any ? And should you commit any, would you like to be cast into prison, or be driven ignominiously from the house of God ? Religious Orders consist not of perfect souls, but of those who are aspiring to become perfect.   Perhaps you think it possible for the height of perfection to be attained in a week.   Examine yourself and see whether you have reached that state, and if you have reckoned the time it took you to become perfect, and calculate how long you will remain so. Supposing you are perfect, are you not forced to acknowledge your success due to the grace of God, and, perhaps the effect of a naturally amiable disposition, which finds no difficulty in the practice of virtue ? Would you compel God to bestow the same graces upon every one ? Or can you expect all to have a disposition like your own ? You do not think of the trouble these poor Sisters take to tame the refractory

19

and rebellious inclinations, to which the exercise of virtue is so distasteful. The slightest indisposition, or the least occurring temptation would at once eclipse the brilliancy of all your virtues and completely change your present state of mind. What excuse could you then plead? You would be obliged to acknowledge, that you were deceived in believing yourself to be possessed of many virtues. You would find, that your state was nothing more than the habitual routine of a naturally amiable turn of mind, in which the will had no other part, than a simple concurrence with the work of nature. You would then beg pardon for your want of charity. As for myself, added he, I have not the least desire to receive such a pardon; I prefer to compassionate their weakness at the proper time, and I would rather gradually lead them back to their duty, or even yield a little to them, than wound the virtues of patience and charity."

The high idea which St. Alphonsus had conceived of the religious calling, caused his affliction to be extreme when he saw his brethren overcome by temptation, and ready to fall back. He would examine their combats from two different points of view, in order to find out whether they were caused by temptation, or by the malice of self-will. He pitied the subject in the first case, and tried to aid him by his prayers and by those of others; he even forgave him some impertinence. The following is an instance of this. One of the Fathers who was still young, fancied that he had been sent to the house at Iliceto

as a punishment.   He informed St. Alphonsus in an
extravagant letter that, if he did not remove him
from that house, he would leave the Congregation.
St. Alphonsus was convinced that this was nothing
but a mere suggestion of the devil ; he therefore
wrote to him in the most gracious language : "St.
Paul, the first hermit, said to St. Anthony the Abbot, who begged him to open the door, or else he
would die on the spot : 'This is a new way of begging : you beg with a menace.'   I say the same thing
to you.   I sympathize with you in the strife which
has arisen in your heart.   Who ever sent you to
Iliceto as a punishment?   And, then, just observe
what you say ; 'otherwise I shall ask for a dispensation.'   This is very well, but, who will give it to
you?   Another time I trust you will not be so angry.
I repeat that I forgive you, for, it is not you who
speak, it is temptation.   But let us have patience
and wait until this noxious influence has passed
away."   Through these words the young Father's
mind was calmed, the temptation driven away, and
peace restored to his heart.   St. Alphonsus employed
another admirable artifice on such occasions.   When
any one came to him for a dispensation from the oath
of perseverance, Alphonsus seeing the temptation,
appeared at first to be quite ready to grant what he
was asked.   And as resistance often makes us obstinate,
this very promptitude put an end to the temptation.
But St. Alphonsus then continued to speak to the
tempted person with mildness ; he made him weigh
the evil consequences of the step he had taken, and

showed him that it was nothing but a temptation ; in this way the subject felt ashamed, and his mind having been enlightened, he saw his error and requested to be allowed to stay.

St. Alphonsus was particularly distressed at the misplaced tenderness of some who, after having shown great fervor up to that time, thought themselves obliged to leave the Congregation in order to assist their parents, when they heard that any reverse of fortune had befallen them. Pitying their distress and wishing to preserve their vocation, St. Alphonsus did not hesitate to relieve their families in spite of the great want under which he himself labored. He did so on many occasions by giving up to them the alms received for their Masses. Some of the brothers thought that such instances of charity were excessive, on account of the poverty of the Congregation ; but St. Alphonsus replied that, "Charity can never fall into excess and that God repays all that is given in His name." Even when he found out that the temptation proceeded from the malice of self-will, he would still make use of all possible means, in the spirit of charity and mildness to make them enter into themselves, and adopt better sentiments. He would bear with the faulty as long as possible. Father Villani having one day informed him of the expulsion of one of the subjects, Alphonsus wished to know all the particulars about it, and having examined into the faults alleged against the guilty one, he did not consider them sufficient, so he answered as follows: "In order to justify the expulsion of a subject, we must have well grounded reasons for it, which must be of such a nature, as to preclude any compassion, after all hope of amendment is gone." Another time he wrote to Father Tannoja : "After a subject has been received as a novice, there must be weighty reasons to dismiss him, and after having taken the vows, there must be *reasons of a most serious nature joined to incorrigibility, in order not to commit mortal sin in sending him away.*" If, however, such a tempted subject profited by the advice and lessons of the Saint, if he knew how to humble himself before him, he at once regained the Saint's good grace, so much so, that Alphonsus became his defender in spite of the dissatisfaction which others showed at it. "*I have added my opinion,*" he writes in one of his letters, "*that it is not right to expel one who truly humbles himself.*" After all means that charity could suggest, had been exhausted, so much so, as to preclude all hope of amendment, then St. Alphonsus made use of severer and more energetic means ; namely, he had such offenders closely watched, or he forbade them the exercise of the sacred ministry, or he permitted them to go and see their relatives, or sent them to houses of his Congregation, which they disliked, that they might thus be induced to lead a better life, or to leave the Order of their own accord. They generally took the latter course : meanwhile St. Alphonsus prayed to the Almighty to enlighten them, or expel them Himself; the prayer for the latter favor, he generally performed in cases, in which, on account of certain circumstances, it was not advisable for him to expel them himself. The Lord never failed to hear this prayer of his.

If any one of those who had lost all love for his vocation and the Congregation, and who gave no hopes of amendment, even after severe punishments, would not yet go of his own accord, then St. Alphonsus dismissed him. Sometimes also he did this in regard to those who obstinately refused obedience and gave great scandal to others, to the detriment of common discipline and regular observances. His principle, which he also inculcated upon others, was that the imperfect and faulty ought to be long borne with, and be treated with the greatest charity, kindness, patience, and meekness, but never with inordinate charity; and, that charity began to be inordinate, and indulgence imprudent as soon as they proved detrimental and ruinous to the well-being of the Order. In this case, — with St. Ignatius and other holy founders of religious Orders, — he considered the dismissal of such subjects one of the most efficacious means provided by God to preserve the Order in its primitive fervor. We read in the life of St. Ignatius, that he used this means without ever allowing himself to be restrained by what he used to call imprudent or indiscreet charity. He did not bear long with those who were obstinate in their opinions, and who would always obey with difficulty. Neither did he ever relent because the blow had to fall upon a great number. Once he expelled nine at a time; another time he dismissed ten. Once on the Feast of Pentecost, he expelled twelve, and it was after this clearance, that he was observed to be in higher spirits than usual, not, of course, on account of the condemnation of these unfortunate men, but on account of the general good which would result to the Society, from his having cut off these rotten members, which infected the body with evil humors. He wished the other Superiors to follow his example. Leonardo Clessilio, Rector of the College at Cologne, sent away more than half of his subjects, though he had but fifteen. St. Ignatius highly praised him, and held him up as an example to other Superiors, if they had unworthy subjects.

St. Vincent de Paul, too, as is related in his life, acted in this manner towards those who gave no proofs of a good vocation, who scandalized others by their bad example, or undermined fraternal charity and union, or did not amend. In regard to these his resolution was soon taken, saying with the Apostle: "Would to God that those who cause disturbance were separated from among you."

"A Superior, then," says St. Alphonsus, "must be firm in regard to the incorrigible, endeavoring to prevent the spread of bad example. If those who are tempted as to their vocation, are treated according to the above principles, and in the manner in which the Saints have acted, then, should they remain incorrigible, they must, like Judas, attribute their perdition to themselves; the Superior may pray with our Saviour: While I was with them I kept them in Thy name; those whom Thou gavest me have I kept, and none of them is lost, but the Son of perdition."[1]

[1] John 17, 12.

CHAPTER XII.

ON THE CARE AND SOLICITUDE OF A SUPERIOR TO PRESERVE THE HEALTH OF HIS SUBJECTS, AND ON HIS CHARITY TOWARDS THE SICK.

A SUPERIOR must remember that he is accountable to God not only for the spiritual health of his subjects, but also for that of their bodies. Hence in trying to advance his subjects in true solid virtue and piety, his spiritual direction should be such as not to prove hurtful to their bodily and mental vigor, but rather to render them more fit for the fulfilment of the duties of their state. The Lord has told us by the Prophet Osee, that He likes the exercise of charitable works, better than any other kind of good works performed in His honor. The latter are even displeasing to Him, if not accompanied by the works of charity. Now the same commandment which obliges us to show our charity for our neighbor by good works, obliges us also, as St. Augustine and St. Thomas teach, to have the same charity for our bodies; but as this charity cannot be found in indiscreet mortifications, the performance and oblation thereof cannot be pleasing to the

Almighty. Hence St. Bernard says,[1] "Discretion must be the guide of all our virtues, affections and manners; it must assign to each virtue its due time and place, and this right order in virtue gives each one its due measure, splendor and durability; virtue, without discretion, is a vice." For this reason he teaches that he who is very indiscreet in mortifying his body, commits four robberies: he robs the body of its strength, the mind of its vigor and affection, the neighbor of good example, God of His honor; from which he draws the conclusion that such a one is guilty of the sin of sacrilege, abusing as he does the living temple of God, and depriving the Lord of His due honor, because the example of one alone suffices to deter many others from walking on the road of perfection, when they see him, on account of his excessive bodily austerities, taken sick and troubled in his mind, unfit for anything and finally die a premature death. A Superior then, in order not to become guilty of these robberies and this sacrilege, should be guided in this point by the principles and examples of the Saints, especially those of the founders of Religious Orders, some of which I will cite here, and in the chapter on mortification.

Although St. Francis of Assisium left nothing undone to induce his brethren in religion to lead a mortified life, yet he wished them to be discreet in the practice of bodily mortification. "In the exercise of virtue, he would say, we must be guided by prudence and discretion, not indeed by that of the

[1] Serm. 49 in Cantica.

flesh, but by that of the Gospel. Let every one have
regard for his own constitution. Should any one of
you need but little food, I do not wish that one who
needs more, should imitate him in this point, but let
him take as much as is necessary; for as we must not
eat too much which would be injurious both to body
and soul, so, in the same manner, we must guard still
more against taking too little, because God is more
pleased with mercy than with sacrifice." "My
brethren," he would say, "if a servant of the Lord
takes food and sleep in sufficient quantity, and his
body is rather slow in prayer and other good works,
he must chastise it and treat it as a horse or an ass is
treated when he does not wish to work though he is
well fed. But if one does not give his body what it
needs, he renders it unfit to carry the yoke of penance
and perform the spiritual duties, and then its complaints are not unjust." St. Ignatius of Loyola entertained the same sentiments on this head. It is related in his life, that he was always very solicitous to
preserve the health of his subjects for the greater
service of God, in order that thus he might have less
difficulty to inspire them with great courage and dispose them to undergo arduous labors for the glory of
God. Such mortifications and works of penance as
were best calculated to subdue human respect, pride,
self-esteem and self-conceitedness, were, in his opinion, far better than excessive fastings, the wearing of
hair shirts, iron chains, and such like austerities. To
the performance of the latter he would not even try
to induce those who were troubled by annoying dang-

erous emotions of the flesh, but would allow them
rather sparingly, especially so, if those who suffered
from these miseries were students. These, he thought,
should apply themselves more to study as long as
they could be noticed to make sufficient progress in
learning and in virtue without any considerable
prejudice to themselves ; whilst on the other hand,
he considered the time before or after their studies
more appropriate for bodily penances. He avowed of
himself that in the beginning of his conversion he
practised greater austerities than after his soul had
been purified from all attachments and irregular
affections. He wished others to act in the same manner. When his nephew, in consequence of having
practised great austerities, had rendered himself very
weak, he wrote to him thus : "I recommend to you
moderation in your labors and in the treatment of
your own person, which does not belong to you, but
rather to Jesus Christ and to the Society ; wherefore
you must take care to preserve your health and not to
ruin it just as if it were your own property. Although
charity induces you to take labors upon yourself
which are above your strength, yet this same charity
united to obedience obliges you also to moderate them,
in order to continue longer in the service of God."

Although he allowed St. Francis Borgia to follow, in the beginning of his conversion, the inspirations of his excessively great spirit of penance, yet,
when he saw him too much attached, and given up to
these austerities, and loving the contemplative life to
the prejudice of the active, and knowing at the same

time that, his spiritual wants no longer required them
in the same degree, he interfered with his spiritual
exercises and regulated them by writing to him the
following very instructive letter : ''When I learned
in what manner you carried on your bodily austerities,
and the spiritual exercises which you prescribed to
yourself for your spiritual progress, I rejoiced very
much in the Lord, it is true, thanking the Divine
Majesty for all the favors which it has been pleased
to bestow upon you, but believing myself enlightened
by the Lord as I do on this point, namely, that certain bodily and spiritual exercises which are useful to
our souls at certain times, are not always so at every
period of life, but must be replaced by others, I will
now tell you in the Lord what I think good for you.
First, as to your interior and exterior exercises, I
think that one half of them may be omitted, for our
ascetical exercises must be adapted to our constitution,
and proportioned to our evil propensities and the
temptations of the devil in order to preserve our will
from giving consent to unlawful things.   But the
more we get rid of our evil thoughts, affections and
inclinations, the more we shall experience holy
thoughts and inspirations for which we must make
room as much as possible, throwing wide open the
gates of our souls.   Now as you no longer need so
many weapons to overcome your enemies, I think,
before your and my God, it would be best for you to
devote, for the time to come, one half of your time to
study,—acquired science being henceforth more necessary than the infused,—to the government of your

province and to spiritual conversations, always taking
care to keep your soul calm, easy and ready to receive
whatever impressions the Lord may be pleased to give
it, for it is, without doubt, a sign of greater virtue
and grace if it knows how to enjoy the Lord in different offices and places than in but one, and with the
help of the divine assistance, we must endeavor to do
what is necessary to advance that far in perfection.

"Secondly, as to your fasting and abstinence,
I think in the Lord, that it is better for you to preserve your stomach and increase what is left of your
natural strength, rather than diminish it, for knowing, as I do, that you would rather die than offend
God, even venially, and that you have not to suffer
from any considerable temptations of the devil, of the
world and of the flesh, I wish very much you should
remember that you have from the Lord both your
body and your soul, and that you are accountable to
Him for both one and the other ; consequently, you
must, for the sake of the Lord, not lessen your bodily
strength ; if your body has become too weak, your
soul will not be able to do much. Hence, if until
now I was edified by your severe fasting and
abstinence and approved of them, I could not do so
for the time to come, foreseeing that your stomach
would become too much deranged, not being able to
digest even common food by which the life of the body
is sustained ; on the contrary, endeavor as much as
possible to eat of everything that is put on the table,
and as often as may be required, without scandal to
your neighbor; for we must wish well to our body

and love it in proportion as it is ready to serve the soul, which, by this very service and obedience of the body becomes more fit for service to the greater glory of our Lord and God.

"Thirdly, as to chastising your body, you should abstain from everything like bloody disciplines, and if the Divine Majesty has hitherto given grace for such like penances, I say now, without giving any further reasons, that it is better for you not to perform them for the future, and instead of seeking for or drawing blood, you ought rather to seek the Lord of all, I mean His holy gifts, as, for instance the gift of tears or the shedding of some—first, at the recollection of your own sins, or those of your neighbor, or secondly, at the meditation on the mysteries of our Lord's life, or thirdly, at the meditation on the love of the three divine persons; these tears are so much the more precious as the thoughts and meditations by which they are produced, are more sublime; and although the tears in the third instance proceed from a more perfect source than those in the second, and those in the second instance from a more perfect source than those in the first, yet, for all that, every one should prefer to meditate upon those subjects to which he feels more attracted by grace and from which he receives more of the gifts of the Lord, Who knows and sees what road is most suited for every-one. In order to find out this road by means of the divine assistance, it is well to try different ways, to see which one may lead us most safely and most happily to the life to come, uniting ourselves, to these most holy gifts and concealing them within ourselves. By these gifts for the possession of which we may lawfully wish, I mean such as are entirely out of our own power; and are altogether gratuitously granted by Him Who is the Giver of all good gifts. Such gifts relative to the divine Majesty are the following: a lively and efficacious faith, hope, and charity, consolation, resignation, divine lights and impressions, and all the other spiritual consolations united to humility and filial love and respect for our holy mother the Church and for those who preside and teach in her. Any of these gifts is better than all acts of exterior austerity, which latter are good only in as much as they are a help to the acquiring of those holy gifts, or at least some of them. However I do not wish to say that we should seek after them merely for the sake of the interior delight which they give us, but rather with the intention of making, by means of them, all our thoughts, words and actions more pleasing to God, and more meritorious for ourselves, and should one endanger his bodily health by great austerities, it will be better for him to seek these gifts by interior acts and little mortifications, for then soul and body retaining their vigor, will be more fit to work together for the greater glory of God.''

When St. Ignatius found that a number of the young students impaired their health by excessive application, he built a house in a vineyard within the city walls, in which they might live for a certain time for the recovery of their health. When it was objected by some, that they were hardly able to support life and could not undertake to build, he answered: "I set more store by the health of a brother than by all the treasures of the world;" nor was any one able to make him give way in this resolution. At the approach of Lent he sent for the physician and each of the students was summoned before him, in the presence of Ignatius to be examined whether they were able to fast, and what was adapted to their strength, and he besought the doctor to forbid those to fast whom he thought in his paternal affection were too weak to do so, or those who could not do so without great difficulty. He would not leave the matter to the care of the Minister, because he had not full confidence in his compassion. When he heard that in the Jesuits' house in Sicily the young men were to live by the same rule as the rest during Lent, he sent a severe reprimand to the Supe.ior. In the year 1545, Pietro Ribadeneira was forbidden by the physician to fast, and when he spoke to the holy father of it, doubting lest this permission might give offence to his companions, the Saint replied: Who ought to be offended? Ought they not rather to give thanks to God for not being under the same necessity? Having heard that some persons had blamed him on that account, he threatened to dismiss from the Society any one who would dare again to blame a permission so justly given and so necessary, and these threats were read in public in the refectory at Toledo as Ribadeneira himself affirms. He anticipated the wants of his children, as well as their requests, and took a memorandum of each particular that it might not escape his memory, and when obliged by important business to commit anything to the ministration of others, he himself declared their wants, so that they might be properly provided for.[1]

"I see that nearly all who die amongst us," says St. Frances de Chantal, in one of her letters to a Superioress of her Order, "die of pulmonary consumption ; and, often, those young sisters who have been raised in the most careful and delicate manner, are attacked by it. I have frequently thought over the cause of this, and to me, it seems to proceed from the fact that the young sisters are too quickly placed upon the routine of exact observance and subjection. They ought to be indulged with a moderate liberty, so that they may take some recreation, and, by degrees, be led to the strict observance of the rule and the performance of the spiritual exercises, in proportion to their increase of strength in mind and body. I have said in our *Answers*, that half an hour's meditation ought to be enough for them, and that they should be made to sleep and eat oftener than the other Sisters. This is, unquestionably, necessary for them ; as are also some little amusements and diversions, until their bodies will have attained their full growth. Superioresses ought to notice those who are predisposed to this disease ; for, fervent religious often hide it and bear with it in silence, until it has reached an irremediable stage. This should be prevented ; and whatever be the age of those attacked by it, they ought to be made to take good broths, to eat veal,

---

[1] Life of St. Ignatius.

mutton, and even poultry, when they do not relish
other food. Very little beef and nothing salted should
be given to them. Attention should be paid to making them sleep comfortably, and to recreating them
by some light exterior occupation. We know by experience that these are the best remedies for this disease. Indeed, the general food of the Sisters ought
to be good, as is marked in the *Customs*. The bread
should be light, the wine unadulterated and never
sour. Moreover, a holy liberty of spirit must be left
to the Sisters, that they may unbend their minds in
the time of recreation. I know this to be not only
useful, but very necessary for Religious. I must now
say a word for those born in warm climates, where
constitutions are bilious, and for those possessed of
violent passions I have observed that when such
persons are pushed on to strict observance, the violence they do themselves, often causes them to fall into consumption and into a state of melancholy, most
prejudicial and painful in its effects. On this account
Superioresses and Mistresses of Novices ought to
direct them with exceedingly great charity and meekness, bringing them gradually into subjection, allowing them a moderate liberty, thus leading them to
conquer themselves and their passions by love, and
not by force. I believe this manner of acting is
absolutely necessary for such souls, not only
for their own good, but in order to train them
to the mild and peaceful spirit of the Visitation.
This will be the work of time and patience ; but
neither ought to be spared. I beg the Superior-

esses who will read these lines, to be attentive to this point.''

"I beg of you,'' wrote St. Vincent de Paul to a certain person, "to take care of your health for the sake of our Lord and His poor members, not doing more than your strength allows.   It is an artifice of the evil one to deceive pious souls by tempting them to do more than they are able, in order to render them by degrees unfit for anything.   The spirit of God, on the contrary, induces us not to be indiscreet by doing more than we can, in order that we may be able to persevere in doing good.   Follow this advice and you will act in accordance with the spirit of God.   Moreover you must not fear to do too much, if you do what is your duty, but beware of wishing to do more than you are obliged to do.   I tremble, if one desires to do more than God has granted him strength for.   This would be a considerable fault in a daughter of Divine Providence.''

"It is in the order of Divine Providence,'' St. Francis de Sales used to say, "that we should treat our bodies according to their weakness, treating them as we do poor sick people, with patience and charity, and this exercise is not of the least meritorious because it mortifies both heart and courage.   If by the exercise of our duties, we contract a sickness or shorten our life, we must bless the Lord for it and suffer with a joyful heart.   As to the rest, love and respect for Divine Providence and charity towards ourselves oblige us to abstain from such practices of penance as would undermine our health ; for as it would betray effeminacy on our part to have too much regard for our health, so on the other hand it would be barbarian pride to neglect it altogether. As the soul cannot carry the body when fed too well, so, in the same manner, the body, when fed too little, cannot carry the soul. Let the body be treated like a child, let it be chastised without reducing it to death." It is related of this Saint that he himself abstained from such fastings as he foresaw would endanger his health. On noticing one day that the Bishop of Belley was fasting, he asked him whether he did not feel too much weakened by it. "I answered him," said the Bishop, "that I scarcely ever had any appetite." "Well," replied St. Francis, "you must then scarcely ever fast." "And why then, my father?" answered the Bishop, "Is not fasting so much recommended in Holy Scriptures!" "of course it is," said St. Francis, "but only for those who have a better appetite than you have." He also recommended to St. Frances de Chantal to have regard for her health and not to lessen it by long night watches.

One day, St. Paul appeared to St. Frances of Rome, and said to her: "The Superior should carefully watch over the wants of her subjects, and see that her daughters have everything that is necessary; for if what is necessary is not given to the body, it will become sick in the end and unfit for the service of God."[1]

In his letters St. Alphonsus recommends to his

[1] Her Life. Chapt. 17, rule 5th.

brethren, and especially to Superiors, to avoid immoderate zeal for giving missions. "If a subject,"
he writes, "becomes sick, it is a greater loss than the
omission of ten missions. Let no father start in
rainy weather, not even if a mission were to be given
at Paris. Hence, I hereby declare that it is my express will which no one must interpret otherwise,
that no father, for the time to come, shall travel in
the rainy season, unless it be only for a short distance,
or on a most extraordinary occasion. I give this
order to quiet the conscience of Superiors."[1]

In another letter he writes: "I recommend to
you not to expose your health on your return, by
travelling in rainy or snowy weather in order to reach
home the sooner. Oh my God! to send in these dog-
days one of our subjects, each of whom is as dear to
us as our own life, to a place where he must die in
consequence of the epidemic which is there prevailing! If there be another priest left in that place
to give absolution you must recall that father at once.
I would not like to have on my conscience the responsibility of having endangered the life of this excellent
subject."

To a Superior who had requested him to permit
him to stay up at night longer than the rest of the
Community, he wrote thus: As to your staying up
longer at night you must have patience, trying to go
to rest at the time appointed by the rule. You may
stay up half an hour longer than usual, but no longer.
This permission, however, is good only when you are

[1] Letter dated Dec. 25th 1771.

at home, for when you are on a mission charity requires that you should go to bed with the other members of the Community.[1] He prescribed seven hours' sleep in the mission as well as in the house. At the mission of Nola, one of the fathers having incommoded the others by getting up before the time, as he did not require so much sleep, St. Alphonsus reprimanded him and made him do penance by eating his dinner on his knees.[2]

"No one must be allowed," says he, "to stay up too long at night without a particular divine grace. We must indeed sleep as much as is necessary, but no more, because if we do not, we shall be unfit to perform our spiritual exercises, as it happened to St. Charles Borromeo, whereupon he resolved to take more rest." He recommended and rigorously exacted that no discontent should be shown on account of inconvenient lodging; he distinguished, however, between what was only incommodious and what was injurious to health. "Health," said he, "is the capital of the Missionary; if that fails, he becomes bankrupt." "I have learned," he wrote to a Superior, "that Brother Michael has returned and looks as well as ever. I beseech your Reverence to inquire carefully about his health. Should it be necessary to forbid him to study, you must do so: should he have a relapse he is gone. I fully authorize you to regulate the studies of our young men and beseech you in doubtful cases, always to prefer health to study." "I have learned," he writes in another letter, "that

[1] Letter Feb. 1st.   [2] Life chapt. 54.

several of our students are unwell.   Let them during
this hot season, take a walk in the morning as long
as the sun is not hurtful.   It is my wish, that our
students should be very healthy, and it matters little,
if they lose two hours of their study time.   Let them
go out in the evening also and have at least one hour's
remission time."   He forbade any part of scientific
courses to be dictated to the students, "because," he
said, "that in writing the chest is injured and time
is lost."   When he was Bishop, the Seminarians
complained, that the cook was not skilful.   Alphonsus sent his own several times to instruct him.   Often,
at the dinner hour, he went to examine the cleanliness
of the dishes, and above all, if the bread and wine
were good.   Once he found the bread was not of a
good quality ; he sent immediately for the Superior
and the housekeeper and reprimanded them for giving
such bad bread to the Seminarians ; he gave orders
that all the bread in the Seminary should be given to
the poor.   "I wish," said he, "the Seminarians
should relish what they eat."   In order to prevent
excess in bodily penances and to preserve the· health
of his subjects, St. Alphonsus forbade every one to
perform any bodily mortifications without having
previously obtained the permission of the Superior.
He also prescribed, that one day of every week should
be a recreation day, in order that every one might return to the performance of his duties with greater zeal
and fervor.   "Superiors," he said, "must moreover,
not permit at all under pretext of saving expenses, or
pra tising holy poverty, that the good spirit or the

health of their subjects should suffer.[1] St. Ignatius
of Loyola is of the same opinion.

If the care and solicitude of a Superior to preserve
the health of his subjects must be great, it must not
be less so to restore it when impaired. Sick brethren
must be as dear to him as the apple of his eye. If his
charity is to shine forth at all times, it is so, particularly at the time of the sickness of his subjects. If it
is truly paternal, it ought also to be most maternal
for the sick. "As long as I know," wrote St. Francis
de Sales to a sick person, "that you are confined to
your bed of sickness, I will always bear you — and I
am sincere in what I say — a great love and affection
as to a person visited by the Lord, Whose spouse she
is, and Whose garment she wears." He must carefully examine into all their necessities and whatever
they can lawfully desire. He should, therefore, often
ask them, whether they do not wish for something in
particular, making it appear that he is always full of
paternal care and solicitude for them. Should it be
necessary for him to refuse them certain things which
may be hurtful or forbidden by the physician, let him
do it with such charity and kindness that, instead of
feeling hurt by the refusal, they may rather feel easy
and consoled, so much so that they themselves, of
their own accord, refuse what has been forbidden by
the physician, or appears hurtful in their present
condition.

Let the Superior also bear with their weaknesses
and human miseries with the greatest patience and

[1] April 21st, 1767.

charity, pretending not to notice them, and not requiring from them the practice of virtue at a time when they feel depressed by miseries. Should it seem necessary to make a charitable correction, let him put it off until after the time of sickness, or make it at a time when he foresees it will be taken well. Let him spare neither expense nor trouble to furnish the sick brethren with all possible comforts, that are compatible with the religious state that they may have no reason to complain, but feel quite at home. Let him also call in due time for the physician, and take particular care that the medicine prescribed may be given at the proper time, as otherwise he would be accountable to God for all the pains and sufferings of his brethren. Should he not have time to attend himself to what has been said, let him charge one of the most charitable, self-sacrificing and judicious subjects to render these services to the sick. The best suited for this purpose are, generally speaking, those who have often been sick themselves. "It is by my own pains, sufferings and infirmities," says St. Frances de Chantal, "that the Lord has been pleased to make me sympathize with the sick, and practise patience and charity towards them, and, had it not been for my own continual infirmities, which the Lord inflicted upon me, it would have proved a difficult task for me to be instrumental to our holy Father St. Francis de Sales to institute our Order in that state of mildness and charity, in which it is now existing ; but the Lord made me understand, that there is nothing equal to perfect charity." Let the Superior remember that

21

his charity and affection for the sick cannot easily go to excess when there is question of procuring relief for them ; in a word, he must be sick with the sick, his care to give ease, assistance and comfort should almost exceed belief, not only when his brethren are dangerously ill, but also when they complain of light indispositions. These indispositions, it is true, may sometimes be nothing but over great anxiety for their health, or may be only imaginary, or too much exaggerated, yet, generally speaking, he should believe what they tell him, according to what St. Augustine prescribes in his rules ; for a slight indisposition may prove serious if neglected in the beginning ; even in imaginary evils there is some reality at the bottom on account of the uneasiness and anxiety which it produces ; besides, should the Superior not believe them, they would be afraid to tell him again when they are really indisposed, thinking to themselves, that it would be useless for them to speak to him about it as he would not believe them anyhow; and this might be followed by evil consequences: finally, it is better for the Superior to be deceived than not to apply remedies to certain evils which possibly may exist. He ought to conceal his hesitation to believe them, should he have even the best reasons for it ; to manifest it, would always hurt their feelings; it is better for him to show himself rather ready to believe them than to expose himself to the danger of violating charity.

To these directions mostly taken from the writings of St. Alphonsus, I will add the example of some other Saints to give them more weight and authority.

In the life of St. Ignatius of Loyola we read as follows: He gave orders that, if any were sick, he should be immediately informed of it, and he generally inquired after them every day. The infirmarian had always to come with the other officers of the house to give his report every evening after supper. He gave command that whatever the doctor ordered should be exactly attended to, and the steward went twice a day to receive his directions, and any one who failed in this duty was severely punished. One night having inquired of the infirmarian if he had provided everything which the doctor had ordered, and the man having humbly confessed that certain things had not been procured for a sick man according to order, he sent him out to search for them with two companions, forbidding his return until he had found them.

Another time the infirmarian and steward having forgotten to send for the doctor in good time for a sick man, he sent them out at midnight, saying that they should not enter the house again 'till they brought the doctor with them. And since this was not possible at that hour, they were obliged to seek shelter in a hospital until the morning. One day when they were in want of money to provide some necessary articles for the sick, he had the pewter plates, dishes and bed coverings sold. To one who was oppressed by melancholy under his illness, he sent some of the novices who were skilled in music, to refresh his mind by their songs. Besides showing these marks of attention to the sick, he used himself to visit them from time to time, and greatly consoled them by his sweet and divine discourses. If the malady increased, or if blood was to be drawn, he used to assist them, fearing lest the bandages might become loosened, or some dangerous accident occur. The General of the Society himself used to arrange the beds, shake mattresses and coverings and take part in all the services of the house however low or dirty. "I have myself seen him," writes Ribadeneira, "cleanse the beds of the sick from vermin that he might relieve the sufferers from this plague." Even when infirm himself he would retain the superintendence of the sick. He used to say that God's providence had made him weak and of feeble health, that he might be taught by his own experience to compassionate the sick. He gave directions that no burden should be imposed upon the newly-recovered without his own permission. Moreover, though they were dismissed from the infirmary, he directed that their meals should be provided by the infirmarian and not by the cook, and that they should remain under the care of the physician until their health and strength were fully established."

Of St. Alphonsus it is related in his life, that when any of the students were ill, he spared nothing in order to facilitate their recovery; he would send for the best physicians in the neighborhood, and if the sick persons were humble and resigned, they obtained a fresh hold on his love. "I am their father," he would say, "and the Society is their mother. Since they have left their parents in order to give themselves up to God, it is right that they should be treated with the greatest charity."

We read in the life of St. Francis of Assisium, that one of his brethren in religion had contracted a sort of consumption in consequence of his immoderate mortifications. Hearing that this sick man had a desire for fresh grapes, St. Francis took him into a vineyard where he sat down with him under a vine after he had blessed it; he then gave him some grapes; no sooner had the sick man eaten them than he felt quite cured; he often related this act of charity to his brethren with tears in his eyes, to show them how much they were beloved by their father.

One night as he learned that one of his brethren could not rest at night feeling exceedingly hungry in consequence of excessive fasting, he sent for him at once ; in order to relieve him from his painful feelings he gave him bread to eat and he himself ate also in order to encourage this man to do the same. Next morning the Saint related to his brethren in religion what had happened during the night and he added : "My brethren, take an example from this, not indeed from my having eaten, but from my having fulfilled the precept of charity."

We read of St. Frances de Chantal, that her first exercise in the morning, after leaving the choir, was to visit the sick, to attend to the detail of their wants, to give direction that every necessary attention should be bestowed upon them, to spend much of her precious time in giving her personal attendance and in performing every species of charitable service. In the execution of these duties she was heard to exclaim: "Had I health and strength I could wish to have no other employment in the Order but to attend to the sick in the infirmary."

One of the principal reasons why the heart, the eyes, the hands and all the energies of a Superior should be directed to give ease, comfort and relief to the sick, is that thus it may be more easy for him to benefit their souls in their pains and sufferings; for a sick man will listen so much the more willingly to the spiritual discourse of his Superior as he notices more his charity and solicitude for him. Many a soul, it is true, is brought to a sense of her duty and has entered into herself by means of bodily sickness; but the number of those who do not profit by their sufferings is far greater, because there are but too many who at the time of sickness, especially when the disease has assumed a chronic form, and also at the time of convalescence, do not combat their disorderly appetites, and, from being servants of God they soon become the slaves of corrupt nature destitute of all zeal and love for prayer and mortification.

To guard the sick against this spiritual lethargy, a Superior will do well to relate to them what Father Surin, S. J., writes in one of his letters: "A young man," he says, "filled with the Holy Ghost, and with whom I had the happiness to travel for three days and from whom I learned more of the spiritual life than ever before, told me among others, that one of our greatest evils was that we did not profit well by our bodily infirmities and indispositions.

"The Lord," said he," inflicts them upon us for ends most wise, uniting Himself to the soul far more perfectly by sufferings than by consolations. Over great care for preserving our health is a great obstacle in the road to perfection."

Should a soul experience a great desire to advance in the spiritual life and to give herself up to prayer but feel unable to do so on account of her bodily infirmities, let her consider that God requires of her an angelic patience, a constant resignation and calm submission to the dispositions of His divine Providence, a generous abandonment of herself to His fatherly care, a perfect holy indifference as to life or death and an utter contempt for all earthly things: if she is thus faithful and if the Lord should wish to make use of her for His glory, He will repair in an hour's time all the harm that a sickness of several years may have caused her to suffer in her body. Hence sick people must be repeatedly exhorted to pray often and most fervently for the grace to profit well by their sickness, and obtain the wise end for which the Lord is accustomed to visit us with different kinds of infirmities, in order that it may be said of them in truth: "This sickness is not unto death, but for the glory of God, that the Son of God may be glorified by it."[1]

A powerful argument to dispose sick people to submission to God's will and to holy indifference as to life or death may be taken from what St. Alphonsus says in his Introduction to his book "Triumphs

[1] John 11, 4.

of the Martyrs," No. 24 and 27—viz: "I must quote here," says he, "a passage of St. Augustine, who says that the martyrs became martyrs not so much on account of the pains and tortures which they suffered, but rather on account of the cause and end for which they suffered.[1] Hence St. Thomas teaches that martyrdom, properly speaking, consists in this, that one should die in order to practise an act of virtue ; the martyrs then obtained the glory of martyrdom by accepting of death for the purpose of pleasing God and doing His holy will.

Death is a tribute, which every one must pay. It is a most painful martyrdom. Even many of the Saints were afraid of it, nay, even our Saviour Himself felt it most keenly. Hence, not only those acquire the merit and crown of martyrdom who die for the sake of faith, but also all those who accept of any other kind of death with all its horrors, with the intention of pleasing God and doing His holy will ; because thereby they perform the greatest act of virtue, abandoning and sacrificing themselves as they do without reserve to the divine pleasure. It follows, moreover, that a soul will obtain as many crowns of martyrdom as she has made sincere acts of abandonment of her will to the divine will concerning her death. Thus we shall see many Saints in heaven crowned with the merit of martyrdom without having shed their blood for Jesus Christ. We should then pray to the Lord most earnestly to grant us the grace to accept death at His hands with the intention of

[1] Epist. 16, 7.

pleasing Him and doing His will.'' From what has
been said it follows also that, as a martyr is admitted
to the beatific vision of God immediately after his
death without passing through purgatory, a soul leaving the world in the above manner, will likewise enter
heaven immediately after her departure, her death
being an act of perfect love for God, by which all sins
and punishments are cancelled.

Although this doctrine is very consoling for sick
persons and well calculated to dispose them to a perfect resignation to God's holy will, yet let it be remembered, that if the Lord does not enlighten his
mind to understand it, and inflame his will to embrace and to love it, he will draw from it but little
comfort and encouragement. In the life of St. Ludwina, who was sick for thirty-eight years in succession,
we read that in the beginning of her sickness she
shrank from suffering. By a particular disposition of
Providence, however, a celebrated servant of God,
John Por, went to see her, and perceiving that she
was not quite resigned to the will of God, he exhorted
her to meditate frequently on the sufferings of Jesus
Christ that by the remembrance of His Passion she
might gain courage to suffer more willingly. She
promised to do so and fulfilled her promise, but could
not find any relief for her soul. Every meditation
was disgusting and unpleasant and she began again
to break out into her usual complaints. Upon being
asked by her director how she had succeeded in her
meditation upon our Lord's Passion, and what profit
she had derived from it: "O my father," she replied,

"your counsel was very good indeed, but the greatness of my sufferings does not permit me to find any
consolation in meditating on my Saviour's sorrows."
Seeing at last that Ludwina derived no benefit from
all his charitable exhortations, the Rev. Father Por
thought of another means. He gave her Holy Communion and immediately after, whispered into her
ear: "Till now I have tried to console you, but in
vain ; but now let Jesus Christ Himself perform this
office." Behold! no sooner had she swallowed the
Sacred Host than she felt so great a love for Jesus
Christ and so ardent a desire to become like unto
Him in His sufferings that she broke ont into sobs
and sighs, and for two weeks she was hardly able to
stop her tears. From this moment she never complained any more but desired to suffer still more for
Jesus Christ.

Hence it is evident that a Superior should direct
that the sick be strengthened by the reception of the
sacraments as often as possible ; for they will derive
more benefit from one single communion than fiom
all the exhortations he may give them, no matter how
pious or persuasive soever they may be.

I feel I must finish this chapter for fear of becoming too tedious to my readers. I have expatiated so
much upon this point from the conviction, that there
is scarcely anything better calculated to draw the
blessing of God upon a Superior and his Community,
and to confirm his subjects in love and esteem for their
vocation than the careful and charitable attendance to
the corporal and spiritual wants of the sick, whilst,

on the other hand, the neglect of this duty is followed by many great evils.

How well the Lord is pleased with a Superior faithfully complying with this duty, and how great a reward is awaiting him in the life to come, may be gathered from what we read in the life and revelations of St. Gertrude. One day after having recited the office as far as the fifth lesson St. Gertrude saw a religious who was ill and who had no one to say matins with her. The Saint, moved by the charity which always animated her, said to our Lord: "Thou knowest, O Lord, that I have almost exhausted the little strength I have in reciting my Office so far ; nevertheless, as I ardently desire Thee to abide with me during these holy days and as I have not a fitting abode prepared for Thee, I am willing, for Thy sake, and in satisfaction for my faults, to commence Matins again." As she began the Office once more, our Lord verified the words which He had said : "I was sick and you visited Me;" and as you did it to one of these My least brethren, you did it to Me[1] by appearing to her and overwhelming her with caresses, which could neither be explained nor understood.

It appeared to the Saint that our Lord was seated at a table in the most sublime glory, and that He was distributing ineffable gifts, graces, and joys to the souls in heaven, on earth and in purgatory, not only for each word, but even for each *letter* which she had repeated ; and she also received an intelligence of the Psalms, Responses and Lessons, which filled her with

[1] Matt. 25, 40.

inexpressible delight. And when she besought
our Lord to pour forth an abundant grace and
benediction on the whole Church, "What do
you desire that I should do, My beloved?" replied He, "for I give Myself up to you with
the same love and resignation as I abandoned
Myself to My Father on the Cross; for even
as I would not descend from the Cross, until
He willed it, so now I desire to do nothing but
what you will. Distribute, then, in virtue of My
Divinity, all that you desire and as abundantly as
you desire."

After Matins, the Saint retired again to rest
and our Lord said to her: "She who wearies
herself in exercises of charity, has a right to
repose peacefully on the couch of charity," and
as He said this, He soothed her soul so tenderly,
that it appeared to her as if she did indeed
repose on the bosom of this heavenly Bride-
groom. Then she beheld a tree of charity, very
high and very fair, covered with fruit and flowers and with leaves shining like stars which
sprang forth from the heart of Jesus, extend-
ing and lowering its branches so as to surround and cover the nuptial couch on which
the soul of Gertrude reposed. And she saw a
spring of pure water gush forth from its roots,
which shot upwards and then returned again
to its source, and this refreshed her soul marvel-
lously. By this she understood the Divinity of
Jesus Christ sweetly reposing in His humanity,

which imparts ineffable joys to the charitable
elect.[1]

"It is my opinion," writes St. Frances de Chantal to a Mother
Superior, "that you should not leave your Community for the purpose
of serving those who are afflicted with a contagious sickness; for
should you be infected, the whole Community would be deranged and
suffer greatly. The Superior should not expose herself, unless the salvation of a sick person would be in danger, which can hardly be the
case with us, as we take care to keep ourselves in such a state as we
wish to be at the hour of our death. Superiors should take a reasonable care of their health which is more necessary to the Community
than that of any other member."

[1] Chap. 36.

CHAPTER XIII.

ON OBEDIENCE.

AVING thus united his children in the bonds of charity, the Superior should also endeavor to unite them to himself by obedience. He should labor strenuously to accomplish this object. It is in obedience that the essence of the religious life consists. This virtue, then, is to be maintained in its full vigor, with all possible strictness. "Obedience alone," says St. Alphonsus, "can preserve the Order and its true spirit ; but I repeat, obedience towards every one who holds the place of the Superior ; for, otherwise, the whole order will be in peril. Hence, any other faults can be more easily forgiven, than those against obedience. If perfect obedience be given up, the Order will be destroyed." In the lives of the holy founders of religious Orders we read, that they were slow to command, but that they were urgent when it was necessary to obtain obedience. Although every other fault found mercy with them, yet their severity was great when even a slight deviation from obedience was in question. Their zeal then became enkindled without any respect of persons.

But as in religion, all should be done out of love, nothing by constraint; the Superior should do all in his power, to make his subjects conceive a great love for the holy virtue of obedience. To accomplish this, he ought frequently to hold out to his subjects, in public and in private, in season and out of season, the excellence, the beauty, the merit and all the advantages of this virtue. The yoke of Jesus Christ is sweet, and easy to carry, if viewed in a proper manner. Let the Superior make his subjects well understand, that there is a great dignity and nobility in carrying this yoke, since it gives true liberty to all those who bear it.

What can be more noble for a soul than to seek her own good? for one thing is good for one, another for another. Now what is the good of every thing? It is that which makes the thing better and more perfect. It is clear that inferior beings cannot make superior ones better and more perfect. Now the soul being immortal, is superior to all earthly, or perishable things. These, then, cannot make the soul better and more perfect, but rather worse than she is; for he who seeks what is worse than himself, makes himself worse than he was before. Therefore, the good of the soul can be only that which is better and more excellent than the soul herself. Now it is God alone who is this good — He being Supreme Goodness Itself. He who possesses God, may be said to possess the goodness of all other things; for whatever goodness they possess, they have from God. In the sun, for instance, you admire the light; in a flower, beauty;

in bread, the savor; in the earth, its fertility. All
these have their being from God. No doubt, God
has reserved to Himself far more, than He has
bestowed upon creatures. This truth admitted, it
necessarily follows that he, who enjoys God, possesses
in him all other things; and consequently, the very
same delight which he should have taken in other
things, had he enjoyed them separately, he enjoys in
God, in a far greater measure, and in a more elevated
manner. For this reason, St. Francis of Assisium
often used to exclaim: "My God and my All" — a
saying to which he was so accustomed, that he could
scarcely think of anything else and often spent whole
nights in meditating on this truth.

Certainly, true contentment is only that which is
taken in the Creator, and not that which is taken in
the creature; a contentment which no man can take
from the soul, and in comparison of which, all other
joy is sadness; all pleasure, sorrow; all sweetness,
bitterness; all beauty, ugliness; all delight, affliction.
It is most certain that "when face to face we shall
see God, as He is," we shall have most perfect joy
and happiness. It follows, then, most clearly, that,
the nearer we come to God in this life, the more contentment of mind and the greater happiness of soul,
we shall enjoy; and this contentment and joy
is of the self-same nature as that which we
shall have in heaven: the only difference is,
that here our happiness is small, whilst there
it will be infinitely great. A truly wise man
then, is he who, here below, seeks God and en-

deavors to be united as much as possible with His Supreme Good.

But now let me ask, what course of life is better calculated to find God and bring about the union of the soul with her Supreme Good, than the religious state? It is precisely this manner of life which aims at nothing else than the service of God, or the exact fulfilment of the Divine will.

What can be more reasonable than always to follow this course of life, to seek this happiness; nay, even to bind ourselves by vows evermore to follow it? Happy fetters, blessed chains these vows! They are not the chains of a slave and the marks of captivity, as the children of the world falsely imagine, from whom the mysteries of the Kingdom of Heaven are hidden; on the contrary, they are the bright ornaments of *those who are truly free*—the children of God, to whom it is given to understand the mysteries of the Kingdom of Heaven.

Certainly, he is free who does what he himself wills. A just man, though he obey the law, or authority, does nevertheless always what he wills, because he desires the good which is commanded, and does it, not induced by force of the outward command, but of his own desire and inclination. When a man directs a traveller in his way, no one can say, that he forces him to go that way, because the traveller desires it far more than he who directs him: so, whatever is suggested to a religious in his spiritual way and journey, either by word or writing, he takes it, as behoves him, for his own good and salvation, of which

22

he is very desirous. The good which he thus does, he does willingly and cheerfully, receiving and performing the commands of his Superior, or of his rules, as if he did it naturally. So that there cannot be truer liberty than that which religious people enjoy; — for their obligations are the result of their own free choice.

But let us make this truth still plainer. No rational creatures enjoy a better and greater liberty than do the Saints in heaven; for they cannot sin anymore. True liberty does not consist in being able to commit sin. The power of sinning is no power at all; it is a mark of weakness and misery, rather than of perfection. God, Who is Supreme Liberty, and Who can do all things, cannot sin. To have the power of sinning, is to be under the power of sin; and this power of sin in a man is in proportion to the power of his will to resist sin. The Saints in heaven, then, who are no longer under this power of sin, are perfectly free and happy. Hence the more we lessen in us this power of sinning by determining our will to what is perfect, the more free and the more perfect we render ourselves. Now we lessen this power of sinning by taking the vows of religion, especially, that of obedience; for by them it is, precisely, that we bind our will always to the will of God. O happy necessity which continually urges us to do what is best! It is, therefore, a great advantage for our free will to be thus bound; for, by this means, far from being destroyed, it is rendered far more perfect, conformed as it is, to the rule of all perfection — the will of God. We have then good reason to rejoice at being thus bound by vows. It is by them that we have renounced that kind of liberty which we could not have made use of without great prejudice to ourselves. Were we to walk towards a dangerous precipice, our friends would do us a great favor by blocking our passage in such a manner as to make it impossible for us to run into the gulf below, though we should be inclined to do so. Now, if we wish to cast ourselves into the gulf of hell, we have but to follow the way of our own will. "If there were no self-will," says St. Bernard, "there would be no hell." Consequently, if the passage.thither be so completely blocked as to prevent us from following it, the greatest good is done us.

Hence a learned doctor says: "The vows are so far from lessening the liberty of a man that, on the contrary, he who binds himself by them enjoys a more perfect liberty than any one else; for true liberty consists in being master of one's self, and he who is thus bound and united to God, is without doubt, more his own master than he who is not thus bound." To illustrate:

Interrogate any one of those who, with an insatiable heart, look after earthly gain, ask him what he thinks of you who renounce all to follow Christ and purchase heaven; ask him, I say, whether you do wisely? Certainly, he will answer, you do wisely. Ask him again, why he does not do himself what he commends in you? He will answer: It is because I cannot. Why can you not? Because avarice will not

let me. It is because he is not free; he is not master
of himself nor of what he possesses. If he is truly
master of himself and of what he has, let him lay it
out to his own advantage; let him exchange earthly
for heavenly goods; if he cannot, let him confess, that
he is not master of himself, but a slave to his love for
money.

Again, your inducement to make the vow of
chastity is, your hope, by the grace of God, to become
so far master of yourself as to keep this virtue. And
what prevents another from taking this vow is, the
fact that he does not believe that he is sufficiently
master of himself to be able to keep it. Thus you
see that you are the person that has the greatest
power of himself to do what you wish, and to do what
you believe you ought to do. But it is precisely in
this that liberty consists. For the liberty which the
other keeps for himself, is not a true liberty; it is a
subjection rather, nay, even a slavery; because, in
reality, like a slave, he obeys his passion which has
acquired the mastery over him, and which drags him
into sin. He is a slave to his passion "which leads
him captive to the law of sin."[1] For he who is overcome, is a slave to him who overcame him; wherefore "whosoever sins is a slave to sin."[2]

It is the same in regard to obedience. What
moved you to make the vow of obedience was, your
confident hope, by the assistance of God, to have so
much power over yourself as to follow always the will
of your Superior. And that which prevents another

[1] Rom. vii, 23.   [2] John viii, 34.

from taking the same vow, is, his conviction that he has not so much power over himself as to be able to renounce his own will, and to submit to that of another. You see then clearly, that you have more power over yourself and more real liberty by subjecting yourself to the yoke of obedience, than has this other person who is not able to do so. As therefore all those are slaves, who can only do as vice suggests, so, on the other hand, all those are truly free, who live according to virtue. Thus there is a real greatness and dignity in carrying the yoke of obedience; it is indeed this kind of yoke to carry which the Holy Ghost exhorts us in these words: "Put thy feet into her fetters, and thy neck into her chains; bow down thy shoulder, and bear her, and be not grieved with her bands."[1] Thrice happy chains, that give liberty rather than restrain it in those who bear them!

It is, then, quite certain, that the greatness of our liberty is in proportion, to the power which our will has *to will and to do* what God wishes us to do. But let it be remembered, that, the greater this power is, the greater is also the goodness and perfection of our will; and the greater the perfection of our will is, the greater is also the perfection of all its good actions; for the goodness and merit of our actions, is in proportion to the goodness of our will. To illustrate:—

A man who is hardened in sin, offends God more grievously when he sins, than another who sins out of frailty or from a sudden outburst of passion, because he sins by a will determined to evil, which is to

[1] Eccles. vi, 25.

sin against the Holy Ghost; so, in like manner, all those good actions which proceed from a will quite determined to what is good, are, doubtless, of a far greater perfection and merit, than all others can be. The greater the artist, the more valuable the work. So before God, the better the will, the better and more meritorious are all its good actions.

Another illustration of what has been said: Every action of Jesus Christ is of an infinite merit, because in Him the Divinity is so united to the Humanity as to make but one person. If we substitute, for our will, the will of God as the rule and basis of all our actions, every one of them will be, as it were, of an infinite value, being as they are, actions of the divine will rather than of our own. Now it is precisely by obedience that we substitute the divine will for our own; and thus acquire infallibly, that constancy and determination of the will to adhere to what is good, which is looked upon by Theologians as one of the chief conditions of virtue.

It is by obedience that we acquire this goodness or perfection of the will far faster than by any other means. Let a soul practise, for a certain length of time, all virtues, without practising that of obedience, and let another soul, during the same length of time, practise perfect obedience, and then let us rest assured, that the latter will surpass the former in merits, in grace, in union with God, and in heavenly glory hereafter, far more than the light of the sun surpasses that of the dimmest star. A soul earnestly endeavoring to practise perfect obedience, will by degrees, become so united with God as not to be able to will except what God wills ; but not to be able to will except what God wills, is, as it were, to be what God is, with whom *to will and to be* is but one and the same thing ; for to whomsoever power is given to become a child of God, to him is also given power, not indeed, to be God himself, but to be what God is.

To a soul thus disposed, the Lord grants such great favors as it is impossible to describe. He gives her a faith so lively, a confidence so firm, a charity so ardent, a zeal for the salvation of her neighbor so burning, a degree of prayer so sublime, a prudence so unusual, a courage in all difficulties so invincible, a peace so profound, a humility and simplicity of heart so admirable, and sometimes even a spirit so prophetic, together with a gift of performing miracles so extraordinary as to make every one exclaim: Truly, that soul can say with St. Paul: "I live, now not I, but Christ liveth in me."[1]

God has an infinite desire to communicate to us all His gifts and even Himself; but it is only the obedient whom He finds disposed to receive them. Hence it is that, when He intends to raise a soul to an eminent degree of sanctity, He gives such a soul particular lights in regard to the virtue of obedience ; He inspires her at the same time with great love for this virtue so as to induce her to practise it in a perfect manner, that is, with promptitude, with simplicity, with cheerfulness, with humility, with fortitude, with holy indifference and with perseverance.

---

[1] Gal. ii, 20.

St. Catharine of Sienna felt an ardent desire to become a great Saint. So she begged our Lord one day to teach her the shortest way to perfection. "Know then," said our Lord to her, "that the salvation of My servants and their perfection consists in this only, that they do My will, and that they endeavor, with their whole strength, to do it always; that they obey, glorify, and look to Me alone at all times. The more carefully they do this, the more they advance in perfection; for, then, they adhere and unite themselves more closely to Me Who am Supreme Perfection Itself. In order that you may understand this sublime truth expressed in a few words, consider My Christ, in Whom I am well pleased. He annihilated Himself, taking the form of a Servant, being made in the likeness of man, in order that, by His example and word, He might lead you back to the way of truth, from which you had gone astray so very far, walking in the greatest darkness of the intellect. He was obedient unto death, teaching you by His persevering obedience how your sa'vation depends altogether on your firm resolution to do nothing but My will alone. He who carefully meditates upon His life and doctrine, will soon come to understand that the summit of perfection consists in nothing else, than the uninterrupted, persevering, and constant, accomplishment of My will. This He has declared repeatedly: Not every one who says to Me, Lord, Lord, shall enter into the kingdom of heaven, but he, who obeys the will of My Father Who is in heaven, shall enter into the kingdom of heaven. He means to say, that no

one, whosoever he may be, and whatsoever exterior
good works he may perform for My Name's Sake,
shall be admitted to the glory of life everlasting, if
he has not performed all, according to My will.

"He has said again: 'I have come down from
heaven not to do My own will, but the will of Him
Who sent Me.' And: 'Not My will, but Thine, be
done.' Now, if, in imitation of your Saviour, you
will do My will, in which alone your salvation consists, you must necessarily renounce your own will in
everything; you must make it die, as it were, having
no longer any regard for it. The more you die to
yourself, the more you endeavor to empty yourself of
what is your own: the more will I fill you with what
is My own. But no one will arrive at this perfection,
unless he constantly renounces his self-will. He,
who neglects this, neglects also this sublime perfection; but he, who practises it, does My will in a perfect manner, and I am well pleased in him. I am
always near such a one; for nothing gives Me greater
pleasure than to be with you, and to co-operate with
you. My delight is, to be with the children of men;
and to change you, by My grace, into Myself, so that
you may become one with Me, by partaking of My
perfections, of My peace, and of My joy. But this I
will not do, unless you so will; for, I will never
violate the privileges of your free-will.

"Now, in order that you may be inflamed with
a most vehement desire of submitting yourself to Me,
and of uniting your will most closely to Mine, you
have but to consider My ardent desire of being with

23

you. This you will understand the better, the more deeply you reflect how I have willed, that My only-begotten Son should assume flesh, that My Divinity, stripping Itself, as it were, of Its Majesty, should be united to your humanity, in order that, by this inconceivable love of Mine, you might be induced, drawn, nay, sweetly forced, to unite your will in the same manner with Mine, and to remain thus always united with Me.

"Moreover, consider how I have willed, that this My Beloved Son, should give Himself up to the horrible and cruel death of the Cross; that, by His sufferings, He might cancel your sins, which had separated you so far from Me.

"Finally, consider how I have prepared for you a precious banquet in the Most August Sacrament, of His own Flesh and Blood, in order that, receiving Him, you might be transformed into Me; for, as bread and wine which you take, become one with the substance of your body, so you, too, by receiving Him become spiritually changed and transformed into Myself, because He is one with Me.

"It is certain, that your perfect welfare depends on your perfect renunciation of self; for, I will fill you with My grace, in proportion as you empty yourself of your will. This participation in My will, effects your perfection by My grace, without which you would be totally destitute of all virtue and dignity. Now, in order to obtain this grace, you must, in profound humility, and in deep knowledge of your own misery and poverty, ardently desire, and strenuously endeavor, to obey Me only, and do nothing, but My will. In order to be enabled to effect this, you must, by means of your memory and intellect, build for yourself a cell out of My will. You must keep this all closed, remaining shut up within it, so that, withersoever you go, you may not go out of it ; and withersoever you look, you may not look out of it. Regulate all your affections according to My will ; speak and do nothing but what is pleasing to Me, and what you know to be in accordance with My will. Then, the Holy Ghost will teach you everything you have to do.

"There is yet another means, by which you may attain to a perfect renunciation of your will, viz : if there are servants of Mine who will teach and guide you to do My will. Submit yourself to them, by giving up, into their hands, your own self, and all that is yours, always obeying and following their advice. You hear Me, if you listen to My wise and faithful servants.

"Moreover, I wish that you should often meditate, with an unyielding faith and an elevated mind, upon Me, your most glorious God, Who created you, in order to make you capable of partaking of My own happiness ; of the happiness of the Most High and Most Powerful Being, doing for you everything that I please ; Whose will no one can resist ; without Whose will, nothing can happen to you, as I spoke by the Prophet Amos. Meditate upon Me, your God, Whose wisdom and knowledge are infinite ; Who sees and penetrates everything at a glance ; Who cannot be deceived, nor disturbed by any error; Who governs you, and, at the same time, heaven and earth; because I am God, the most Wise Being.

"And in order that you may understand something of the effects of this My Wisdom, you must know, that, from the evil of guilt and punishment, I can draw a good which far surpasses the extent of the evil itself.

"Furthermore, I wish, that you should meditate upon Me, your God, as being most perfect in love and in kindness; whence I cannot will anything but what is good, salutary, and profitable to you and to others; for no evil can go out of Me. I hate nothing, and, as I have created man through love, so do I continue to love him with infinite love.

"To these truths, you must always cling with steadfast faith. From a constant meditation upon the same, it must be clear to you, how, under My Wise Providence, afflictions, temptations, hardships, sickness, and other adversities are permitted to befall you for no other reason, than for your own good, in order that by them, you may be induced to amend what is bad in you, and begin to walk in the road of virtue, which leads you to Me, your Supreme Good.

"If this light of Faith shines on you, you will also understand that I, your God, know better how to promote your welfare, and wish for it more than you do yourself; and that, without My grace, you would be ignorant of it, unable to promote it, nay, unable even to will it.

"This being true, you must endeavor, with your

whole strength, to submit your will to Mine; then
peace will always reign in your heart; for I will be
with you; because My habitation is in peace. There
will be no scandal of sin for you, that is to say, no
occasion of sin; for, great is the peace of those who
love My Name; they shall not fall, because they love
nothing but My law, that is to say, My will. My
law is that rule, according to which all things are
directed. Their union with Me is so close, and their
delight in doing My will, so great, that, happen
what may, nothing but sin is able to disturb or disquiet them. Their souls being purified, they see
without deception, that from Me, the Ruler of the
Universe, Who govern all things with wonderful
wisdom, charity and order, nothing but good can
proceed, and that consequently, I can take care both
of their temporal and spiritual welfare, far better and
with more salutary effect than they can themselves.

"Persevering in the consideration, that all things
which happen and which they may endure, proceed
from Me, and *not* from their neighbor, they feel animated with unconquerable patience, baffling every
attack, so that they suffer everything, not only with
a tranquil mind, but also with a cheerful heart, because, in all things, whether exterior or interior,
they taste the sweetness of My unspeakable love.

"And this is to give true honor to My goodness,
namely, to believe and consider, with a thankful and
cheerful heart, in all difficulties and adversities, that,
I order all things sweetly, that everything proceeds
from the profound source of My love, and that noth-

ing but your own will and self-love hinders and destroys the fruit of this consideration, and the union of your will with Mine. Were you to do away with these obstacles, there would be no longer any hell for you, either in the world to come, with its perpetual torments of body and soul, or in this world, by continual disquietudes of mind and the ever recurring anxieties of exterior and interior troubles.

"Well, if you wish to live, endeavor to die to this life, drowning yourself in the unchangeable life of perpetual glory, and doing away with your own self-will. 'Blessed are the dead that die in the Lord,' and, 'Blessed are the poor in spirit.' These see Me in mutual love, in their earthly pilgrimage, and will see Me in heaven, in everlasting bliss and glory."

Such were the lessons that our Lord gave to St. Catherine of Sienna. He also gave similar lessons to Blessed Margaret Alacoque. It was God Himself, says the writer of her life, Who prescribed to His servant, blind, entire, universal obedience towards all her Superiors. He exacted from her, that she should not only renounce, her lights, and her judgements, but even what He Himself prescribed to her. He did not wish to interfere with the ordinary rules of obedience. He required that she should even submit to her Superiors the Divine lights with which He had favored her. Upon this subject, she thus writes. "Though my Divine Saviour constituted Himself my Master and Director, yet He did not wish me to obey His commands without the consent of my Superiors to whom He wished me to yield, if I may say so, a more implicit obedience, than to Himself. What He particularly taught me, was to distrust myself, as the most cruel and powerful Enemy I could possibly have ; but He promised, that, should I place all my confidence in Him, and obey perfectly, depending in all things on the will of my Superiors ; He would protect me. Moreover, He forbade me to trouble myself about anything that might happen to me. He wished me to regard all the events of life as occurring in the order of His Providence and Will, for the greater honor and glory of His Name. Finding myself engaged in an employment which often prevented me from going with the Community to meditation ; a feeling of discontent arose in my mind one Easterday. I was immediately reproved by my Divine Master Who said : 'Know that the prayer of submission and of sacrifice, is more agreeable to Me, than contemplation and every other meditation, however holy it may appear.' These words caused in my soul, so deep a feeling of peace, that, from that time, I have never been troubled in the least by anything that my Superiors exacted from me." It sometimes happened, that her love of mortification led her, not indeed to violate the orders of her Superiors, but not to wait their permission before mortifying herself. Her Divine Master again reproved her for this very severely. "Thou deceivest thyself," said He to her one day, "in thinking to please Me by practising this kind of mortification which has been chosen by self-will rather than by the will of Superiors. Know that I reject all such things as fruits which self-will has turned to rottenness. Self-will in a religious soul, excites my abhorrence. It is more agreeable to Me that such a soul should remain in ease and quiet through obedience, than load itself, through caprice, with austerities." When Margaret once prolonged a penance beyond the appointed time, God said to her, as if angry with her: "What you did at first, was for Me ; what you are doing now, is for the devil."

Blosius[1] relates, that our Lord said one day to St. Gertrude: "Whosoever wishes Me to enter his heart, and take up My permanent abode within him, must give up to Me the *key* of his own will, and never require it back." We read in the life and revelations of this Saint as follows : A certain religious died, who had always been accustomed to pray very fervently for the souls of the faithful departed ; but she had failed in the perfection of obedience, preferring her own will to that of her Superior in her fasts and vigils. After her decease, she appeared adorned with rich ornaments, but so weighed down by a heavy burden which she was obliged to carry, that she could not approach God, though many persons were endeavoring to lead her to Him. St. Gertrude marvelled at this vision ; she was taught, that the persons who endeavored to conduct the soul to God, were those whom she had released by her prayers ; and that the heavy burden indicated the faults which the soul had committed against obedience. Then our Lord said: "Behold how these grateful

[1] Morrit. Spirit. C. 11.

souls endeavor to free her from the requirements of My justice, and show these ornaments : nevertheless, she must suffer for her faults of disobedience and self-will." The Saint replied : "But, Lord, did she not repent, when admonished of these faults before her death ? Did she not perform penance for them ? And does not the Scripture say : 'When man confesses, God pardons ?' Our Lord answered : "If she had not acted thus, the burden of her faults would have been so heavy that she could scarcely ever have come to Me."

After this, our Lord showed St. Gertrude the path by which the souls ascend to heaven. It resembled a straight plank, a little inclined, so that those who ascended, did so with difficulty. They were assisted and supported by hands on either side, which indicated the prayers offered for them. Those who were assisted by the Angels, had a great advantage, as they repelled the dragons who flew around it, endeavoring to prevent their prayers. The religious who had lived under obedience, were assisted by a kind of railing placed on each side of this plank, so that they were both supported and protected from falling. In some places, these railings were removed, as a punishment to those Superiors who had failed to govern their subjects by the rules of obedience. But all the souls who had been truly obedient, were assisted and supported by the Angels who removed every impediment from their path.

One day the soul of Brother Hermann appeared to St. Gertrude, in great sufferings. The Saint asked him : "For what fault have you to suffer most?" He replied : "For self-will and obstinacy. When I did any kindness for others, I would not do as they wished, but as I wished myself. So much do I suffer for this, that, were the mental agonies of all mankind united in one person, he would not endure more than I do at present." She replied : "What remedy will be most efficacious for you?" He answered : "To perform acts of the contrary virtue, and to avoid committing the same fault."[1]

Another time our Lord appeared to St. Gertrude and said to her : "Since you have renounced your own will in all things, I will pour forth on you, all the sweetness of My Divine Heart." As the Hebdomadaria recited the Chapter at Matins by heart, it was revealed to Gertrude, that she acted thus to satisfy a precept of the Rule, which requires that it should be thus recited, and that she acquired as much merit by this, as if as many persons as there were words in what she chanted, interceded for her with God. She remembered what St. Bernard said would happen at the hour of death, when our actions will address us thus : "You have produced us, we are your work, we will never leave you, but will abide continually with you, and appear with you at the day of judgement." Then God will permit all the actions of the obedient to appear as so many persons of distinction, who will console him, and intercede with him for God, so that each good action performed through obedience, with a pure intention, will obtain

[1] Revelations C. 10, p. 520.

the pardon of some negligence, and thereby afford extreme consolation to persons in their agony.

One day this Saint prayed to our Lord that he might vouchsafe to correct a fault in one of her Superiors. She received the following reply: "Do you not know, that not only this person, but also all those who have charge of this My beloved community, have some defects; no one can be entirely free from them in this life. And this happens by an excess of the mercy, tenderness, and love, with which I have chosen this Congregation, that, by this means their merit may be greatly increased. For it is something far more perfect to submit to a person whose faults are apparent, than to one who always appears perfect." To this, the Saint replied: "Although I am full of joy at perceiving great merit in inferiors, I ardently desire, that Superiors should be free from faults, and I fear they contract them by their imperfections." Our Lord answered: "I know the weaknesses of every one; I sometimes permit Superiors, in the diversity of their employments, to be sullied by some stains, as otherwise they would never attain to so high a degree of humility. Therefore, as the merit of inferiors is increased both by the perfections and imperfections of the Superiors, so, the merit of Superiors is increased by the perfections and imperfections of inferiors."

From these words, Gertrude learned to admire the infinite wisdom of God, manifesting Itself even in the very defects of the elect; so that, were there no other subject than this wherein the mercy of God shows forth, the united thanksgivings of all His creatures would not suffice to praise Him for it.

It is thus that the Lord has often vouchsafed to instruct His Saints on the virtue of obedience. Hence it is, that the maxims of the Saints on this subject, are all the same, and that they abhorred nothing so much as disobedience.

One day St. Magdalene appeared to St. Frances of Rome, and spoke to her on obedience thus: "By means of obedience, the soul carries out the decrees of the Divine Wisdom, and by this virtue, she infallibly reaches her last end, no one being able to put an insurmountable obstacle in her way: an obedient soul is always sure, that God governs her, and she will easily overcome every revolt of corrupt nature. She feels a firm confidence in God, and bears all adversities in the spirit of humility; she knows that nothing can befall her without the permission and will of Him, in Whom alone she feels delight, and into Whose hands she has irrevocably given up her entire will."[1]

"Poverty," says Pope John XXII.,[2] "is a great good, chastity is a greater one, obedience is the greatest of all. By poverty we rule over riches, by chastity over the flesh, by obedience over the spirit." St. Augustine, and St. Thomas Aquinas say the same. Our Lord did and said many things during thirty years, but all this is comprised in this one sentence of St. Luke: "He was subject to them." What greater praise can be bestowed upon a religious than this:

[1] Life Chapt. 22.   [2] Extrav, Quorumdam.

He was always submissive and obedient to all his Superiors. St. Gregory says : "Obedience alone is that virtue, by means of which, all other virtues take root in the soul, are perfected and preserved."[1] "So great are the advantages of obedience ;" said St. Francis of Assisium, "that for those who submit to it, no moment of time passes by without gain."

You must surrender yourself entirely into God's hands, and trust to His sweet Providence which confers grace on every man, according to his condition. As He guides the Superior that he may command rightly, so He assists the subject that he may obey well.

You must keep your eyes firmly fixed on your vocation ; and, not look upon him who governs, but upon Jesus Christ, in Whose place he governs.

You must not listen to those reasons which are suggested by the sensual part of your nature, but piously search out those which induce to obedience.

On your first entrance into religion, and at all subsequent times whatsoever, you ought to resign yourself into the hands of the Lord, your God, and of him who governs you.

You ought to desire to be ruled by a Superior who endeavors to subjugate your judgement, and to subdue your understanding.

In all things, except sin, you ought to do the will of your Superior and not your own.

You ought not to look to him who gives the order, whether he be the Chief or the deputy, or an

[1] 35. Moral C. 10.

inferior; but to God alone, Whose place he holds; otherwise the merit of obedience is diminished. "Keep a careful watch over yourself in this matter," says St. John of the Cross, "and do not reflect upon the character, ways, or conversation, or habits of your Superior. If you do, you will injure yourself, and you will change your obedience from divine into human, and you will be influenced by what you see in your Superior, and not by the invisible God Whom you should obey in him. Your obedience will be in vain, or barren in proportion as you are troubled by the untowardness of your Superior or pleased by his favor. I tell you, that a great many Religious in the way of perfection have been ruined by not looking upon their Superiors as they ought to have done; their obedience was almost worthless in the eyes of God, because it was influenced by human considerations. Unless you force yourself, therefore, to be indifferent as to who your Superior may be, so far as your private feelings go, you will never be spiritual, neither will you faithfully observe your vows."

When it seems to you that you are commanded by your Superior to do something against which your conscience revolts as sinful, and your Superior judges otherwise, it is your duty to yield your doubt to him, unless you are constrained by the evidence to believe that what he commands is sin. If submission does not appease your conscience you must impart your doubts to two or three persons of discretion, and abide by their decision. If this does not content you, you are very far from having attained that perfection which is required in the religious life.

"It is more meritorious," says St. Alphonsus, "to pick up a straw in obedience to the will of God, than to convert the whole world without it. By practising obedience, we gain more, than by performing many penances and devotions of our own accord. One act of this renunciation of self-will is of greater merit before God, than the erecting of many hospitals. A religious must do those good works which are prescribed in his rules, or by the precepts of his Superiors. The gratification of self-will, is death to the soul. My brethren; consider well, God requires of you, obedience and submission, far more than a hundred sacrifices and a thousand other good works. A soul that has given herself up to God without reserve, lives without loving, seeking, or asking for anything else."

"To perform holy actions in disobedience to one's Superior," says Cassian, "is very hurtful; for such as act badly, under the pretext of good, generally remain incorrigible."

"Do not murmur at the actions of Superiors," says St. Gregory, "even should they seem to deserve censure."

As one, by putting off his religious habit in order to leave the Order, apostatizes exteriorly, so in like manner, he apostatizes interiorly, who, instead of following the will of his Superior, contradicts him, or murmurs against him in public and in private.[1]

[1] St. Vincent de Paul.

Obedient souls need have no fear of the judgement of God ; for, they shall not be judged. So said our Lord one day, to St. Juliana Veronica.

The true perfection of the religious life consists in the renunciation of self-will.[1]

God requires of a soul that is determined to love Him, nothing more than *obedience*.[2]

For our own advantage and security, God wishes the Superiors to be, as it were, equal to Himself ; hence, He looks upon the honor and respect, or the contempt shown them, as shown to His own Majesty.[3]

In order that we may gain greater merit, God wishes us to be guided by faith, and to act up to its principles ; for this reason, he makes known His will to us by our Superiors, and not by Himself. Go to Ananias, said Jesus Christ to Saul, and he will tell you what you must do. Banish from your mind all temptations against your Superiors, as quickly as those against the virtue of holy purity. As to offices, neither refuse, nor ask for any ; prefer that office which is less honorable and more arduous. Do not imagine to find an excuse with God, for refusing an office, through fear of committing faults. It is your duty to serve the Order. Trust in the power of holy obedience, and the Lord will assist you. Only those offices with which your Superiors entrust you, are acceptable to God. Although it may sometimes seem to you, that certain arrangements and dispositions are not altogether prudent and discreet, yet, do not

[1] St. Bonaventure.   [2] St. Teresa.

[3] St. Bernard.

on that account complain and show dissatisfaction, but obey ; and, for the sake of obedience God will grant a happy issue.

"It is no great thing if I am obeyed," wrote St. Alphonsus to his brethren in religion, "but, I wish an equal submission to be shown to him, whosoever he be, that presides over any exercise ; for, whatever may be his personal merits, he holds the office of Superior. If this be not attended to, mischief is done, and we shall see nothing but confusion and disorder. On the day of judgement, religious will be accused only for that which they have done against obedience — but not for the works which they have performed *out of obedience.* Let him who wishes to glorify God, do so by renouncing his will."

Such are the principles of the Saints concerning obedience. Their lives were in strict conformity to these principles.

When St. Joseph Cupertino, one of the most extraordinary Saints of the Church, was enraptured and altogether absorbed in God, one word from his Superior would suffice to draw him out of this state. The Lord has so great love and respect for obedience, that He never detains a soul enraptured in the contemplation of His holy perfections, against the will of those who hold for her His place on earth. Obedience was the virtue of predilection of St. Joseph of Cupertino. He was wont to say: "I would rather die, than not obey."[1]

When St. John of the Cross needed a change of

[1] Brev. Rom. Sept. 18.

24

air for his health, he purposely chose that house, the Superior of which, he knew, was very much opposed to him, and would make him suffer a good deal.

St. Francis Regis was called home in the middle of a mission, and, notwithstanding all the efforts which the clergy made to retain him, he could not be prevailed upon to stay.

We read in the life of St. Juliana Veronica, that the devil made all possible efforts to induce this Saint to disobey her Confessors and Superiors. But all that he effected with her was, that she became so much the more obedient, writing her name from that time forward Veronica Juliana, daughter of obedience in spite of the devil. In reward for her great love of obedience, God manifested to her even such commands of her Superiors as were given only mentally. She executed them quite as promptly as those which were expressed.

We read the same of Blessed Girard, a lay-brother of the Congregation of the Most Holy Redeemer.

When St. Francis de Sales had resolved to tender his services to all those who were lying ill of the epidemic at Annecy, and to leave the continuation of the mission at Chablais to his fellow-laborers, his Bishop, Mgr. Granier, commanded him under obedience not to carry out his resolution. Francis obeyed most willingly, because to refuse obedience, was, in his eyes, a crime deserving great punishment. He understood, that it was an illusion of the devil for one to fancy, that he had a vocation for certain functions to which he was impelled only by self-love and self-will.[1]

St. Gertrude was of a rather delicate constitution. For this reason, she was treated by her Superiors, more indulgently than the other religious. Now, what did she do to keep pace with her other Sisters in religion, on the road to perfection? Nothing else than to submit, in all simplicity, her will to that of her Superior and to suffer herself to be guided by her in everything. Though her zeal enkindled in her an ardent desire to do what the rest of the Community did, yet she would be careful not to let this appear. When she was told to retire earlier than the other Nuns, she would go, without the least objection, being firmly persuaded, that if, through obedience she was lying on her bed, she would enjoy just as well the presence of her Divine Spouse Jesus Christ, as when present at the Divine Office in the Choir. Our Lord was so well pleased with this submission of Gertrude, that He revealed to St. Mechtilde, that, if any one wished to seek Him in this life, he would find Him in the Blessed Sacrament, and in the heart of Gertrude, in which He remained with delight.

St. Dorotheus relates of Dositheus, his scholar, the following. One day when he was reflecting on the rigorous account which he would have to give of himself before the tribunal of God, he was seized with a great fear of the Eternal Judge. In order to have good reason to be less afraid of Him, he embraced the religious life. But as his health would not allow him

[1] Life by Clavus.

to rise at mid-night for matins, nor eat the ordinary diet, nor comply with all the regular observances of the Community, he made up his mind to devote himself to the practice of perfect obedience, and to serve in the infirmary in the lowest offices. After having spent a life of perfect obedience for five years, he died of consumption. God, then revealed to the Abbot of the Monastery, that Dositheus was as high in glory as St. Paul and St. Anthony, the hermits, were. When the other religious heard this, they murmured and complained, saying: "Where is God's justice, if a man who never fasted, and who always eat of what was best, be equal to us who perform all duties of religion, and *bear the heat and burden of the day?*[1] What are we the better for all our austerities?" Whilst they were thus complaining, God made known to them that they did not understand the merit and excellence of obedience, a virtue which was so great and meritorious in His sight, that Dositheus had gained more by it in a short time, than many a one of them had done by his long and rigid mortifications.

The Saints went still farther in the renunciation of their will. They used to condescend to their equals, nay, even to their inferiors, whenever they could do so without violating their duty.

Condescension, it is true, cannot properly be termed obedience, because it is not practised through justice towards Superiors, but, through humility and charity towards equals, nay, even towards inferiors.

[1] Matt. 20, 12.

The humble man looks upon every other person as better than himself, and considers each one, in some degree, as his Superior whom he is to obey, or whose will he is to comply with.

This condescension, — which is no obligatory obedience, — is a virtue most amiable and acceptable to God. It may be practised in all *indifferent* matters. But that which is of obligation, or of greater benefit, must not be omitted for the sake of condescension. In such a case, the necessary remonstrances should be made in all humility. To give an example; I intend going to a certain place; but some one else requests me to go along with him to another place. As it is all the same to me whether I go or not, I conclude that it is God's will for me, rather to do the will of the other person, than my own, and I go with him. This manner of practising condescension was quite familiar to the Saints.

St. Anselm, during the whole course of his Priorship, was exceedingly loved by every one on account of his great condescension towards all, both Clergy and laity. When one came to him and said: My father, you ought to take a little broth, he would take some; when another came and said: My father, this will not agree with you, he would take no more. Thus, in all things wherein God was not offended, he submitted his will to that of his brethren, and even to that of secular persons. This exceedingly great condescension of the Saint, however, was not approved of by all. Some represented to him, that he should not yield so easily to the will of others, but that it was rather a duty for others to accomodate themselves to his will. "Alas! my dear children," exclaimed the Saint, "I suppose, you do not know my intention in thus acting. Know, then, that I firmly believe, that the will of God, and whatever is pleasing to Him, cannot be better manifested to me, than by the mouth of others. The Lord does not speak to me in person, nor does He send His angels to indicate to me, what is acceptable to Him. Stones, plants, and animals, cannot speak; it is, therefore, by men only, that I can learn the will of God. For this reason, I do what they tell me as well as I am able, and, in obeying men, I believe I obey God Himself, Who, by them, manifests His will to me.

"Moreover, God commands us to keep up charity and union with all men. Now, in my opinion, there is no means better calculated to effect this than condescension; gentle humble condescension must appear in all our actions.

"Besides, has not our Saviour said, that unless we become like unto children, we shall not enter into the kingdom of heaven? Be not astonished, then, to see me, like a child, so ready to comply with the will of others. In doing so, I do no more than what my God and Saviour requires of me. And after all, what does it matter whether I do this or that; whether I go to this place or that? But it would be indeed a great imperfection, if, in matters of so little importance, I could not comply with the will of my neighbor."

Behold how yielding this Saint was in everything

that was not contrary to the commandments of God, to the precepts of the Church, or to his rules, the observance of which must, of course, be preferred to everything else. Had any one required him to do something contrary to his rules, he would not have done it. These excepted, he had made it a rule, always to accommodate himself to the will of others.

The second example is that of St. Pachomius. Once when engaged in making mats, a boy said to him: "My Father, you do not do your work right; you must do it this way." Although the Saint knew, that he was doing his work right, yet he at once gave up, and made the mat just the way the boy showed him. One of his disciples said: "My Father, you commit two faults by doing what the child tells you. You expose the boy to vain-glory, and you injure your mats, which would be better if made according to your own way." The Saint replied: "My Son, should God permit this boy to be tempted to vain-glory, He will grant me so much humility, that the boy will be edified by it, and thus partake of it. What gain or loss can there be, if I make the mats in this or that way? But, no doubt, the loss would be great, were we to make but little account of these words of our Saviour: 'Unless you become like unto little children, you shall not enter into the kingdom of heaven!'" Oh! how profitable is it not for us, to be possessed of this Spirit of Condescension!

The Saints found holy obedience very easy and delightful, because they kept their eyes constantly fixed upon their divine Model Jesus Christ. His

whole life was one of constant obedience. But this
virtue shone forth most brightly when He was to be
crucified on Mount Calvary. There it was, that He
gave us the most touching lesson on obedience. There
He obeyed all, not only His Eternal Father, but even
Pilate, the soldiers, the executioners, although they
had no power over Him. He obeyed in everything,
even the most difficult things. At the first order
given Him, He laid down upon the cross and presented
His sacred hands and feet to be pierced with nails.
He obeyed in the most perfect manner, without contradiction, without resistance, without protestation,
without appealing to a superior tribunal; He obeyed
blindly, promptly and entirely, so much so, that He
preferred rather to lose His life than the merit of
obedience.

Happy he who understands and knows how to
profit well by this lesson of obedience, which the Son
of God gave us under the most difficult and most trying circumstances of His life. Our Lord Jesus Christ
has declared, that he who imitates Him perfectly in
this virtue, is His brother, His sister and even His
mother. "Whosoever," He says, "shall do the will
of My Father Who is in heaven, he is My brother and
sister and mother."[1] O what a happiness! to have it
in our power to become a brother and sister and even
a mother to Jesus Christ. As it was by a *fiat*, that
the Blessed Virgin became the mother of God, so it is
by a *fiat* (voluntas tua, Thy will be done,) that we,
too, obtain a similar happiness. Let us rest assured,

1 Matt. 12, 50.

that he is the greatest Saint, who excels most in the virtue of obedience. As all religious are called to great sanctity, which of them can have a lawful excuse for not being truly good and holy? — obedience being a virtue which can be practised by every one, everywhere and under all circumstances.

It was for his obedience to the will of God, that Abel obtained from the Lord the testimony that he was *just*; that Henoch was translated by God, in order that he should not see death. On account of his obedience to the will of God, Noah and his family were saved from the deluge; Abraham became the father of many nations; Joseph was raised to the highest dignity at the Court of the King of Egypt. Moses became the great Servant, prophet, and lawgiver of the Land, and the great performer of miracles with the people of God. Obedience to the will of God, was for the Jews, at all times, an impregnable rampart against all their enemies; it turned a Saul, a persecutor of the Church, into a Paul, the Apostle of the Gentiles; it turned the early christians into martyrs. For martyrdom does not consist in suffering and dying for the faith; it consists rather in the conformity of the martyr's will, to the Divine will which requires such a kind of death and not another. The conversions of thousands of sinners wrought by St. Francis Xavier, St. Francis Regis, St. Alphonsus and other eminent Saints and holy Missionaries, are they not the children of their obedience?

What madness in a religious to deprive himself by disobedience, of all these blessings of God! Let

25

him remember our Lord's words: "Every tree that
bringeth not forth good fruit, shall be cut down, and
shall be cast into the fire."[1]　A tool which no longer
corresponds to the end for which it was made, is cast
away; a wheel in a machinery, which prevents others
from working, is taken out and replaced by another;
a limb in the body, which becomes burdensome, and
endangers the functions and life of the others, is cut
off and thrown away; a servant who does no longer
his master's will, is discharged; a rebellious citizen
violating the laws of the state, is put into prison;
a child in an unreasonable opposition to his parents,
is disinherited.　Thus men naturally hate and reject
what is unreasonable, or useless, or opposed to, and
destructive of, good order, whether natural or moral.
What more natural then that the Lord of heaven and
earth, the Author of good sense and of good order,
should bear an implacable hatred to disobedience to
His holy will.

Disobedience turned the rebellious Angels out of
heaven; it turned our first parents, Adam and Eve,
out of Paradise; it made Cain a vagabond and a
fugitive on earth; it drowned the human race in the
waters of the deluge; it burned up the inhabitants of
Sodom and Gommorrha.　Disobedience to the will of
God lead the Jews so often into captivity; it buried
Pharaoh and all his host in the Red Sea; it turned
Nabuchodonosor into a wild beast; it laid the City of
Jerusalem in ashes; it has ruined and will still ruin
whole nations, empires and kingdoms; it will, finally,

[1] Matt. 7, 19.

put an end to the world, when all those who always rebelled against the will of God, will, in an instant, be hurled into the everlasting flames of hell, by these irresistible words of the Almighty: "Depart from Me, ye cursed, into everlasting fire which was prepared for the devil and his Angels,"[1] there to obey the laws of God's justice forever.

Man, then, when in opposition to God's will, is altogether out of his place; he suffers as many pangs as a limb which has been dislocated; he is continually tormented by evil spirits who have power over a soul that is out of its proper sphere of action; he is no longer under the protection of God, since he has withdrawn from His will, the rule for man's guidance, and has voluntarily left his watchful Providence. Oh Jonah! God sent you to Niniveh, and you wish to go to Tarsus! you were buffeted by the tempest, cast into the sea, and swallowed by a monster of the deep! Behold, what shall come on those who abandon God's will, to follow their own passions and inclinations. They shall be tossed like Jonah, by continual tempests: They will remain, like one in a lethargy, in the hold of their vessels, unconscious of sickness or danger, until they perish in the stormy sea, and are swallowed up in hell! "Know thou, and see, that it is a bitter and fearful thing for thee to have left the Lord thy God, when He desired to lead thee in the way of salvation, and that My fear is not with thee, saith the Lord God of Hosts."[2]

God grants to the devil great power over the dis-

[1] Matt. 25, 41.   [2] Jeremias II.

obedient.　As the Lord permitted a lion to kill a prophet in Juda in punishment for his disobedience to the voice of the Lord,[1] so in the same manner, He permits the infernal lion to assail the proud and dis- obedient religious everywhere with the most filthy temptations which they feel themselves too weak to resist, and thus fall a prey to his rage.　Unless they repent soon, like Jonas, of their sin of idolatry, as it were, they will not be saved as was the Prophet, but will perish in the waves of temptations, and sink into the fathomless abyss of hell.

In the ecclesiastical history of B. Kastell, 74th Book, we find the following: Two religious Priests, in company with several others, set out for Japan, in order to strengthen the Christians in their faith dur- ing the time of persecution.　Many, at that time, ob- tained the crown of martyrdom.　But these two Priests were not among their number; for they did not stand the trial at the decisive moment.　When prisoners with many others, they obstinately persisted in their own opinion contrary to that of their Superiors, re- fusing the obedience due to them.　Although it was not a matter of importance, yet several of their com- panions entertained great fear about their persever- ance and constancy, knowing from experience, the course of the decrees of the Divine Providence.　This fear was but too well grounded.　These two priests were sentenced to a slow death by fire; and, while tied to the stake, they showed themselves more and more impatient as their pains increased.　At last

[1] III Kings, 13, 20-30.

they gave way to despair, tore their fetters and ran to the judge craving pardon in the name of the false gods upon whom they called as loud as possible. But the judge did not listen to them, but had them cast into the flames, in which they ended their lives in complete despair.

A certain missionary priest of a religious Order was one day witnessing the execution of a person in the Indies. "You must know, Father," said the criminal, "that I was once a member of your Order. My life was happy as long as I observed the rules, but no sooner had I relaxed in their strict observance, than I felt unhappy in everything, so much so, that I abandoned the religious life and gave myself up to vice, which has at last reduced me to the melancholy pass in which you behold me here. I tell you this, in order that my example may be a warning to others."

"My brothers," wrote St. Alphonsus one day to his brethren in religion, "I feel an extreme compassion when I think of those who were once our brethren, and who lived in peace, and under obedience, united to God and contented with everything that happened to them : and now they are in the midst of the world, in confusion and disturbance. They have, indeed, the liberty to go where they like ; but do what they may, all is without regularity, without interior spirit, and without quiet. From time to time, they will think of making meditation ; but when their infidelity to God, and their ingratitude to Him in having abandoned their vocation, stares them in the face, the remorse of conscience which they feel is too sharp ; and hence it comes to pass that, in order to avoid the bitterness of that remorse, they often give up prayer ; and so their lukewarmness and their disquiet of mind increase more and more.

"Their misfortune did not begin with grievous faults, but with little defects ; and the devil made use of these to bring them, little by little, to the loss of their vocation. I repeat, I pity them from the bottom of my heart ; for I am certain that their whole life is nothing but confusion and disquiet, and if their life is full of straits, much more so will be their death. Some years ago I had hard work to comfort one of these, who at the thought of the loss of his vocation became crazy, and cried out in a frenzy that he was damned, and that there was no salvation for him, because he had voluntarily lost his vocation."

"Listen well," said our Lord, to St. Margaret Alacoque, "to these words from the lips of Truth. All religious separated and disunited from their Superiors, ought to regard themselves as vessels of reprobation, in which the purest waters turn to corruption, the rays of the Sun of grace producing on them the same effect as does the natural sun upon muddy waters. These souls are rejected from My heart. The nearer they endeavor to approach Me, by the means of the sacraments, prayer, and other exercises, the farther I withdraw from them through the horror which I have of them. They will go from one hell to another. Such disunion has already ruined numbers ; it will ruin many more in the end ;

for every Superior holds my place, no matter whether
he be good or bad. For this reason, inferiors, for
merely thinking of resisting authority, cover themselves with so many fatal wounds. It is in vain for
them to knock at the door of My Mercy: they will
not be listened to, unless they hear the voice of their
Superior."

"Hear, O Israel," said our Lord through the
Prophet Baruch:[1] "how happeneth it, that thou art
in the land of thy enemies? that thou art counted
with them that go down into hell?" It is because,
"thou hast forsaken the fountain of wisdom (holy
obedience.) For if thou hadst walked in the way of
God, thou hadst surely dwelt in peace forever."

From the punishments, which the Lord is accustomed to inflict upon the rebellious, let us draw, for
the obedient, a very encouraging conclusion. It is
the following: If God created hell for those who go
against His will in a grievous matter, what must be
His reward for those who comply with His will in
matters of importance! God being more inclined to
reward liberally, than to punish severely. Again, if
by committing a venial sin, we could convert and
save all men, we should not for all that, be allowed
to commit it—so great a dishonor and offence to God
is even one venial sin. He detests it infinitely. How
great in the sight of God, must then be all acts, how
little soever, done according to His will. He loves
and rewards every one infinitely. "Well done, good
and faithful servant, because, thou hast been faithful

[1] III, 9.

over a few things, I will set thee over many things ;
enter into the joy of thy Lord.''[1]

How much, then, should we love and esteem
even the smallest rule and the least act of obedience.
Truly, we should not call anything in religion small ;
everything in it is great, bearing, as it does, the
stamp of the divine will from which it draws all its
greatness, value and merit. Hence it is that the
Saints were so scrupulously exact in the performance
of all their actions small and great. Some even used
to get into ecstasy at the very word: 'Divine will.'
Their most ardent and most constant prayer was,
that they might be able to do the will of God under
all circumstances, even the most difficult. St. Gertrude prayed for this grace three hundred and sixty-
five times a day. It was thus, that they placed themselves in perpetual rest and security ; that they
obliged the Wisdom of God to govern them ; His
power to defend them ; His goodness to console them ;
His grace to sanctify them ; His mercy to encompass
them ; His sanctity to purify them ; His happiness to
defend them from evil, and to sustain them in good
and to make all succeed and go well with them, for
time and eternity.

The same blessings are prepared for all religious.
But it is only the obedient who will receive them.
"Thou hast chosen the Lord this day, (on the day of
thy profession) to be thy God, and to walk in His
ways, and keep His ceremonies and precepts, and
judgements, and to obey His commands. And the

[1] Matt. 25, 23.

Lord has chosen thee this day, to be His peculiar people, as He hath spoken to thee, and to keep all His commandments, and to make thee higher, than all nations which He has created, to His own praise and name, and glory, that thou mayest be a holy people of the Lord, as He has spoken.[1] Now, if thou wilt hear the voice of the Lord thy God, to do and keep all His commandments, the Lord thy God, will make thee higher, than all the nations that are on the earth, and all blessings shall come upon thee, yet so if thou hear His precepts.[2] For, I am the Lord, thy God, mighty, jealous, in showing mercy unto thousands to them that love Me and *keep My commandments.*[3]

[1] Deut. xxvi. 17. 19.   [2] Chapt. xxviii.

[3] Exod. 20, 5–6.

CHAPTER XIV.

ON THE MARKS OF A RELIGIOUS VOCATION.

WHEN a King levies soldiers to make war, his foresight and prudence require, that he should prepare weapons to arm them ; for what sense would there be in sending them to fight without arms. If he did so, he would be taxed with great imprudence.

Now God acts in the same way. "He does not call," says St. Bernardine of Sienna," without giving, at the same time, to those whom He calls, all that is required to accomplish the end for which He calls. So that when God calls a person to religion, He furnishes him with the physical, intellectual, and moral qualities necessary for the religious life. In other words, God not only gives him the *Inclination*, but He also endows him with the *Ability* for the performance of the duties annexed to that state of life.

As regards *Ability*, the physical constitution of the postulant should be such as to aid rather, than prevent, the development of his intellectual and moral faculties ; it should be sufficiently strong to endure the hardships of the religious life ; and it should, moreover, be free from any hereditary disease. The mind of the postulant should be calm and deliberate; it should be strong, so as to be able to apply, if required, to study, or to many spiritual exercises, without danger of being deranged thereby. Weak minds will always be in danger of derangement from much mental application. This danger is so much the more to be apprehended, if, at the same time, these persons are of a very nervous temperament, or of a rather scrupulous conscience, or if they are bound to fast too much, or if they have led for a time, a very sinful life; on account of which they will, in the ordinary course of Providence, sooner or later have to suffer many great temptations which will bring upon them many hard mental afflictions and combats. Now all this, weak minds cannot endure long, especially if guided — which may easily happen — by unexperienced, or indiscreet spiritual directors.

With regard to the intellectual faculties, the postulant need not have talents so brilliant as to make him a great mind; but he should have a sound, practical judgment, that is, common sense. *"Moins d'esprit, plus de jugement,"* as the French say. Neither great talents for some certain branches of science, nor piety and the spirit of devotion, can make up for a deficiency in judgment or common sense. Subjects of medium talents, yet gifted with a sound, practical judgment, are generally best suited for religious Communities; because they are humble and docile. "Men of superior talents," says St. Vincent de Paul, "not possessing at the same time an unusual disposition to advance in virtue, are not good for us; for no solid virtue can take root in self-conceited, and self-willed souls."

In reference to the intellectual faculties of the postulant, St. Francis de Sales expresses himself thus: "If I say that, in order to become a religious, one should have a good mind, I do not mean those great geniuses, who are generally vain and self-conceited, and in the world are but the receptacles of vanity. Such men do not embrace the religious life to humble themselves, but to govern others, and direct everything according to their own views and inclinations, as if the object of their entrance into religion, was to be lecturers in philosophy and theology." "These great minds," says St. Frances de Chantal in one of her letters, "when they are not given to devotion, submission, and mortification, serve to ruin a whole religious community, nay, even a whole religious Order." "We must pay special attention to these," says St. Francis de Sales, "I do not say, that they should not be received, but I do say, that we should be very cautious about them; for in time and by the grace of God, they may greatly change; and this will undoubtedly come to pass, if they are faithful in making use of those means which are given them for their cure.

"When, therefore, I speak of a good mind, I mean well regulated and sensible minds, and also those of moderate powers, which are neither too great, nor too little; for such minds always do a great deal without knowing it; they set themselves to labor with a good intention, and give themselves to the practice of solid virtue. They are tractable, and allow themselves to be governed without much trouble; for they easily understand how good a thing it is to let themselves be guided.

"Good understandings" says St. Frances de Chantal, "are always capable of the religious observances, whilst the weak are liable to relaxation. Believe me, dear Sisters, I conjure you, to look well to the natural dispositions of those whom you receive; for I know, that nature ever remains, and will, every now and then, burst forth. There are very few who dispose themselves to receive grace sufficient, to overcome a bad natural disposition, and rarely do we see a person of good understanding and of good dispositions perverted.

As to the moral qualities of the postulant, they should be such as to suit a life in common. Hence he should easily agree with, and yield to others, and be of a cheerful, happy, gay, affable and sociable disposition. St. Francis de Sales says: "He should have a good heart, desiring to live in subjection and obedience." Cardinal Wiseman says in his Book on Pius VII.: "If one sees the youthful aspirants to the religious institutes, here or abroad, in recreation or at study, he may easily decide who will persevere by a very simple rule. The joyous faces and the sparkling eyes denote the future monks far more surely than the demure looks and stolen glances."[1]

"There are many thus far qualified, but,

[1] Recollections of Four Cath. Popes. B. 39.

for all that, they are not called to religion, unless they experience, at the same time an *Inclination* for the religious life. Now this *inclination*, is nothing else than the firm and constant will to serve God, in the *manner* and in the *place* to which His Divine Majesty calls him. In many, the will is so inflamed with the love of the religious life, that they embrace it without any question about it, and with exceedingly great pleasure. In others, and perhaps in the greater part of those who are called to religion, this love or *inclination* for the religious state is not so strong, but their understanding is so much enlightened by the grace of God, that they discover the vanity and dangers of this world, seeing also clearly, at the same time, the quiet, the safety, the happiness, in a word, the inestimable treasures of the religious life, though perhaps, as I have just said, somewhat dull in their affection, and not so ready to follow that which reason shows them. This latter manner of *inclination*, or love for the religious life is better than the former, and is more generally approved by those who are experienced in this matters, than the other, which consists only in a fervent motion of the will ; for being grounded in the light of reason and faith, it is less subject to error, and more likely to last."

Now in the opinion of St. Francis de Sales, *this firm and constant will* of a person to serve God in the *manner* and in the *place* where God calls him, is the best mark of a good religious vocation. "But observe," adds this enlightened Saint, "that when I say a *firm and constant will* of serving God, I do not

say, that a person should from the beginning, perform everything required by his vocation, and that
he should be perfect at once, and never feel tempted,
unsettled, and unshaken in his undertaking; that he
should never experience any doubts as to his religions
calling, or should not waver, at times, in a kind of
irresolution about his vocation: for this may happen
from the weakness and repugnance of human nature,
and the temptations of the devil, the arch-enemy of
all good. Oh no! that is not what I mean to say;
for every one is more or less subject to passions,
changes, and vicissitudes; and a person will love one
thing to-day, and another thing to-morrow. No two
days of our life are alike. To-day is different from
yesterday, and to-morrow will be unlike either. It
is not, then, by these different movements and feelings that we ought to judge of the *firmness and constancy of the will*, but we should consider rather,
whether amid this variety of movements, the will remains firm and unshaken, so as not to give up the
good it has embraced; so that to have a mark of a
good vocation, we do *not* need a *sensible* constancy;
but a constancy which is in the *superior part of the
soul*, and which is *effective*.

Therefore, in order to know whether God calls us
to religion, we must not wait for Him to speak to us
sensibly, nor to send us an Angel from heaven to
make known to us His will; still less do we need to
have revelations on this subject; nor do we require
an examination by ten or twelve divines, to ascertain
whether the inspiration be good or bad; whether we

ought to follow it, or not; but we ought to correspond to it well, and cultivate the first movement of grace, and then not to distress ourselves if disgusts and coldness arise concerning it; for if we always strive to keep our will very firm in the determination of seeking the good which is shown to us, God will not fail to make all turn out well to His glory." Such a will is found in those young persons who, quietly and with consideration, prepare themselves for their retreat from the world, by trying to be given more to patience, prayer, penance, fasting and the frequent reception of the sacraments. They are in earnest about the affair, and do not play, or if they do, it is at a good game, in which they can only be gainers. They will not act as Lot's wife, who looked back, nor as the children of Israel, who longed for the flesh-pots of Egypt."

"To find out this good will," writes St. Frances de Chantal in one of her letters, "we must inquire of the postulant, how he has profited by the desire of embracing the religious life, that is, whether he has been more fervent in approaching the sacraments, and reading pious books; in drawing his affections from the world; in becoming more meek in his conversations, and more obedient to his parents; and similar things."

On the contrary, if young persons were mentioned to St. Francis de Sales, who, before their entrance into religion, gave themselves up to the vanities and pleasures of the world, to take — to use their own expression — a last farewell, he considered their call to religion extremely doubtful. When it was remarked to him, that they only retrograded a little, in order to take a fresh and better start, he replied, "that they might easily go back too far, and then make such a violent start, as would make them loose breath, before they could come to take the leap. Experience teaches, that such characters seldom persevere through the year of probation ; because any one who thus abuses and trifles with the **grace** of a religious vocation, deserves to lose it."

When the austerities and trials of a religious life have been fully represented to a postulant ; when his admittance has been delayed, discouraged, nay even refused for the sake of trial, and he still perseveres in his entreaties to be received into the Order, saying with St. Paul: "I can do all things in Him Who strengthens me:" such a postulant, may also be considered to have a good and firm will and a true vocation to the religious life.

One day a young man came to Don Bruno d'Affringues, requesting to be received into his Order. The venerable Superior seeing, that he was of a delicate and weak constitution, represented to him the great severity of the Order. The young postulant replied, that he had previously taken that point into consideration, and that God would be his strength. The Superior, finding him so resolute, addressed him in a very sharp tone of voice, saying: "What are you thinking about, in wishing to enter our Order? Are you aware, that every postulant, before he can be admitted, must perform a miracle? Can you perform

26

it?" "Of myself I cannot," replied the young man, "but the power of God in me can. I have a firm confidence in His mercy, and hope, that, having called me to His service in this Order, having instilled into my mind a great aversion for the world, He will certainly not permit me to return to the same, as I have sincerely forsaken it. Demand of me venerable Father, what you please, God will accomplish it through me, as an evidence of my vocation." At these words, he appeared quite inflamed, and his whole countenance was brightened. Don Bruno, astonished at such firmness, embraced the young man, and with tears in his eyes, he said to those present: "Behold, my brethren, a vocation, that has undergone the Ordeal!" He then turned to the young man and said: "Have confidence, my son, God will ever assist and love you, and you will love and serve God, which is worth more than a miracle."

When a postulant is wealthy, or has good temporal prosperity, and might enjoy the comforts of the world, yet nevertheless wishes firmly to renounce everything, in order to embrace a religious life, he must be considered to have a very good vocation.

"What I am about to say," writes St. Frances de Chantal in one of her letters, "is worth notice, it is, that those who come from amidst the delights of the world, and who, by their station in life, enjoyed much temporal convenience, when in the monastery, generally embrace the austerities and humiliations of the religious life with more rigor and determination, than those who were poor before they came. These latter, if they be not blessed with a sound judgment, and powerfully moved by God, frequently fall into desires and excessive study of their convenience and sensuality, and become mere phantoms of religious, calculated only to exercise the patience of others; for they are incessantly wishing for this or for that, complaining and murmuring and noticing what is done for others, which is an intolerable imperfection. Let us endeavor, I beg of you, to avoid, as much as possible, receiving any such characters, for they do no good to themselves and greatly prejudice others."

Those who, in order to become religious, make great sacrifices, or suffer patiently unjust contradictions and ill treatment from their friends, should be considered to have a true call.

The family of St. Thomas Aquinas, used all possible means, to prevent him from carrying out his resolution of entering into religion. They endeavored to drag him into the world, as it were, by main-force. They imprisoned him, and sent a woman of bad character, to entice him to sin, but he put her to flight by seizing a fire-brand to hurl at her. They then surrendered him into the hands of his worldly-minded sister, hoping, that she might succeed in changing his mind, by flattery and kind persuasions. But the contrary happened; for he inspired her with so great a love for the religious state, as to induce her to embrace it herself. Having, by these trials, become only more firm in his resolution and desire of entering into religion, he, at last, succeeded in his undertaking.

When St. Columbian was on the point of carrying out his resolution of entering into religion, his
mother threw herself across the threshold to obstruct
his passage; but he courageously stepped over her,
and hastened to the place of his vocation.

This good and firm will may also be easily supposed in those postulants whose parents and ancestors
are distinguished for their virtue and piety. The
good fruit of the old tree before us, encourages us to
hope, that the same kind of fruit will, in due time,
follow the blossoms of the young tree: it being a law
of nature, that a good tree brings forth good fruit.

"There are many persons, says St. Francis de
Sales, "who feel the first inspirations to the religious
life rather strongly; nothing appears difficult to them;
they seem to be able to overcome all obstacles ; but
when they meet with these vicissitudes, and when
these first feelings, are not so sensible in the inferior
part of their soul, they imagine that all is lost, and
that they must give up everything; they will, and
they will not. What they then feel is not sufficient
to make them leave the world. 'I should wish it,'
one of these persons would say; 'but I do not know
whether it is the will of God that I should be a
religious, inasmuch as the inspiration which I now
feel does not seem to me strong enough. It is quite
true that I have felt it more strongly than I do at this
moment; but as it is not lasting, I do not think it is
good.' Certainly when I meet with such souls, I am
not astonished at this disgust and coolness ; still less
can I for that reason think that their vocation is not

good. We must, in this case, take great pains to assist them, and teach them not to be surprised at these changes, but encourage them to remain firm in the midst of them. Well, I say to them, that is nothing; tell me, have you not felt in your heart the movement or inspiration to seek so great a good? 'Yes,' they say; 'it is very true, but it passed away directly.' Yes indeed, I answer, the force of the sentiment passed away, but not so entirely as not to leave in you some affection for the religious life. 'Oh no!' the person says; 'for I always have a sort of feeling which makes me tender on that point; but what troubles me is, that I do not feel this inclination so strongly as would be required for such a resolution.' I answer them, that such persons must not be troubled about these sensible feelings, nor examine them too closely; that they must be satisfied with that constancy of their will, which amid a'l this does not lose the affection to its first design; that they must only be careful to cultivate it well, and to correspond with this first inspiration. Do not care, I say, from what quarter it comes, for, God has many *ways of calling His servants into His service.*

Although it be most desirable, and should be held as a general rule, that a person should embrace the religious life from the motive of securing better his own salvation and sanctification, of working more profitably for the salvation of others, and above all, from the pure intention of serving God more perfectly and of belonging to Him alone, yet it cannot be denied, that God does not draw all whom

He calls to His service, by the same ways and means.

He sometimes makes use of preaching; sometimes of the reading of good books. Some are called by hearing the sacred words of the Gospel, as St. Francis, and St. Anthony were, by hearing these words: "Go, sell what thou hast, and give to the poor, and follow Me;"[1] and, 'If any man come after Me, let him deny himself and take up his cross and follow Me.'[2]

Others have been called by the annoyances, disasters, and afflictions which came upon them in the world, which caused them to be disgusted with it, and to abandon it. There are but few who enter the service of God, from the motive of belonging to, and serving, Him alone.

Among the women whose conversion is related in the Gospel, St. Magdalen was the only one, who followed our Divine Saviour through love. The adultress came on account of her public disgrace; the woman of Canaan came that she might obtain relief in her temporal distress. St. Paul, the hermit, and Arsenius withdrew into the desert to escape persecution. St. Paul, the Simple, became a hermit on account of the unfaithfulness of his wife. Blessed Consalvus resolved to become a Dominican, because while riding gaily and swiftly through the streets, he was thrown from his horse into a mud-puddle, and was laughed at by all those who were eye-witnesses. While yet in the mud-puddle, he said to himself: "Is it thus, treacherous world, that you treat me? You now deride me,

[1] Matt. 19, 21.   [2] Matt. 16, 24.

but I also will laugh at you." This said, he abandoned the world, and embraced the religious life.

Nicholas Bobadilla, a poor student of Paris, often went to see St. Ignatius Loyola, for the sake of relief in his temporal wants; but he soon felt attached to St. Ignatius, and became one of his first and most zealous companions.

The venerable Bernard of Corlione, in trying to escape the hands of human justice, fell into those of Divine Mercy by going to join the Capuchins.

Thomas Pounc, an Englishman, fell most awkwardly, while dancing at a ball of the Queen of England. "Get up, you fool," said the queen to him. The young man feeling highly offended, resolved to avenge himself on the world, by quitting it. He entered the Society of Jesus, where he led a holy life; and after having suffered in a dungeon for twenty years, during the time of the religious persecution in England, he finished his life, by sacrificing it, at last, for the sake of the faith.

"There are even others," says St. Francis de Sales, "whose motives for embracing the religious life, were still worse. I have heard on good authority, that a gentleman of our age, distinguished in mind and person, and of good family, seeing some Capuchin Fathers pass by, said to the other noblemen who were with him, 'I have a fancy to find out how these bare-footed men live, and to go amongst them, not meaning to remain there always, but only for three weeks or a month, so as to observe better what they do, and then mock and laugh at it after-

wards with you.' So he went and was received by
the Fathers. But Divine Providence, Who made use
of these means to withdraw him from the world, converted his wicked purpose into a good one; and he
who thought to take in others, was taken in himself;
for no sooner had he lived a few days with those good
religious, than he was entirely changed. He persevered faithfully in his vocation and became a great
servant of God.

There are again others, whose vocation is no better than this; those who go into religion on account
of some natural defect, for instance, because they are
lame, or blind of one eye, or ugly, or have some other
similar defect.

Thus many enter religion through disgust or
weariness, or on account of disappointments, or misfortunes. Such disappointments and troubles detach
them from the love of creatures; they preserve them
from the delusion of false appearances, and force them
to enter into themselves; they purify their hearts;
they cause goodness to take root in their souls; they
give them a distaste for a life in the world. Would
such souls have sought consolation only in God, if the
world had loved them? Would they have known the
sweetness of God, if the world had not maltreated
and banished them from its society? It is God Who
permits such harsh treatment and refusals to befall
them. He causes thorns to spring over all their
pleasures, in order to prevent their reposing thereon.
They would never have belonged to God, had the
world desired them; and they would have been ad-

verse to Him, had the world not been adverse to them. It is thus that the Lord breaks the fetters, by which the world held them in bondage.

"There are souls," says St. Francis de Sales, "who, were the world to smile upon them, would never become religious; yet by means of contradictions and disappointments, they are brought to despise the vanities, and all allurements of the world, and understand its fallacy."

"Our Lord, has often made use of such means to call many persons to His service, whom He could not have otherwise. For though God is all-powerful and can do what He wills, yet He does not will to take away the liberty which He has given us; and when He calls us to His service, He will have us enter it willingly, and not by force or constraint. Now, though these persons come to God, as it were, in anger against the world, which has displeased them, or on account of some troubles and afflictions which have tormented them, yet they do not fail to give themselves to God of their own free will; and very often such persons succeed very well in the service of God, and become great Saints, sometimes greater than those who have entered it with more evident vocations, or with far purer motives. God, very often in these cases, shows the greatness of His Wisdom and Divine Goodness. He draws good from evil, by employing the intentions of these persons, which are by no means good in themselves, to make, of those persons, great servants of His Divine Majesty. Those whom the Gospel mentions as having been forced to

27

partake of the feast, did not, on that account, relish it less.

"The Divine Artisan takes pleasure in making beautiful buildings with wood that is very crooked and has no appearance of being fit for anything ; and, as a person who does not understand carpenter's work, seeing some crooked wood in his shop, would be astonished to hear him say it was meant for making some fine work of art (for he would say, how often must the plane pass over it before it can be fit for such a work?) so Divine Providence, usually makes master-pieces out of these crooked and sinister intentions. He makes the lame and the blind come into His feast, to show us, that we need not have two eyes or two feet to enter Paradise ; that it is better to go to Heaven with one leg, one eye, or one arm, than to have two and be lost. Now this sort of people having entered religion in this way, have often been known to make great progress in virtue and persevere faithfully in their vocation. It cannot be expected, that all should commence with perfection. It matters little in what manner we begin, provided we are resolved to attain our end by strenuous efforts. We must then revere and esteem the incomprehensible ways and inscrutable judgments of God, in this great variety of the vocations and means of which He makes use to draw His creatures to His service.

"Now, from this great multiplicity of vocations and variety of motives, it follows that it is often a difficult matter to form a correct judgment, as to whether a person is called to a religious life. This difficulty, however, vanishes in a great measure, if we apply the mark above given, viz, that, among the several marks of a good vocation, the best and surest of them all is, *the firm and constant will to serve God in the manner* and in *the place* to which one feels called by His Divine Majesty."

The *Inclination*, then, for the religious life, implies not only the firm and constant will to serve God in religion in general, but it implies also the particular attraction to a life either exclusively contemplative, or active, or mixed. This attraction must be well inquired into, as it cannot be expected, that a man will faithfully persevere in a manner of life, for which he feels no particular liking: it being almost impossible for human nature to go, for a life time, against a torrent.

Although *Ability* and *Inclination*, taken in the sense just explained, generally suffice to prove the religious vocation of a person, yet there are better and more evident marks, than these, viz:

1 — *Divine revelation.* St. Paul the Apostle, St. Aloysius de Gonzaga, St. Stanislaus, and other Saints, are examples of this kind.

2 — *Special Inspirations*, by which a person is suddenly enlightened, and vehemently urged on to a life of perfection, and sweetly forced, as it were, thereto.

WHAT DISPOSITIONS ARE REQUISITE IN A NOVICE TO BE ADMITTED TO THE VOWS?

In replying to this question, we must chiefly keep in view what the religious life is, and what it requires.

The essence or spirit of the religious life, consists in sacrificing ourselves to God without reserve, and in aspiring earnestly to religious perfection. A novice cannot, it is true, be expected to be perfect; but he is required to be willing to make sacrifices, and to cherish, in his heart, an ardent and effective desire of becoming perfect. "Be firmly persuaded," writes St. Alphonsus, "that God does not wish to have those in the Order, who have not an ardent desire to sanctify themselves." A novice, then must be ready to make such sacrifices as are required by the spirit of his Order: he must be willing to renounce the gratifications and luxuries of the world, to undergo labor and toil, to be contented with plain and poor accommodations, food, and clothing. Although a novice should not be required to perform great and severe penances, yet, from a true penitential spirit, he should be desirous to practise little ones. But above all, a novice who asks to make his vows, must earnestly have labored, in the course of his noviciate, cheerfully to sacrifice his will, easily to resign his judgment, his views, opinions, and notions to his superiors, and even to his equals and inferiors. He must have endeavored to put off the old man, and put on the new, by entirely conforming himself to the spirit of the Order. He should understand, that it is not enough to possess virtues, but that he must have the virtues and spirit of the Order, into which he is to be admitted. He must have especially the virtues of humility and simplicity, a love of community-life, a disinterested charity, a blind obedience to the rules and superiors. "For to the spirit of the Order, must be subjected all our inclinations and dispositions,'' says St. Frances de Chantal. —

"If we know,'' says St. Francis de Sales, ''that a novice earnestly endeavored, during the time of his noviciate, to do what was required of him, and to make good use of the means prescribed to him to conquer his evil inclinations &c. &c. (for the time of the noviciate is allotted for this end,) if we know that he has remained faithful in striving to reform himself, and to keep his resolutions, and that he desires to become still better, and to conform himself in everything to the rules and constitutions; then we may conscientiously vote for him, even though he may have committed faults, even of some moment, during the time of his probation; for he must not be expected to be perfect at the end of his noviciate.

The Apostles were truly called by Jesus Christ, and had taken great pains to change their lives, nevertheless, they committed many faults, not only in the first year, but also in the second and third. Religion is a school in which we are to learn our lesson. The master does not require his scholars to know their lesson without making a mistake; it is enough, if they pay attention to learning it as well as they can. Thus we must do what we are able, and God will be satisfied, and superiors also. Religion does not consider it a great triumph to fashion a mind already formed, a soul sweet and tranquil in itself, *but* it greatly esteems the reducing to virtue souls that are strong in their inclinations; for those souls, if they are faithful, will outstrip the others, acquiring by the point of the spirit what the others possess without any trouble. It is not required in religion, that we should have no passions (that is not in our *power*, and God wills that we should feel them till our death), nor is it required that they should not be strong; for that would be saying that a soul with bad habits cannot be fit to serve God. The world is mistaken in this idea. God rejects nothing where malice is not found. How can a person help being of such and such a temperament, subject to such or such a passion? The whole, then, depends on the acts which we make in consequence of a rising passion — acts always being dependent on our will; for sin is so voluntary, that without our consent there can be no sin. God has left power to the will to resist passions, otherwise, in requiring perfection of us, He would require of us an impossible thing, and this would be an injustice, which cannot be found in God. In religion, then, we must do what is in our power to acquire perfection. Religion, indeed, tolerates our bringing with us our bad habits, passions and inclinations, but not our living as they would lead us to live. It gives us rules to serve as a constraint to our hearts, and to drive out everything that is contrary to God.

We should not, then, refuse to admit a Novice to the vows on account of certain faults, provided he possesses and preserves a firm and good will of correcting himself, and of making good use of the means given him for this end. And, in a letter to a Superioress, the same Saint says: "Though a daughter should naturally have a bad disposition, if, in her general and essential deportment, she acts by grace, and not by nature, she is worthy of being received with love and respect, as the temple of the Holy Ghost. Wolf by nature, but lamb by grace."

St. Alphonsus, expresses the same sentiments, when writing of a young man of this description, he says: "I recommend this young man to you. Let him receive the habit, and always listen to him with kindness, and always help him. He is full of talent, and has, certainly, a good intention now, but he is dreadfully tormented by temptations, because he has led an extravagant life. Should he be so unhappy as to fall sometimes, you must, it is true, show him his errors, and try to move him to repentance, but at the same time, endeavor to inspire him with confidence. In the meantime be not discouraged yourself. Tell this also to Father Ginsone, and to any other, to whom he may perhaps go to confession."

Hence very little or no account, is to be made of a great exterior piety and love for corporal penances and mortifications that a novice may evince, if it can be seen, that he combines with them singularity of character, not to say selfishness; that he is eccentric in his manners; singular in his habits, opinions, or pious performances; that he does not endeavor to destroy what we might call *selfish individuality;* not trying to conform his notions, actions, language, in a word, the entire man, to the spirit and ordinary mode of action of the Order. For, a religious as I have said, must endeavor to attain perfection. But the foundation of all perfection is humility, which consists in self-contempt; in the denial of our own will and judgement; in a ready submission to every one; in conformity to the manner of thinking and acting peculiar to the Order; and in child-like sincerity towards our Superiors and in humbling ourselves for faults committed, acknowledging and avowing them frankly, and with sorrow for God's sake. Now a novice must have endeavored to attain all this, through a spirit of faith, and with the full conviction of its necessity, or, as St. Frances de Chantal says, "through true fear of God, and a desire of pleasing Him."

But should a novice continue to cling to his own opinions, not easily yielding them up to those of his superiors, showing himself unwilling to obey with simplicity, reasoning about everything, and betraying a strong inclination to criticise the actions of others, especially of superiors; he would be wanting in humility; that is, in the first and most essential quality for a Religious, without which he will never be truly obedient, and consequently, cannot persevere to the end in the Order.

[1] Letter dated April 7, 1758.

CHAPTER XV.

PRACTICAL CONCLUSIONS FROM THE FOREGOING CHAPTER.

ENERALLY speaking, Novices of ill health should be dismissed, because they will ultimately become unable to endure the regular observances of the Order, always requiring exemptions and dispensations from the rule, to the great prejudice of the spirit of discipline.

For female religious Orders I add here a remark of St. Frances de Chantal — "Dear Sisters, there is an evil much to be feared ; this is '*mal de matrice.*' Truly I would wish you would never receive any one, violently afflicted with it; for this infirmity weakens the mind and fills it with a thousand foolish and melancholy ideas, so much so as to make these persons incorrigible and greatly prejudicial to communities. But such as have a good mind and are not much affected with it, should not be refused."

A Novice, however, who is of less service to the Order, in consequence of a natural defect as for instance, deafness of one ear, may be admitted to the vows, provided his learning and knowledge, and above all, his solid piety supply for such a deficiency.

Novices, whose constitution is delicate, or whose health has been so impaired during the time of their probation, as to leave no hope of recovery, may be allowed to remain, provided they be generous souls. Now generous souls do not easily complain ; they earnestly try to be patient and resigned to the holy Will of God ; they tell their sufferings without exaggerating, leaving the care of applying the remedies to the one charged with it, and contenting themselves with suffering lovingly and keeping close to God. Such souls as these show, that they are in earnest in applying to perfection ; they give edification to every one, and draw down the blessing of God upon a whole community. They ought to be suffered to remain in the Convent.

If we read in the lives of some holy founders of religious Orders, that weak, delicate, and infirm and deformed persons may be admitted into their Orders, they had in view no other, but generous souls of the above description, who, at the same time, had a strong mind, a firm, determined will and a very good heart, as has been explained above, and as is quite evident from letters written on this subject by St. Francis de Sales, St. Frances de Chantal and others.

We read in the life of St. Alphonsus that he was greatly afflicted at seeing a good Novice sick, and when the Fathers, at times, wished to send him home, the Saint himself became his Advocate. There is no law excluding from the house of God one who has left all to follow Him. If the physicians employed, and the remedies used in the Order, cannot restore his health, it is not probable, that it will improve under the paternal roof, and if God wills, that he should soon die, it is better for him to die in religion, than in the midst of the world. What mother was ever so unnatural, as to expel her child from the house for being sick. It was the opinion of the Saint, that those novices, who were pious and patient in illness, assisted the Order by their example; for as they were themselves pleasing to God, they drew down the blessings on others, and when a fervent novice was at the point of death, St. Alphonsus was never distressed, but rejoiced in the assurance, that such a one was happy. But when a sick novice wished to leave the Order, he granted the permission only with pain.[1]

2.   Novices, who are *naturally* inclined to melancholy, should also be dismissed, because they are a burden to themselves, and insupportable to others. "Truly, these sad and melancholy minds," writes St. Frances de Chantal to a Superioress, "are incurable, without an extraordinary grace; therefore, when we see, that this is the disposition of subjects, we must not admit them."

3.   Neither should those be admitted to the vows, whose temperament is excessively choleric, unless it can be seen, that they have an extraordinary assistance from God and they faithfully correspond with it; otherwise they will violate charity but too frequently. "Truly," says St. Frances de Chantal, "mutinous, violent and head-strong minds, are never cured but

[1] Tannoja's Life of St. Alphonsus II. Vol. Chap. 63

by an extraordinary grace from God, and as such gifts are seldom bestowed, such evils are seldom cured.''

4.   Those novices ought to be dismissed of whom the Master of Novices is compelled to say: "They might be admitted, if they could always be under a Superior, who would suit their disposition, or if they could always remain under my direction." Such as these must be sent away without a moment's hesitation. "Take care," says St. Frances de Chantal, to a Superioress, "not to receive one difficult to manage, for all Superioresses have not the address to keep them in their place."

5.   Novices of a selfish, unsociable and sensitive disposition, with whom it is difficult to get along, on account of their pride and self-conceit, should also be dismissed, because they do not suit a life in common.

6.   There are certain novices who are delighted only with the learned men and great Orators of the Order, and who take particular complacency in associating with them, flattering themselves, that the time will come, when they will be their equals, and who, when saluted by these celebrated persons, readily come forward to speak to them, wishing always to converse on scientific matters and showing contempt for men of medium talents, however pious these may be.   If at the expiration of their noviciate it be not fully evident, that they are more humble and truly called to the religious state, they should be dismissed even if it be the eve of their profession.

7.   To admit novices to the vows, whose char-

acter, disposition and custom it is to criticise and
censure others, unless they give evident proof of being, by the grace of God, radically cured of this vice,
is, according to St. Vincent de Paul, "to receive
domestic enemies into the Order, or to admit wolves
into the fold; for those whose custom it is to censure
and criticise, can never be at rest because they will
always and everywhere find something to blame."

8.   Novices who are too easily discontented, who
murmur, complain and fret at the least inconvenience,
who are too much concerned about their health and
too tender of themselves will never make good members in religion.   This tenderness or superfluous love
for their bodies makes them too attentive not only to
the least evil which they may feel, but will also fill
them constantly with foresight for all those which
might happen, causing them to lament and murmur
that they are not well treated and assisted, that they
want this or that.   Such like reflections are far from
generous minds.   Hence "it is an infallible maxim,"
says St. Frances de Chantal, "that persons tender
for their bodies are so also for their minds.   This
proceeds from a want of generosity.

"See what our blessed Father has said of it in our
rules: 'To say a word of this evil, which is often
secret, such persons generally fill the monastery with
tears, complaints and lamentations; they are generally melancholy and fretful, very often discouraged,
taking difficulties for impossibilities and believing
everything that is disagreeable to be insupportable;
and to maintain their cause; they form many sad

and scandalous complaints against the rules, and those who govern. If they are reproved for their tenderness and their tiresome humor, they redouble their complaints, murmuring that there is no charity because others do not weep and lament with them, or pity them, and they protest that they have very great cause to be afflicted. Should they be sick, and others are not occupied with describing the immensity of their sufferings, and with running up and down to seek every remedy that their fancy suggests, then they look upon themselves, as of all others, the most miserable and neglected; then they think every one is devoid of pity. In fine, persons of this description are always on the watch to see if more be done for others than for themselves, self-love suggesting to their fancy that there is not as much done for them as is requisite. This tenderness both of body and mind is one of the greatest evils in the religious life; and we must be very careful not to receive those who are considerably attacked with it, because they do not wish to be cured, refusing to make use of what could give them health.' ''

9. Novices who do not readily and cheerfully obey not only the Superior, but also the Capo-Novice, or any one else presiding, should be considered to have no vocation for a religious state.

10. Novices who show no zeal to advance in perfection, easily violating the rule of silence, feeling too much pained when humbled, trying to escape humiliations, allowing themselves to be often reprimanded for the same faults, without making proper efforts to

correct them, should also be dismissed. "You say also," writes St. Frances de Chantal to a Superioress, "that there are some, who are so tender as not to be able to bear being corrected without troubling themselves so as often to render themselves sick. Now if that is so you must open the door to them; for since they are sick and do not wish to be treated nor to receive the remedies given for their cure, we see clearly that they are incorrigible and give no hope of being cured." St. Paul one day said to St. Frances of Rome, "There should never be among you such souls as are addicted to sloth, for the spirit of darkness rapidly leads them to the loss of their vocation. Despising God's honor as they do and regretting having even given themselves to the religious life, they become incorrigible and put a wrong construction on everything."[1]

11. Those novices should not be admitted to the vows whose disposition is fickle and capricious, who one moment desire one thing and the next moment another, always commencing and never accomplishing anything; who are at one time sad and morose and then excessively gay and joyful even to dissipation, and who are at the same time sensitive, self-conceited and addicted to singular opinions and views.

12. "Novices who are subject to be easily troubled and whose minds are often filled with chagrin and disquietude, who show but little love for their vocation, but when all is over, promise to do wonders, are no proper persons for religion. If after having

[1] Life of St. Frances of Rome, Chap. xviii., Rule 4.

been told what they must do for their amendment,
they remain incorrigible, they must be rejected."[1]

13.   Novices who are always vacillating about
their vocation should be sent away; "for so long as
a postulant (and the same should be said of Novices)
remains firm," says St. Alphonsus, "there is nothing to fear, because God will certainly assist him, but
when he begins to waver saying one day 'yes' and the
next 'no' he should be told that under such circumstances he cannot be allowed to remain."   "You
ask," writes St. Frances de Chantal to a Superioress,
"what we should think of a person who testifies by
her words that she repents of having entered religion.
Certainly if she perseveres in her disgust for her vocation and if you see that it makes her tepid and negligent in forming herself according to the spirit of her
vocation, you must send her away; this, however,
may happen by a simple temptation or as a trial, and
this you may know by the profit she makes of such a
thought, disgust or repentance, when she discovers it
with simplicity and is faithful to employ the remedy
that will be given her; for God never permits anything for our trial without wishing us to profit by it,
which we always do if we are faithful in discovering
it, and as I said, simple in believing and doing what
we are told; and this is a proof that the trial is from
God.   But if this person uses her own judgment and
her will is not firm and if she perseveres in her disgust, that is a bad sign and it is almost without remedy, you must send her away."

[1] St Frances de Chantal·

14. Novices of a giddy and frivolous character and who are naturally inclined to excessive levity are not good subjects for a religious life.

15. Novices who are not ingenuous, open-hearted and sincere, whose language is equivocal and untruthful; and those from whom it is difficult to obtain an answer save an unsatisfactory 'yes' or 'no,' should be dismissed, for such characters are always deceitful and can never be trusted. Let them be sent away without the least scruple or hesitation. "Persons of deceitful and false dispositions," writes St. Frances de Chantal to a Superioress, "will never be corrected and will do much harm in religion, unless they are open in declaring this evil, and very courageous in remedying it."

16. Those novices should be dismissed who although they came to religion with the laudable intention of escaping the dangers of the world, and securing their salvation, yet never have any high aspirations, or great desire to attain perfection, never thinking of performing any particular mortifications or refraining from any lawful pleasure or innocent amusement for the good of their soul and trying at most to avoid what is evidently sinful.

17. It may be justly concluded that those novices have no religious vocation who, though apparently striving in earnest to attain perfection, yet do every thing according to their own views and notions contemning the path to sanctity pointed out by the rule and the voice of obedience, loving singularity and avoiding as much as possible the community life, re-

28

tiring into a corner during the hours of recreation, or withdrawing from labor in common, and appearing on such occasions with a sad and dejected countenance, and never knowing how to rejoice with others, or take upon themselves what is painful and unpleasant to their natural inclinations, feeling troubled, uneasy, and discontented when interrupted in their exercises · of devotion and told to do something else, obstinately persisting in performing devotions and mortifications of their own choice and preferring them to those prescribed by the Rule of obedience and caring but little for the observance of what they call, small points of the Rule &c. &c.

18. Those novices should not be allowed to remain in the Order, who evince no love for the spiritual life, not even in the superior part of the will, being disgusted with spiritual conferences and conversations and soon becoming wearied with discussions on spiritual matters and on that account withdrawing as much as possible from those who delight in spiritual discourses, showing however on the other hand great eagerness to acquire profane science and feeling, on this account very anxious to exchange the Noviciate for the house of studies, wasting meanwhile their precious time in trifles and frivolous amusements.

19. Those novices will never become good religious who observe the rules only exteriorly, according to the letter, without love for them, and in whom you can never discern any interior spirit.

20. Of novices who do not endeavor to amend their faults after having been repeatedly reprimanded

for them and are incorrigible, St. Alphonsus says: "The Congregation is free, and God only desires voluntary sacrifices. The novice who does not amend after having been reprimanded shows that he did not come to religion with a right intention, and he should be dismissed from the Congregation. At the commencement some faults may be tolerated in a novice, but if he does not correct them, after having been duly reproved for them, he should be dismissed at once, especially if these faults are of a serious nature and dangerous in their consequences; for a vicious subject causes more evil by his bad example than a heretic. When you see one who has this fault, do not allow him to frequent the society of others; his conversation will do more harm than a hundred demons." "It is true," writes St. Frances de Chantal to a Superioress, "if things are little, we must not for that fail to do them with much care and affection; for there is nothing little in religion, and those who neglect small observances, will soon contemn the greater. But we must know if such a novice does not wish to amend; for if in these little things, she should render herself incorrigible, that would be very bad."

21. Those novices are not fit for religion in whose manner of acting, speaking and judging every thing they see or hear in religion, you can always discover a worldly spirit.

22. The Master of Novices can never be too guarded, too much on the alert, too prudent, or too circumspect to hypocritical novices, or corrupt, run-

away students, school-teachers, theatre-actors, idlers, dissolute apprentices, and similar characters who present themselves in sheep-clothing generally with no other intention, than to find a home for a time *gratis*, or to acquire education without any expense to themselves. This not unfrequently happens in this country where so many emigrate from all parts of the world to seek their fortune.

23. "A subject capable of troubling, overthrowing and defaming a house and who has already done so, we must never keep."[1]

24. All novices after having been well instructed for six or eight months and plainly told what is required of them in conduct and in spirit, in order to labor seriously to acquire it, and who give no positive proofs (in accordance with their abilities) of their earnest desire to advance in the way of religious perfection, but are found to be still such as described in any of the articles from the first to the twenty-third, inclusively, should be dismissed without a scruple, or rather, it should be a matter of scruple to retain such characters, for reasons already alledged as well as also because they have not, nor, is it to be hoped that they will ever have, the true idea of a religious life, for want of a good religious soil, or root, or true seed from which a solid and true religious can spring, grow and attain the maturity of a religious life; and because in the practice of religious virtues they have not made, nor is there reason to hope that they will make, sufficient progress, in order that one may be-

[1] St. Frances de Chantal.

lieve and say with a safe conscience that they will do better in future; for putting as they do so many obstacles to grace, they will never understand, much less lead an interior life. Hence they will never aim properly at perfection; they will always be disedifying members and finally leave the Order.

"All the daughters of the Visitation," says St. Francis de Sales, and his saying is also applicable to other religious Orders, "are called to great perfection and their enterprise is more elevated than we can think; for they tend to a union not only with the Will of God, as all creatures should, but even to a union with His desires and intentions, even before they are signified to us, and if they knew of any greater perfection than conformity to the will, desires and intentions of God, they should undoubtedly aspire to it, their vocation obliging them thereto."

But as this is not done by such characters, as I have just said, we must say with St. Alphonsus: "Be firmly convinced that God does not wish any one to live in a religious community who has not a sincere desire to sanctify his soul," and in his instructions on the religious state he says, "I would advise any one who is desirous of entering religion to resolve to become a Saint, and to endure all sorts of sufferings exterior or interior, rather than prove unfaithful to God, or abandon his vocation; and if he cannot determine to do this, I exhort him not to deceive the Superior and himself by entering, for it is a sign, either, that he is not called to it, or that he is not willing to respond to his vocation as he ought to do, which is worse still. In so unprepared a state of mind, it would be better for him to wait till he is better able to resolve at giving himself entirely to God, and suffering all things for him. If he should, however, determine to make the experiment, he will injure both himself and the community, for he will most probably soon leave it, and thus he will disgrace himself in the eyes of the world, and render himself guilty before God of the greatest unfaithfulness to his vocation, and would render himself unable to take a single step in the way of God, who alone knows to what ruin he would expose himself." Nay in his Circular of the 8th of Aug. 1754, he even doubts the salvation of such as wish to be saved in a religious Order, but not as Saints." This assertion is indeed very hard, yet very true, provided by sanctity we do not mean those miraculous deeds of the Saints, or the so-called "gratiæ gratis datæ" granted to them by the Lord and that we understand by aiming zealously at perfection nothing else than that *firm, unwavering will* to acquire sanctity which every religious must aim at, in proportion to the gifts and talents bestowed on him by his Creator. So great is our frailty that our deeds are always below what we propose to ourselves. Hence, "if we do not aim high," says St. Alphonsus, "we shall easily miss our mark entirely." Besides, by embracing a religious life, we take upon ourselves so heavy a yoke and so great a burden, that if the sublime end to which we aspire is not kept constantly in view to cheer, inflame and strengthen our hearts to continue, renew, and confirm the sacrifice of ourselves, disgust and repugnance of soul, sloth and tepidity of spirit and discouragement of heart will overwhelm us, and finally all regular observance, all desire of advancing in perfection and even all efforts to attain salvation will be neglected and abandoned.

25. Should a novice appear to be called to perfection by extraordinary ways, he must be well tried, especially in obedience and humility; for these virtues are indeed the touchstone by which it can be easily seen, whether these extraordinary ways proceed from the Grace of God, or from the illusions of pride and the imagination, or from the craft of the devil. If such a novice after having been well tried, is evidently humble, without dissimulation and obedient without any hesitation, nay, if in proportion as he is tried he becomes more solidly grounded in virtue and in the interior peace of soul, which is generally granted to those thus favored, then it may be safely concluded that he is guided and influenced by the Spirit of God.

On the other hand, should the obedience and humility of such a novice not be so perfect as should be expected from one extraordinarily favored by Almighty God, his extraordinary ways are not to be trusted, and he cannot be conscientiously admitted to the vows. "Above all," writes St. Francis de Sales to a Superioress, "you must avoid those who play the saint and ecstatic. Deep humility and submission accompanied by a holy joy in the common life is a beautiful sanctity."

26. If a novice, for a considerable time, has led a very extravagant life in the world and is either of a frivolous, light-minded and inconstant disposition, or has an excitable imagination and is easily given to melancholy and scrupulosity, it would be rather hazardous to allow him to make his profession ; for in the first instance he would scarcely be able to keep the vow of chastity, in consequence of his character and the many hard and frequent temptations of the flesh consequent upon his former life and permitted by Almighty God for wise ends to return, not unfrequently in the most frightful manner and with the greatest, and as it were, almost irresistible violence. And in the second place, these temptations will easily cast r novice of such dispositions into an abyss of sadness or some other evil, especially if he is not perfectly sincere and obedient to his Confessor, in consequence of which he will finally return to the world, or become an insupportable burden to a religious community.   There would indeed be less danger in admitting such a novice to the vows, if it could be foreseen that he would always be under the direction of an enlightened and discreet Confessor, nay, there would be no reason to fear for him if from the commencement an extraordinary grace, and co-operation thereto on the part of the novice could be seen.   Should this not be the case, it would be more advisable not to admit him to the vows.

27. It is not advisable, or prudent to admit converts to the vows within one or two years after their conversion, however exemplary their conduct may

have been during the time of their noviciate; for they are generally supported by a strong sensible grace; everything in religion being new to them, they are always more or less in a pious excitement or religious enthusiasm, and as long as this lasts, they obey willingly and cheerfully, exhibit great humility and edify every one by their whole deportment. Experience, however, teaches that in many cases, in proportion as sensible grace withdraws, they lose courage and fervor, they feel overwhelmed by the religious life, as by a burden too heavy for them to carry and finally cast it off and return again to the world. It is not, however, necessary to be so rigorous with those who are converted to the faith when very young, or even with those who have fervently persevered in the practice of religion for four or five years after their reception into the Church.

28. "Extremely great precaution" says St. Frances de Chantal, "is to be taken in receiving those who have quitted other religious Orders; generally, there is something in them, which renders them unfit for the religious life; bodily weakness is often the pretext for dismissal, though in reality the bad dispositions of their mind is in most cases the true cause of their leaving." The general experience is that out of a hundred, there is not one who perseveres.

29. There are some novices, especially certain young ones, who seem to have very little or no difficulty in their noviciate, none on account of food, habitation, or other inconveniences of the religious
29

life, perhaps because in this, they are better off, than they were at their own homes; nor any difficulty on account of obedience, probably because both at home and at the parish-school they were accustomed to it, nor any difficulty on the part of their natural dispositions or passions, because they seem not as yet to be fully developed. They go when they are told to go; they come when they are told to come. When called upon to render their account of conscience, they scarcely ever have anything to tell. Of temptations, they seem to have no idea, their answer to questions proposed to them is an unmeaning yes, or no, just as it may seem to suit them. In a word, their manner of conduct is such as to make it impossible for one to say they are good or bad. You cannot accuse them of exterior faults, nor notice in them, any special inclination to advance in virtue. They seem to be neither one thing nor the other, their whole character being so undecided, that you know them and know them not, feeling perplexed as to whether they act from grace or nature, whether they do or do not understand the difference between the piety and virtues of the religious or of the secular life, placing one in extreme embarrassment as to their true call to the religious life, because there seem to be no positive reasons either for rejecting or admitting them.

Novices of this description must, according to the advice of St. Frances de Chantal, be closely watched for some time by one of sound judgment, yet in such manner as not to be noticed. Let him pay particular attention to their words and actions; let him ask them at times, when the subject of conversation leads to it, such questions as relate to certain essential points of the rule and the spirit of the Order ; they will then give their answers according to their views and opinions. If, after they have been for some months in the noviciate, these their answers and opinions are such as to show sufficiently that they have no true idea of the religious state but are worldly-minded, then nothing is to be thought of their faultless conduct in the noviciate and they should be considered unfit for the religious life.

Should they, however, answer in such a manner as religious of a good spirit would do, then you may conclude that they act in a right spirit through the grace and love of God and consequently you may be easy in conscience about their religious vocation.

Another means to be adopted by the Master of Novices, when the vocation of a novice is doubtful, is prayer, *"Ostende, Domine, quem elegeris;"* Let me know, O Lord, in some way whether this one is called to the Order; if he is really called, then give me a sign, an occasion by which I can convince myself of the spirit of this novice and of his vocation; for I would not wish to dismiss him if Thou hast called him ; but if Thou hast not called him, or if Thou foreseest that he will not co-operate with Thy grace, oh! then let me see a way, a means, an opportunity by which I may better know his spirit, and convince myself as to whether he is called or not.

If after using similar means, you are still unable to discern the spirit of a novice, or to determine the

principle of his thoughts, words, and actions, perhaps
in consequence of the duplicity or subtlety of his deportment, then let him be dismissed as one not fit for
the religious life, although his conduct may be blameless in other respects.   It matters very little whether
this deficiency in the novice, arises from his want of
a true appreciation of the value of the spiritual life,
or from an unwillingness to exert himself to advance
in the path of virtue.   *"Qui potest capere, capiat;"*
"Let him that can receive, receive it."   To comprehend the secrets of the Kingdom of God is a favor not
granted to all, neither is this hidden treasure found
by all who have the means given them to discover it
and enrich their souls by the heavenly mysteries, nor
"are all those who are called," says St. Frances de
Chantal, "faithful to correspond to grace, persevering
in that which might preserve their vocation and render
it good and secure."   The remarks made on page 23
and 24, are also applicable to this sort of novices and
those whose opinion on the subject is different, form
a very incorrect judgment.

If a novice evidently has any of the deficiencies
mentioned above, it will prove useless for the Master
of Novices to retain him on trial any longer than six
or eight months, deferring his profession in hopes of
any better assurance of his vocation.   "Experience
has taught us," writes St. Frances de Chantal to a
Superioress, "that those subjects whom the Chapter,
(say also whom the Master of Novices), has a difficulty
in admitting, occasion much trouble after their reception.   I really believe there are few of our houses that

have not learned this truth at their own expense. The Spirit of God presides over Communities (and does not fail, I add, to enlighten and assist the Master of Novices in his important office.)   Great regard must be paid to his sentiments.   Up to this day we have been too easy, let us henceforward be more choice of our subjects and be careful not to admit to the profession any who seem unfit, through human respect, or human considerations ; and remark this well, my dearest daughter, that we should never admit any one to the profession with the hope that she will do better for the future ; for we must consider the present condition of the mind, because we must rely upon what we see at present and not on the future, not being obliged to know it.''

The longer a novice remains, the more difficult it becomes for the Master of Novices to send him away, and he may, in the end, be falsely induced to compassionate him, allowing him to make the religious vows, especially if he is not guilty of any great exterior faults.

Besides, under such circumstances, human prudence will urge such a novice to be more fervent and appear to amend his faults.   Such an amendment will scarcely ever be a true radical cure, a real change of heart and interior sentiments and dispositions operated by the grace of God ; consequently it will not last long, and a sad, though frequent experience, teaches, that if such characters are admitted to the vows, they sooner or later leave the Order, or become very tepid and relaxed members, troublesome to

Superiors and burdensome to the Order and causing much spiritual harm to their brethren in religion, for want of a true religious spirit, especially if their health becomes impaired by a chronic disease, which God often permits for their amendment, but which they seldom profit by, allowing the flesh easily to triumph over the spirit, in consequence of which they will soon prove religious by name only desiring to have every thing in accordance with their own unmortified desires and caprices.

"But this novice may perhaps have a religious vocation," the Master of Novices may sometimes say to himself, "and may do better after awhile; if I send him to the world where he is exposed to so many dangers, he may be lost and his soul may be required of me at the judgment seat of God." Such doubts, fears, and perplexities must be overcome by the following considerations.

The great dangers of salvation to which novices if dismissed, are exposed in the world, must not at all be taken into consideration in deciding their vocation, because the holy Will of God and the general good of religion, requires that no novices should be admitted to profession whose Divine Call, is not beyond all doubt. As for the salvation of such novices, we must truly believe that, should they be really called, if otherwise disposed to make the sacrifice of themselves, Almighty God, in His infinite mercy and liberality, will not fail to recompense their good will, by other efficacious graces.

If we lived in a Catholic Country, surrounded by

a Catholic atmosphere, influence and spirit, some indulgence might perhaps be granted to some novices
of the above description, but living as we do in
America, where the spirit of infidelity so much reigns,
where the spirit of independence and freedom of
thought, word and action, has become the rule of the
day, as it were, where the greater mass of the people
are in the habit of judging and censuring Superiors,
both ecclesiastical and political without impunity, a
thing diametrically opposed to the spirit of God and
His religion; where religious are so much exposed to
the dangerous allurements of the world and are,
though very young and inexperienced, but too often
employed in the sacred ministry, or in the service of
their neighbor on account of the greatness of the
harvest and small number of the laborers, and where
the religious training is very often too deficient and
superficial; under such circumstances, I say, it is of
the greatest importance that the vocations of novices
should be very solid and beyond all reasonable doubt,
as otherwise, they will not persevere to the end; for
the greater the dangers are from without, the greater
also must be the interior spirit, strength and courage
of religious in order not to succumb amid so many
trials and temptations.

"In deciding upon the solidity of a novice's
religious vocation, and in admitting him to membership in religion, we must never be guided by human
respect or considerations," says St. Frances de Chantal; "O God! what an important point this is, viz—
that no human respect enter into the consideration of

the admission of subjects, but only divine inspiration be attended to.   What is human respect? It is to see if the person, be noble, rich, beautiful and agreeable; if her parents will be a support to the house; if they will be afflicted and offended if she be sent away;" it is also human consideration, I add, to think, that a novice is very talented and may bring great celebrity upon the Order, or that the harvest is so great and the laborers are so few and that on this account, allowance is to be made for certain defects in such individuals, and that they will be better afterwards. "But such and similar considerations," says St. Frances de Chantal, "must have no power when the persons have not the spirit and qualities required by the Rule; for then they must be dismissed."

"God will not demand of us an account of their salvation, but most certainly of the evil, which they would bring upon religion should they be suffered to remain through human prudence.   Hence be firm in never admitting anyone who has not the true dispositions requisite for the spirit of our holy vocation, and God will bless you more and· more for it.   I have nothing so much at heart after holy humility and dependence on God, as that we should make a good choice of subjects.   Sisters, the happiness and preservation of our Congregation depend on this good choice of subjects and on the care taken to ground them well in solid virtue.   In the name of God, let us remain firm in this point, I repeat never let any human consideration, but only divine inspiration guide us in their admission to membership.   So im-

portant is this point, that, if I could, I would write
it with my blood in indelible characters on the hearts
of all our Sisters, but especially of Superioresses. As
when we find good souls we must cultivate and serve
them carefully, cherish and guard them preciously,
so when the contrary is the case, we must dismiss
them generously and promptly after having, by a
sweet patience, tried to render them capable of the
vocation.   To burden convents with subjects altogether unfit, is to bring a wordly spirit among us.
We should guard well against this miserable world,
and greatly guard lest it should enter our Convents;
may God in His mercy preserve us from it.   In a
word, my dear Sisters, if you wish to preserve the
spirit of your holy vocation, be faithful and firm never
to admit to the profession those who have not the
requisite dispositions ; otherwise you will destroy
yourselves and the good and repose of your houses."
    Hence it is a principle of Moral Theology that no
one should be allowed to embrace a higher state, unless it be morally certain, that such is the Divine
Will; for this reason, no one must be permitted to
take religious vows, unless it be beyond all reasonable
doubt, that he is spiritually and corporally suited to
carry the yoke and burden of religious life, which
certainly cannot be expected of a novice whose vocation is doubtful.   It should therefore ever be remembered, that a novice who is not evidently called to
religion by our Lord, will never become a good and
true religious, nor can it be reasonably hoped that
without a particular grace from God (which is

not so easily obtained) he will persevere in the religious life until the end.

St. Alphonsus says: "Let us have charity towards all, but no false compassion," or as St. Ignatius expresses it, "no imprudent charity."

Now according to the sound principles of Moral Theology, a novice of a doubtful vocation is unfit to embrace a higher state; therefore if through a false compassion and indulgence, a novice whose religious vocation is not morally certain, should be allowed to make vows, this would indeed be misplaced compassion and indulgence and imprudent charity; for experience sufficiently teaches that to impose the yoke and burden of the religious life on one of a doubtful vocation, is *cruelty* rather than charity; because, though Almighty God does not refuse the necessary graces to fulfil the duties and obligations of the religious life to those who without a true vocation take the religious vows in *good faith*, yet there are very few who profit by those graces, and the greater number, especially in a Country like America, sooner or later return to the world with a guilty and troubled conscience, miserable here below and with but little hope of happiness hereafter. It is therefore necessary to be rigorous in admitting novices to their profession, admitting those only to the vows whose vocation, as has repeatedly been said, is beyond all reasonable doubt, for it is much easier to dismiss them before their profession than after it.

Hence the advice of St. Francis de Sales to the Sisters of the Visitation, should be applied to all

religious Orders and Congregations, viz : "It is better
for the Sisters to increase in solid virtues than in number of houses." St. Alphonsus speaking of the Congregation of the Most Holy Redeemer, expresses himself in a similar manner. "God does not will," he
says, "that we should be great in number, but that
we be great in goodness and holiness." Again,
"God is more pleased with two or three truly humble
and mortified men than with a thousand who are imperfect. God does not wish us to have many members, but is satisfied with a few good ones. The
Congregation does not need a large number of subjects, it needs only such ones as truly desire to sanctify
themselves; ten who really love and serve God will
be enough, and these few will do more good than
many proud and disobedient spirits." Hence it is
not the great number of members that must be considered in religious Orders, but the solidity of their
vocation. "*Non multa, sed multum,*" otherwise the
saying of the Prophet Isaias will be verified : "Thou
hast multiplied the nation and hast not increased
the joy."[1]

Almighty God is the grand Institutor and Promoter of all religious Orders, and as such, He has
from all eternity, chosen those who are destined to be
the members of them. "For these," says St. Francis
de Sales, "we must wait." He is the Sower of the
seed of true, solid vocations, He sows it and will
always sow it abundantly in the manner, time and
place most pleasing to Him, provided religious Orders

[1] Chapt. ix. 3.

use no other means to draw members than fervent
prayer and good example, and the Lord will not fail
to mark with unmistakable signs those whom He has
called, and if these marks are not sufficiently visible
within six or eight months, it is useless as I have
said above, to wait any longer for their appearance.

These instructions and principles have been
drawn from men of great sanctity, learning, experience,
prudence and discretion both in the religious and
spiritual life. The experience of several years has
thoroughly convinced the writer of their truth.
Would to God, they were all rightly understood and
applied by all those who have to decide religious vocations. Certainly the honor and glory of God would
then be greatly promoted, the true religious spirit increased, the salvation of many more souls secured and
the number of bad religious diminished, and with an
easy conscience we could see and hear of how many
who forsake their religious calling; we could say with
St. Alphonsus: "I am not sorry if on account of his
faults one ceases to be a member of our Congregation,
on the contrary, it affords me great consolation, because a diseased member is removed from among us,
who might have infected others." Our Lord Jesus
Christ was the best of Masters, and yet many of His
disciples abandoned Him; even one of His Apostles
apostatized. Thus it has been in ages past, thus it
will be in time to come. The precious grace of a
religious vocation is not granted by God in such a
manner as would make it impossible for one to lose it,
through his own faults and infidelities. "A religious

vocation," says St. Alphonsus, "is the work of grace rather than our own; the little that remains to be done, must be done in such a manner as though all depended on *us* and nothing on grace." This being forgotten and neglected by many even of those whose vocation is truly divine, accounts for the great number of bad religious and deserters of religious Orders and Congregations.

CHAPTER XVI.

ON RECREATION.

S the body requires rest to enable it to work, so also does the mind. It cannot always be recollected; it is necessary to unbend it from time to time, and it is on this account that the founders of religious Institutes have established regular hours for recreation. "God wishes," says St. Alphonsus, "that souls consecrated to His service, should recreate themselves from time to time, in order to give some relaxation to their mind." St. Frances de Chantal was very careful to insist with the Superiors of her Institute upon the great necessity of recreation to their daughters, especially to such, as were called to lead a strict retired and interior life. One day a certain Superior requested her, to give orders, that the hours of recreation should be spent in a more serious manner; as for her, she did not like to see the Sisters laugh in recreation, considering that St. Benedict never laughed. "Dear daughter," the Saint replied, "we must, indeed, respect whatever the Saints have done. Were you a Benedictine nun, I would ask of you an explanation of this passage of St. Benedict's life; but being a Sister of the Visitation of Mary, you must try to understand the spirit of your Founder, who, I assure you, was a Saint, whom sanctity did not prevent from carrying into recreation a joyful spirit which he communicated to others also, and who would laugh in a most hearty manner, if there was occasion for it. Not long ago I read in Holy Scripture, that Sara, on conceiving a Son in a miraculous manner, said: 'The Lord hath made me laugh,' I then thought to myself: the spirit of God makes us rejoice, and divine Providence having been pleased to subject us to food and drink and recreation, we should say: the Lord makes me eat, the Lord makes me drink, the Lord makes me sleep, the Lord makes me laugh, and recreate myself; and thus everything is done out of obedience, and in the name of the Lord. "Take care, my daughter, not to deprive your Sisters of the liberty which is granted them by the rule, and do not be too rigid; be easy, provided recreation be carried on according to the spirit of the rule. We of course who are Superiors, after having spent part of the day in transacting business, in conversing with the Sisters, or with Seculars in the parlor, believe, that we lose our time by going to recreation, and we would prefer to spend it in interior recollection; but for our Sisters who did not leave the choir and their cells, it is necessary that, — to use the expression of our holy Father,—they should unbend the bow."

We read, it is true, of St. Frances de Chantal, that, either on account of the pressure of her occupations, or the greatness of her interior sufferings, or the intensity of her interior recollection, or of her continual disgust for this life, or finally on account of the infirmities of her old age, she could not, for the space of some years, be so cheerful as she used to be in her younger days; she would, however, give full liberty to her Sisters to recreate and amuse themselves, and when she noticed that they did not speak on her account, she would exhort them to talk, and in order to encourage them to do so, she would now and then relate a little story for their amusement.

"The Superior," she writes in another letter, "must take particular care to make well the recreation with the Sisters, contributing towards it as much as possible by her sweet and holy joy in the Lord. Hence she ought to beware of sadness which is a great fault in a Superior. Our blessed Father St. Francis de Sales — told me one day that the most desirable qualities in a pastor were *humility, holy joy and meekness.* Be then very humble and cheerful and you will find it easy to guide the flock of Jesus Christ confided to your care. Be also very careful. to keep our Sisters cheerful and content; then the burden of the religious life and everything connected with it will be light for them. In recreation say nothing to them that might mortify them, except what is absolutely necessary, always giving the preference to meekness and charitable forbearance."

When St. Francis de Sales learned that in a certain Convent of the Visitation of Mary, the whole time of recreation was spent in spiritual discourses, he deemed this zeal rather excessive, and he gave orders that they should not speak so much on serious subjects such as interior recollection &c., but should recreate their minds more by conversing on subjects rather indifferent, less serious and requiring less attention.

All the Saints found it necessary to take some sort of recreation. We read of St. John the Evangelist, that now and then he would amuse himself by playing for a while with a little partridge. Rt. Rev. John P. Camus, Bishop of Belley, relates of St. Francis de Sales as follows: "When I was on a visit to him, he used to seek to recreate me after the labor of preaching. He would take me out in a boat on that beautiful lake which bathes the walls of Annecy, or to walk in some pleasant gardens on its fair banks. When he came to see me at Belley, he did not decline similar recreations, in which I invited him to indulge, though he never proposed them, or sought them of his own accord."

St. Frances de Chantal, speaking one day to a religious priest, who was remarkable for the severity of his conduct, and wishing to turn him from that mode of acting, addressed him in the following manner: "At the age which I have attained, and in the situation in which God has placed me, under a pressure of business which absorbs my thoughts, I have no inclination to indulge in laughter, or to give any time to recreation. Were you, however, to see me among our young Sisters, you would observe, that I talk, that I listen to them, and that I laugh, generally without experiencing any joy at what they say, for
30

the sole purpose of helping them to enjoy that recreation, which to them is absolutely necessary.''

The Rev. Father Mantone, C. SS. R., who received the religious habit at the hands of St. Alphonsus, and who had the happiness of living with this
illustrious Saint for four years, related to Abbe Gaume
about this great Saint what follows: ''Notwithstanding his continual infirmities,'' he said, ''St. Alphonsus was the most cheerful, most amiable, and most
affable man in the world. In recreation, he would
never omit playing on the piano to recreate the
Fathers and Brothers. He was the very soul of
recreation and conversation. However, after he had
become Bishop, he would no longer play on the piano,
for fear of giving scandal. But after his resignation
had been accepted, he returned to us and played for
us again as before.''[1]

It is then not at all contrary to perfection and
the spirit of the Saints to take innocent recreations,
provided they are taken in a proper manner and spirit,
in order to obtain the two lawful ends for which they
are permitted, namely, the relaxation of the mind and
the promotion of mutual *fraternal charity*. It is the
duty of the Superior to see that this two-fold end may
not be frustrated.

Hence he must direct that, as St. Paul says, ''all
things should be done decently and according to
order.''[2] To comply with this injunction of St. Paul,
two extremes are to be avoided; we should be careful
not to say anything unbecoming a religious, such as

[1] Rome 2 Vol. Jan. 13.   [2] 1 Cor. 14, 40.

words of self-praise, or cutting words, not to indulge
in disputes, too loud laughter and cries; not to inter-
rupt others in their conversation in an impolite manner, or seek to be chair-man, as it were, all the time.
Railleries above all are to be avoided and banished
from recreation, as they wound charity in the end.
If one religious ridicule another, they rarely separate
in charity with each other; the most innocent mirth,
if it be carried too far, or repeated too often, becomes
offensive in the end. At first it is borne patiently,
afterwards it is taken to heart, then the ridiculed person testifies his pain by a sad or offended air; at last,
he is irritated, answers sharply, after which charity
disappears to make room for anger; persons thus
amusing themselves at the expense of others, destroy
the two principal ends of recreation, make it degenerate into an abuse, and injure charity, and conscience
very much. How great a misery is it not, and how
blameable are not those who wound charity by the
very means which have been established to maintain
it! Let those who believe, that to have wit, and employ it in annoying their fellow-religious by raillery,
be firmly persuaded that they have a bad heart
destitute of that charity which St. Paul styles benign,
since they make such a malicious use of their wit in
tormenting those to whom they should testify cordiality and try to recreate them in an innocent manner.

The other extreme to be avoided and guarded
against is, not contributing our mite towards keeping
up recreation, saying either nothing, or scarcely anything, or appearing melancholy and sad, or too serious

and too much recollected, just as we would be in the
refectory or chapter.   "As it would be unbecoming,"
says St. Francis de Sales, "to burst out into laughter
in a conversation upon serious subjects, so it is disagreeable to see one never laugh in time of recreation."
"I do not wish to say," says St. Alphonsus, "that,
when in recreation, you should always speak upon
subjects of a serious nature; no, at such a time you
ought to be cheerful, rejoicing and laughing with the
rest; speak on such topics as are calculated to cheer
your companions."   "When in recreation," says St.
Francis de Sales, "we ought to be very charitable,
affable, sweet, cheerful, condescending to such a degree
even as to say insignificant things, if they contribute
towards recreating others."   "There are some," says
St. Leo, "who believe that, in order to preserve a
proper decorum and religious recollection, it is necessary for them to walk about with an inclined head
and a sour face; but they are greatly mistaken; the
religious must not put on a melancholy, but a cheerful and holy appearance, he must unite to modesty, a
certain cheerfulness, and to cheerfulness a certain
modesty."   Let us add that, as recreation is an exercise of the community, to which each religious should
repair through a principle of regularity and charity,
it would be wrong for him to retire to his cell through
a misplaced desire of retreat, or, through mistaken
devotion, there to take this time to make his spiritual
reading or meditation.   Each exercise in religion, has
its fixed hour, not indeed for the purpose of gratifying
the desire of any one in particular, but that they may

render what they owe to each other. Hence if the particular employment of any one, or obedience do not call him elsewhere, charity and his rule oblige him to rejoice in the Lord with the rest of the Community at the time of recreation. It is not less wrong for religious to form separate parties in recreation. Those private recreations always denote some division, or at least that some do not sympathize with the others, and have not sufficient virtue to bear charitably with their conversation. Ah! how misplaced and disedifying is such conduct! But how edifying is it not on the other hand, to see all the members of a religious Community come to recreation, and rejoice together in the Lord!

Religious should then endeavor always to avoid those two extremes and walk in the middle way, which is always the way of virtue. This will be done if they attend to what the Saints say on this head. "Recreation," says St. Alphonsus," must be a relaxation, but not a dissipation for the mind. The recreation of a religious is to differ from that of a secular. He must, it is true, have some honest and innocent recreation; but at the same time, he must know how to seek and find God even in this exercise. He must perform it with the intention to do God's holy will. He must then not lose, at such a time, his interior recollection; he should make, now and then, an act of love, and send up to the Lord some ejaculatory prayers; let him from time to time, say something about God, and when convenient, throw into the conversation on indifferent subjects, some seasonable and useful remarks," according to the example of St. Francis de Sales who, when persons spoke to him of buildings, paintings, music, hunting, birds, plants, gardening, flowers, did not blame those who took an interest in these things, but would desire that they should make use of these occupations as so many means to raise themselves to God; he himself set the example, by drawing from all these subjects motives for heavenly aspirations. If beautiful plants were pointed out to him, "we are" he would observe, "the field which God cultivates." If some magnificent and splendidly adorned church, "we are the temples of the living God; O that our souls were as richly adorned with virtues." If flowers, "when shall our flowers yield fruit?" If rare and exquisite paintings, "there is nothing so fair as the soul which is made to the image of God." If taken into a garden, he would exclaim: "O when shall the garden of our soul be sown with flowers, and filled with fruit, weeded, dressed and trimmed? When shall it be fenced in and closed against everything that is displeasing to the heavenly Gardener?" On beholding fountains, "When shall we possess within our hearts the source of living water, springing up to life everlasting? How long shall we forsake the source of life, to dig for ourselves leaking Cisterns? O, when shall we draw, to our content, from the Saviour's fountains?"

It was especially in the evening recreation, at least towards the end of it, that St. Alphonsus required his brethren in religion to relate something edifying, and if this point of the rule was not observed, he did not fail to remind the Superior of it.

Something similar is recorded in the life of St. Frances de Chantal. This Saint would watch those of her Sisters whose duty it was in recreation, now and then to remind the other Sisters of the presence of God, and she herself would do this sometimes by mingling some pious reflections with the conversation; especially towards the end of recreation she would relate or speak on something spiritual, in order that the Sisters might return to holy silence with sentiments of piety and love for God. In Advent and in Lent she wished recreations to be of a more spiritual character than at other times. At such seasons she would sometimes say to her Sisters, without making, however, a custom of it: "Rejoice as much as you can for half an hour, and then let me have the other half to speak upon our Lord."

Jesus Christ takes great delight in such conversations, associating Himself to such as speak of Him. "At the conversations of the servants of God," says St. Teresa, "Jesus Christ is always present." Of this Father Gisolfo, of the Congregation of the Pii Operarii, relates a memorable example in the life of the venerable Father Anthony de Collelis, chapt. 31. Father D. Constantine Rossi, the Master of Novices, saw, one day, two of his young disciples, F. D. Anthony Torres and F. D. Philip Orlia, conversing together, and with them a young man of most beautiful aspect. The Master of Novices was surprised at seeing two novices whom he considered to be most exemplary, speak to a stranger without permission. He therefore asked who the stranger was. They replied that they had been entirely alone, and upon explaining the nature of their conversation, the Master readily understood that the person whom he had seen was our divine Saviour. Our Lord also manifests His pleasure in such conversations, by enkindling divine love and fervor in the hearts of those who are engaged in them. St. Alphonsus says: "It often happens that good religious, after speaking on Jesus Christ, feel more fervor and ardor than after mental prayer." Witness the disciples who went to Emmaus. "And they said to one another: Was not our heart burning within us, whilst He spoke in the way and opened to us the scriptures?"[1]

It is related of St. Aloys. Gonzaga, that by his pious conversations he changed the college in which he was living into a church, as it were, for his brethren in religion often left recreation with greater fervor for the service of God than when coming from meditation. Happy the man who understands how to entertain his fellow-men in a recreating, yet spiritual manner! and blessed that religious Community which harbors such a man! To him may be applied what is said of St. John the Baptist; or of the Prophet Elias: "He stood, as a fire, and his word burnt like a torch."[2]

[1] Luke 24, 32. [2] Eccles.- 48, 1.

CHAPTER XVII.

ON MORTIFICATION.

BEYOND a doubt, mortification is a necessary means for acquiring perfection. "He who disregards mortification," says St. Francis de Sales, "will never be able to raise his soul to the contemplation of God." And St. Teresa adds: "It is folly to suppose that God admits immortified souls to His friendship." St. John of the Cross warns us not to give credit to any one who rejects penitential exercises, were his doctrine confirmed even by miracles. Hence St. Alphonsus admonishes Confessors to do their utmost to implant the love of mortification in souls.

In the practice of bodily mortifications, however, great discretion is required. "No sooner," says St. Alphonsus, "does the devil perceive that a soul has devoted herself to God, and that she is enjoying the first fruits of heavenly consolation, than he urges her to the practice of excessive austerities, fully aware that the indiscreet soul will soon sink under the combined weight of bloody disciplines, rigorous fasts, hair-shirts and other painful works of penance. This is an artifice of the devil which he veils under the

31

cloak of fervor. His real design is to make the soul
unfit for the exact performance of her allotted duties,
and, to reduce her, if possible, to a state of utter
prostration. In such a state, as he knows by experience, the soul will easily give up her pious practices with the risk of never relishing them again ;
especially so, if, at this period, the dew of heavenly
consolations should dry up, in consequence of which
the soul will quickly tire, and soon discontinue, one
by one, her usual mortifications, devotions, commun-
ions, and all other practices of piety, fancying that
the spiritual life is too irksome and too tedious.
Lamentable in the extreme would it be, if at this
period such souls had the misfortune to be guided by
indiscreet confessors, who, not satisfied with practising such austerities themselves, should recommend
them to their penitents. A certain Superior of Carthusian Monks, chastised his body by such revolting
austerities, that one would have been tempted to
believe that he had either quitted the body, or dwelt
in one of iron. St. Francis de Sales said of that
Superior, "that he might be compared with those
physicians who people the graveyards. For, beyond
question, he had been instrumental in the untimely
death of many of his brethren in religion, who regardless of their weak constitutions, had overdone themselves, under his direction, in works of penance, and
had sunk into an early grave." "His successor on
the contrary," adds the Saint, "united mildness and
moderation with austerity, and thus he was enabled
to preserve his Community in excellent health both

of body and soul. We must employ discretion, and bear in mind that God always requires reasonable service at our hands. Indeed, our method of glorifying God, must ever be regulated by sound judgment. St. Bernard came well-nigh being wrecked on this reef in his youth. In riper age he bewailed his youthful austerities: indeed a sinner could not have deplored his waywardness more sincerely. He was wont to call his untimely austerities 'the errors of his youth.' I once knew a distinguished scholar, who, in a short time, completely undermined his vigorous frame by rigid austerities, and thus rendered himself not only useless but even entirely helpless. He only became aware of his mistake when the evil was beyond cure. I had left no means untried to moderate his overstrained fervor — but to no purpose. My repeated counsels and warnings were alike unheeded."

Misguided by a false zeal for corporal austerities, a certain Nun chastised her flesh by the severest penances to such a degree, that her health was placed in imminent jeopardy. St. Francis de Sales gave her the following counsel, which is an admirable expression of his habitual mildness and sound judgment. "Do not subject your feeble body to greater rigor than the rules of your Convent prescribe. Be at much pains to preserve your bodily health, for a good supply of vigor is necessary to perform all our exercises well. We shall surely be wanting in strength if we waste our body by indiscreet austerities. Very few, observed the Saint, know how to avoid extremes. The spirit is willing — hence the first impulse of our fervor always exacts too much from the frail flesh. But we ought to bear in mind that as the spirit cannot support a well-fed body, in like manner, a half-starved body cannot support the spirit.'' In order to guard against extremes in this particular, St. Alphonsus admonishes spiritual directors to inculcate upon their penitents the necessity of abstaining from all austerities for which they have not obtained the sanction of their Confessor. Hence, too, arises a new source of merit for the penitent — the merit of obedience.

St. John of the Cross asserts that they who perform mortifications against obedience, may be said to advance rather in vice than in virtue.

First: It is a general rule, says St. Alphonsus, that external mortifications are only to be permitted when the penitent petitions for them; otherwise they would avail but little, in as much as their merit almost entirely depends upon the degree of fervor with which they are practised.

Secondly: It suffices for a beginning to allow or prescribe easy practices, such as the little Cilicium, discipline, etc., in order rather to increase in souls the desire of mortification than to give a real occasion of mortifying themselves.

Thirdly: Let the director be cautioned not to deviate from this rule, until the penitent is well grounded in the spiritual life; for it is then only, that the duty arises for the Confessor to grant more effective mortifications.

Fourthly: The director must be especially on his

guard in prescribing severe austerities to beginners,
who are usually favored with extraordinary fervor
and consolation. The safest way is to admonish them
to patience in suffering contempt and adversity, to
obedience, to bridling their curiosity etc. He may,
however, accompany the refusal with the promise to
grant their petition as soon as they have brought the
inner man under their control.

Fifthly: It is advisable occasionally to refuse
every kind of exterior mortification, until the penitent
has mastered the predominant passion, as vanity,
selfishness, self-esteem, self-will, and the like.

Sixthly: St. Alphonsus cautions directors to be
extremely sparing when there is question of retrenching the usual amount of rest; for nothing is more
calculated to injure both body and mind. If the
necessary amount of sleep is denied to the body, head-
ache is the natural consequence; whereupon a person
becomes unfit to perform his own peculiar duties.

Seventhly: "As regards fasting, I should like,"
says St. Francis de Sales, "to see the sentiments of
St. Jerome adopted. The holy doctor expresses
himself, in the following strain, to the devout matron
Laeta: 'Prolonged and excessive fasts are extremely
hateful in my eyes, especially in such as are still
young. I am convinced by my own experience that
a young jackass, when jaded, easily turns from the
road; I mean young people, who have contracted
some malady by rigorous fasting, are in danger of
falling a prey to effeminacy.' Beyond a doubt, fasting is the most painful of austerities, in as much as it

places the axe at the root: Surely that which attacks
the root of a tree is far more effectual than that which
hardly penetrates the bark, or softly brushes its
boughs. The deer is known to lose its fleetness on
two occasions — when it is too fat, and when it is too
lean. We are exposed to great temptations both
when the body is well fed, and when it is emaciated.
On the one hand, the body becomes overbearing by
indulgence, and on the other, it gives way to peevish-
ness, and dreads to encounter difficulties; and as little
as we can hope to bear a pampered body, just as little
can we expect a wasted frame to support us. It is a
melancholy fact that many a devout person has been
reduced to the condition of a cripple in the bloom of
youth, by rigid fasts, scourges, hair-shirts etc. as the
case of St. Bernard proves but too clearly. At last
such persons are usually forced to discontinue their
penances and give their whole attention to the restoration of their health. Surely they would have acted
more wisely had they consulted the duties and obligations of their vocation. Labor tends nearly, and perhaps equally as much as fasting to subdue the flesh.
Hence, if your labor is obligatory and conducive to
the greater glory of God, I should gladly see you prefer labor how irksome soever, to prolonged vigils and
unmerciful fasts. The Church, too, has nothing else
in view, when she exempts hard-toiling laborers even
from the regular fasts. One, for instance, experiences
great difficulty in fasting; another's feeling of deli acy
is sharply mortified by serving the sick; a third is
weighed down by the duties of the Confessional, of

preaching, praying etc. The pain and disgust a person has to contend with in fulfilling "duties of this nature, are far more meritorious than the most rigid fasts. For, not to mention the mortifications connected with preaching, catechising, confessing and the like, they are productive of the most desirable fruit in our neighbor. Hence it may be admitted as a general maxim that it is proper to allow the body a greater amount of strength than is absolutely requisite for the moment. It will be no arduous task to reduce the body if necessary, but we cannot restore our wasted strength at pleasure. A wound is soon inflicted, but a cure is not as easily effected. The spirit must make some allowance for the body, treating it as a father does an obedient son. But if the flesh revolt, we must employ the rod, according to the advice of the Apostle. 'I chastise my flesh, and reduce it to slavery.' "

Eighthly: It will not be amiss when granting leave for a mortification, to give the penitent to understand that every pain we can inflict upon ourselves is far below the heroic endurance of the Saints, and infinitely less than the torments our dear Lord chose to undergo for our sake, and that our best endeavor is utter impotence, when compared with one single drop of His Precious Blood shed for our redemption.

Note: Be it borne in mind, that they, whose duties require extraordinary application of the mind, as the pursuit of science, spiritual exercises, especially if the persons are still young, always need their proper nourishment. This is of great importance inasmuch as such persons would otherwise soon lose their mental energy, especially so if they should add loss of sleep to the want of proper food. Should they, in addition to all this, be troubled with violent scruples, they would soon be plunged into a most deplorable condition. The inevitable result would be, extreme prostration both of body and soul — nervousness would follow in the train, and the fancy would be worked up to such a pitch, that the devil would find it an easy task to fill the imagination with a host of ugly and shameful phantoms. In a word, the whole human system would become a prey to the impure suggestions of the devil, and the body having been reduced to so helpless a condition as even in no small degree to affect the mind, there would arise for the soul the greatest difficulty, in resisting and repelling the attacks of the evil one; in consequence of which the poor soul easily imagines that all is lost, being no longer able to distinguish between temptation and the consent of the will. Hence it is necessary to refuse scrupulous persons such extraordinary mortifications. Spiritual directors should even be very backward in allowing other souls rigorous austerities; and should they ever find mortifications of this kind necessary, even then they should grant them for a short time only. The reason for so doing is evident, namely, lest so much rigor impair the penitent's bodily or spiritual health, or lest the practice of such austerity render such persons in any way unfit for the punctual performance of more important duties. They might, however, except one case, i. e.

when God requires an extraordinary sacrifice of a soul. Still directors should not scruple to delay their consent until they have evident reason for recognizing the will of God. They should not entertain the slightest fear of thwarting the designs of God by a refusal. For it must be taken for granted that souls are to be directed according to the ordinary rules of spiritual direction, until the contrary is proved. As soon, however, as they discern the finger of God, they not only may, but they must grant the request, fully assured that God will supply every deficiency, nay, that He will render the soul sufficiently vigorous to practise every austerity without the least danger to her allotted duties. The devil is deceit itself. He places some particular good before our eyes to be obtained by austerities, fully aware that in striving for the secondary good we become incapable of achieving the common good, which after all must be preferred to every private consideration. As regards Religious, the best advice for them is to take the food and rest allowed by the rule of their Institute, in order thereby to be able not for a time only, but for many years, nay for a whole life, to keep the rules, to serve their fellow-religious, and to promote the well-being of their neighbor for the greater glory of God.

A Sister of the Visitation once expressed a desire to practise greater austerities. "Be satisfied," said St. Francis de Sales, "with the mortifications connected with the punctual observance of the rule. The devil is highly delighted to see one undertake a multiplicity of corporal penances. It is madness to seek perfection in a way different from that one which all your companions pursue. Never fear, God will furnish you with abundant means of mortifying yourself provided you are faithful in making a proper use of the occasions offered. Be on the alert, and offer an open heart to the inspirations of the Holy Spirit.'' This was not merely the doctrine of the Saint, but his own special practice also.

Ninthly: Although we must esteem exterior mortifications even to the degree of rejecting the contrary doctrine, were it accompanied even by miracles, we are not to measure our advancement in perfection either by the number or severity of our penances; for bodily austerities do not constitute the true spirit of mortification, inasmuch as they are not so necessarily and immediately connected with sanctity of life as is interior mortification; it is in the latter that the real progress of the soul consists. It is by obedience and the suppression of the passions that we gain most. Were we only at some pains to acquire these virtues, we should never lack occasion for exercising them. The more a soul practises self-denial, the more speedily will she soar above the things of earth and be raised to union with God.

Tenthly: The following are very salutary and harmless mortifications.

1. Endeavor always to preserve your whole exterior perfectly recollected, agreeable and modest. Never allow a word to escape your lips which is not spoken with calmness, discretion, gentleness and modesty, in a moderate tone of voice, yet so loud as

to be understood. Never show in your looks any freedom, which causes distractions and satisfies your curiosity on all sides, nor have in your exterior any habit which is disorderly, or which might be said to arise from your love for ease, always try to keep your whole exterior the same, easy but dignified out of respect for the presence of God. All this is certainly a great mortification for human nature. This very same kind of mortification was one of those which St. Francis de Sales imposed upon himself as we read in his life.

2. You can mortify your appetite in a most advantageous manner and without danger by being indifferent in regard to all kinds of food, of whatever quality it may be and in whatever manner it may be prepared, never complaining or saying anything against it. All should be according to your taste, be it cold or warm, salted or unsalted; eat whatever is placed before you, without making any remark, because, in the opinion of St. Francis de Sales we should have a great reverence for these words of our Lord: "Manducate quae apponuntur vobis." "For, in my opinion," says the Saint, "it shows greater virtue to eat of whatever is placed before you and in the order in which it is placed, without choosing whether it be according to your taste or not, than always to select the worst; because, though the latter may seem to be more rigorous, yet with the former there is united more self-denial, because you do not only deny your taste, but also your choice. Moreover, to select the worst dishes betrays a kind of spirit which is only as-

far away from pride, as smoke is from fire. It is, besides, no small mortification to form your taste, according to the will of everybody and to subject it on every occasion, by accommodating yourself to that which you do not like, and by denying yourself that which you desire. I esteem St. Bernard much more for having drunk oil instead of wine or water, than if he had intentionally drunk worm-wood water, because he thereby showed that he did not care what he drank. To select the food would show a spirit which pays attention to the dish and the sauce. To eat what is good without wishing to please yourself, and what is bad without showing any repugnance, and yet to be wholly indifferent in regard to the one as well as the other — is true mortification. In this very indifference in regard to what you eat and drink consists the perfect accomplishment of these words: "Eat whatever is placed before you." From this I except however all food which is hurtful to health, or which causes depression of the mind, as happens to many when they take warm, highly seasoned, creamy, or flatulent food. I likewise except those occasions when nature stands in need of help and refreshment, in order that afterwards it may be able to endure great labors for the glory of God. In short a constant and prudent temperance, is better than a rigorous abstinence which is often interrupted by intemperance in eating. Those who are abstemious by nature, have great advantages, even in regard to science. Their body is like a bridled horse, which is kept in obedience without much difficulty." St.

Francis de Sales usually drank but little wine and this he mixed with much water; he was also accustomed to eat only very common meat, and if any one made remonstrances on this point, he alleged as a reason that he preferred to live as the poor, that he had a farmer's stomach which relishes common food best. "One day," says M. de Belley, "when at table, I had given him a very delicate meat; I remarked how he dexterously placed it to one side and in its place eat a piece of quite ordinary meat. Now I have caught you in the act, said I to him, reminding him of the rule: "Eat whatever is placed before you." "Do you then not know, he answered, "that I have a farmer's stomach which stands in need of nourishing food; your delicate meats would give it no nourishment." "My Father, I replied, these are but evasive answers, by these artful words you wish to conceal your mortifications." "In truth this is no artfulness at all and I speak to you in all the sincerity of my heart. I grant that my palate would experience greater delight in delicate food, but, since we go to table for the sake of nourishment and not to please the appetite — since we eat merely in order to live, I take whatever I know will best nourish me. To select the food according to its taste would be to live only in order to eat. However, in order to do honor to your table, I will, if you have a little patience, first lay the foundation of the dinner with nourishing food, and then cover it with that which is delicate."

3. Especially love and practise those mortifica-

tions, which are inseparably united with the exact observance of the rules and the faithful fulfillment of the duties of your state of life, because these are most in accordance with the will of God and consequently most pleasing to Him. For this reason St. Frances de Chantal wrote to one of her Sisters in religion as follows: "When we see a tender conscience, subject to scruples, they say, it is a mark of a good conscience; but if such a soul does not submit to the advice given her, it shows obstinacy, and a secret presumption, and she will, surely, soon fall into great disquiet of mind. I say the same of your inclination for mortifications, that shows, that the fire of divine love is in your heart; but if this inclination is not absolutely submitted to your Superior, if it trouble you, make you eager, withdraw you from the sweet and tranquil attention which you owe to the presence of God, be assured, that you are drawn by your human spirit, and that the devil has something to do with it; for the Spirit of God draws to perfect submission. He acts in us gently and sweetly, He makes us prefer the uniform life and actions of our Sisters, to all those imaginary and pretended virtues, which we expect to find in the exterior mortifications that we desire. If then you will believe me, you will mortify yourself by not practising the mortifications which you desire. Thus you will practise the true virtue of mortification and zeal which God desires of you."

4. Great account is to be made of the practice of small mortifications, since for these, occasions present themselves most frequently. Their constant

practice becomes, in the end, a great mortification for human nature. As a light but lasting rain is much more apt to penetrate the ground than a heavy shower, so small mortifications, if performed with perseverance, are better calculated to nourish the spirit of mortification, than great austerities performed only now and then.

5. Rejoice when something is wanting to you, even though you should deem it necessary. "Never am I better off," says St. Francis de Sales, "than when I am badly off." Never complain of the inconveniences of the weather and the like. "Those mortifications which God sends us or which come to us on the part of men by His permission, are always more precious than such as are the off-spring of our own will. These prove a stumbling block to many who embrace with eagerness the mortifications which their inclination suggests, and which nothwithstanding their apparent severity, are no great trouble to them, on account of the facility which their own predilection imparts; but when they encounter some which proceed from another cause, they find them insupportable, how slight soever they may be. For instance, one will have a strong inclination for the discipline, for hair-shirts, fasts and sack-cloth, but will be so sensitive with all about his reputation, that the most trifling jest or unfavoroble observation will put him out of breath and will trouble his peace of mind and prejudice his reason, carrying him on to deplorable extremities. Another will apply himself with ardor to the exercises of prayer and penance and

the practice of silence, who will give way to excessive impatience and anger and fly out into unmeasured lamentations at the loss of a law-suit, or some trifling damage to property. A third will give alms and found magnificent charitable establishments, who will break forth into groans and tremble with fear at the slightest infirmity or sickness and from whom the most trifling bodily pain draws untold and interminable lamentations. According as each is more or less closely attached to the good things which minister to honor, profit, or pleasure, they bear with more or less patience the ills which are contrary to these kinds of goods, without considering that it is the hand of God which bestows and takes them away, according to His pleasure. It is, in fact, that we wish to serve God, not according to His will, but according to our own ; in our way, not His. Do you think this is just?"[1]

Remark. We should remember ever to perform the mortifications prescribed by the rules and by obedience, in the true spirit of penance, because if performed by way of routine, they are of little profit. The use of the discipline or the little cilicium for a short time is not hurtful to our health ; a large cilicium, on the contrary, made of wire or horse hair is hurtful, especially if worn for a considerable length of time.

6. Above all, practise interior mortification, i. e. the mortification of the intellect, of the judgment, of the will, and of self-love. According to the doctrine

[1] St. Francis de Sales.

of St. Francis de Sales, a single ounce of this kind of mortification is worth more than a whole pound of the other. This Saint mortified his spirit by rejecting all vain imaginations, all strange and useless thoughts, which cause a loss of time, expose the soul to distractions, produce aversion for labor and all serious employments, and become the source of thousands of distractions in prayer and of thousands of temptations in the service of God. He mortified his judgment by avoiding stubborness in his ideas, as well as in his opinions and assertions. It is remarkable that in all the discussions that arose in his presence, he was never to be seen over-hasty in giving his opinion; he allowed all the rest to speak first and by thus preferring their judgment to his own, he never entered into disputes, unless forced to speak or give his opinion in matters concerning office; in such cases, he would agree with those whose opinion seemed to him the best, and then he remained firm and unyielding. He mortified his will by constantly acting in such a manner as he deemed pleasing to God, and to be in the order of Divine Providence, not considering whether it were pleasing to himself or not, whether it agreed with his inclinations or not. He daily received a number of letters, some of which were twelve or fifteen pages long, often difficult to read; nevertheless he answered each. Being told that this was too troublesome, he replied: "What matters that, whilst doing this I need not do something else." He wrote to St. Frances de Chantal: "Every day I learn how to deny my own will and to

32

do that which is repugdant to it." It was in this
constant sacrifice of his own will, in this denial of his
most natural desires and wishes, that this holy Bishop
placed his virtue. "The devil," he wrote to one of
his penitents, "cares little if you lacerate your body,
provided you do your own will; he does not fear bodily mortifications, but he truly fears obedience. No
mortification or bodily austerity can equal the sacrifice of the will which lives in constant subjection.
Do therefore never desire to be anything else than
what you really are; of what use is it to build castles
in Spain, if you have to live in France? As to myself, I know only the last verse of the Lamb which to
some may seem somewhat sad or melancholy, still
how full of sweetness and harmony is it not for the
heart: "Father, may it be done to me, not as I will,
but as Thou wilt!" Would that our hearts were always united with His heart, and our will with His
will!"

Finally he was not less ever ready to mortify
self-love, which, in all things seeks but itself, flies
all unpleasant things, follows its own inclination,
and avoids everything that may cause repugnance.
He himself tells us, that he waged a continued war
against his own inclinations and his temperament,
until he had gained the victory. "There are two
passions," he tells us in his candor, "the extirpation
of which has cost me much, viz: Love and anger."
He conquered love by directing it all towards God;
over anger he gained the victory, by taking — these
are his own words, — his heart into his hands, in

order to repress the violence and impetuosity of his temperament, and it was through this especially that he gained so many graces, according to his favorite saying: that he who mortifies and subdues his natural inclinations most, will most abound in supernatural inspirations. "For a long time," says St. Frances de Chantal, "he had to fight against his passions; yet, by his generosity he so subdued them that they obeyed him, as slaves do their master, and afterwards scarcely a vestige of them remained." By God's grace he so ordered all his natural inclinations according to reason and the Gospel, that he performed no action which was not accompanied by some act of christian virtue; and to such a degree that he purified his heart from all earthly inclinations, that he could in truth say: "I require but little, and the little which I require, I require but little. I have scarcely any desires, and should I have to begin my life anew I would have none at all. If God should come to me, I would also go to Him; but if He should not come, then I will conduct myself in such a manner, as neither to ask for, nor to refuse anything, so that I would occupy myself with no desire except with that of willing only what God wills. Often have I debated with myself as to what was the greatest mortification ever performed by any of the Saints whose lives I have read, and this one seems to me to be the most incomparable one. "For twenty-five years St. John the Baptist lived in the wilderness, and my God! with what love for his Redeemer did not his heart burn from the very womb of his mother! How long did he not sigh to enjoy His sacred Presence, and nevertheless, fully determined to do God's holy will, he continued in the office which God had confided to him, without even once coming to visit Him, and he continued in it until Christ Himself deemed it expedient to go to him. Then, having baptized Christ, he never followed Him, but continued in his office as he had done before. What heroic mortification of the spirit was not this! To be so near to God, so near to the Redeemer, and still not to allow himself the satisfaction of going to see Him! To be near Him, and still not to enjoy His sacred Presence! What else does this prove, but that his heart was disinterested and detached from everything, and, in this case, detached from God Himself; that he renounced all the spiritual encouragement and all the spiritual good which he might have drawn from the presence and company of Christ, solely in order to fulfil His holy will and to attend to His service. This example of liberty of spirit so much exceeds all conception, that I cannot speak of it but with the greatest wonder and admiration."

This doctrine the Saint often tried to inculcate upon the hearts of his beloved daughters of the Visitation — he often told them: "We must renounce everything; first of all, we must renounce all exterior goods, such as houses, property, parents, friends, acquaintances; then the goods of the body, that is to say, health, beauty, ease, the pleasures of the senses; then all the ideal goods, those which depend on the opinion of our neighbor, and which we call glory, honor, or good name; finally the goods of the heart, such as spiritual consolations; all these things we must deliver up into the hands of our Lord, that He may dispose of them according to His good pleasure, and then we must serve Him without these goods just as if we possessed them, and all these renunciations must not be made out of contempt, but through self-denial, solely for the pure love of God. Never, He added, will we attain perfection, if we still retain some affection for an imperfection, however small it may be, even though it be but a useless thought, and we cannot comprehend how much harm this does to a soul. Our affections are precious, because all of them should be employed in loving God, so that we must be careful not to let them rest on useless things; a fault however small it may be, if committed with affection, is more detrimental to perfection, than a hundred others committed through surprise and without affection.

7. Do not complain of contempt, of persecution, of pain or sickness. Rejoice in spirit when you are despised, ridiculed, and considered the worst of all. How beautiful are not the prayers of a soul which joyfully accepts contempt! This virtue is one of the most excellent, especially if you live in a community; remember, at the same time, that in imitation of the Saints, you should cherish a particular affection for those who despise and oppose you, being kind towards them, doing good to them, honoring them, speaking well of them, and especially recommending them to God. For this love you should beg God in an

especial manner; you should particularly pray
for it as soon as your nature feels an aversion
for these your adversaries.   To pray for this
grace is especially pleasing to God, and He
never leaves us unheard.   St. Francis de Sales
having once been calumniated, and this calumny
having been spread far and wide, he simply said:
"I humbled myself and did not tell the good
reasons which I might have brought forth for
my defence; but I contented myself with confining
my sorrow in the interior of my heart.   The fruit
which this patient suffering produced in me, was
a still greater love of God and greater fervor
in meditation."   To a soul, who took a great
part in his contempt, he wrote: "Divine Providence well knows what reputation I need in order
to fulfil well the office for which It intends to
employ me, and I want neither more nor less
than is pleasing to It."   "We must die," said the
Saint, "in order that God may live in us; for it
is impossible that a soul should attain to the
union with God in any other way.   These words—
we must die — are hard, but they are followed by
great consolations, for, we die to ourselves, only
in order that by this death we may become united to God.   We must die to every other love,
in order to live for the love of Jesus Christ,
that we may not die the eternal death.   Heavenly wisdom and prudence, a high degree of contemplation, an heroic constancy in adversities, an
admirable presence of mind in unforseen events,

and a most astonishing facility in the practice of virtue, are, O Lord, the gifts and favors which Thou art accustomed to bestow upon those who, for Thy sake free themselves from all inordinate attachments and affections. My God! how gladly would I die for my Redeemer, still, if I cannot die for Him, I will at least live for Him alone!''

CHAPTER XVIII.

RULES OF PRUDENCE FOR THE MANAGEMENT OF TEMPORAL AFFAIRS.

§ 1. *In what Spirit they ought to be Conducted.*

"THOSE who often eat honey, or any other sweet things," says St. Francis de Sales, "find sour ones sourer, and bitter ones bitterer, and easily become disgusted with them. The same happens to a soul that frequently applies to spiritual exercises in which it experiences heavenly consolations. It loathes exterior occupation and returns to them with great reluctance, wherefore it often grows impatient." This not unfrequently happens also to those who have charge of others. But a Superior must firmly believe that he pleases God not only by taking care of the spiritual welfare of his subjects, but also by attending properly to the temporal affairs of his community; for, according to St. Francis de Sales, true piety consists in discharging, for God's sake, the duties of our state and vocation with promptitude and charity of spirit. As God's power and wisdom appear equally great and admirable in little plants and insects and in the majestic cedars of

Lebanon, or in the sun, in the moon and in the stars, so in like manner is His will not less great, or less adorable and amiable when it commands the care of temporal affairs, than when it enjoins that of the spiritual welfare of others. Hence St. Ignatius was right to say that as much devotion and fervor should be displayed in the one as in the other, because in either we should seek nothing but God's holy will and good pleasure. Very consoling is what we read on this subject in the life and revelations of St. Gertrude. As this Saint prayed one day for a person who found great difficulty in a work which had been commanded her, our Lord instructed her thus: "If any one desires, for love of Me, to undertake any painful work, by which he fears to be hindered from his devotions, I will so esteem the purity of his intention, as to consider it as if it had really been carried into effect; and even if he never commences what he has undertaken, he will not fail to obtain the same reward from Me as if he had accomplished it, and had never committed the least negligence in the matter."[1] Another time when the convent was much burdened by a heavy debt, the Saint prayed to God with more devotion than usual that the convent procurators might be able to pay their debts. Our Lord replied tenderly: "What advantage shall I gain if I assist them in this?" The Saint replied: "They will then be able to occupy themselves with more fervor and recollection in their spiritual duties." "And what advantage will this be to Me," continued our Lord,

[1] Chap. 72.

33

"since I have no need of your goods, and it is equally the same to Me whether you employ yourselves in bodily or in mental exercises, provided you refer your intention to Me? For if I only took pleasure in spiritual exercises, I should have so reformed human nature after its fall, that it would no longer have needed food, or clothing, or any of the other necessaries of life, which are now obtained with so much labor. And as a powerful emperor is pleased not merely with bringing up noble ladies in the court of the empress, but also brings up in his own court nobles, captains and soldiers, who are employed in different ways, that they may serve him when occasion presents itself, so also I take pleasure, not only in the interior lights of contemplation, but also in the different exterior affairs and occupations of the children of men, with whom I love to dwell when they labor for My love, and for My glory, because in these occupations they are so much exercised in charity, patience, humility and the other virtues."

After this the Saint beheld the person who had the principal charge of the temporal affairs of the monastery as if he were resting on the left hand of the Lord, and it appeared to her that he often rose with great pain, and offered Him a piece of gold enriched with a precious stone. Our Lord then said to her: "Know that if I lessened the troubles of him for whom you pray, I should be deprived of these precious stones which are so acceptab'e to Me, and the recompense which awaits him would also be less; for he would only be able to offer Me with his right hand this piece of gold, who, without suffering any adversity, refers all his actions to God according to His adorable will ; but he who is constantly suffering and still conforms himself to the decrees of Providence, offers Me gold enriched with very rare and precious stones."

Nevertheless, the Saint still continued to pray that the convent procurator might be relieved from his difficulties. But our Lord said to her : "Why does it seem hard to you that any one should suffer these inconveniences for love of Me, since I am the one true Friend whose faithfulness never changes? For when any one is deprived of all human help and consolation, and is driven to the last extremity, those who have formerly received kindness from him are sorry for his misfortunes, and yet their sorrow is often fruitless and can afford no assistance to their friend. But I am the only true Friend Who, in such dire necessity, will console the afflicted with the merit and glory of all the good works they have practised during their whole life, whether by thoughts, words, or actions ; and these shall appear scattered over My vestments like roses and lilies ; while the delightful vision shall revive in the soul its hopes of eternal life, to which it beholds itself invited in recompense for its good works. Then the soul disposes itself in holy contentment to depart from its mortal body and to enter eternal felicity, so that amidst its joys it may say : 'Behold, the smell of my beloved is as the smell of a fertile field.'[1] For even as the body is composed

[1] Gen. 27.

of many members united together, so also the soul
consists of affections, such as fear, grief, joy, love,
hope, anger, modesty; in the exercise of each of
which the more man acts for My glory, the more he
will find in Me that incomprehensible and ineffable
joy, and that secure delight which will prepare him
for eternal happiness.   For in the resurrection, when
the body will be raised incorruptible, each of its members will receive a special recompense for the labors
and actions which it has performed in My name and
for My love.   But the soul will receive an incomparably greater reward for all the holy affections which
it has entertained for My love, for its compunction,
and even for having animated the body for My service.''   Once again, as the Saint prayed that the faithful procurator might receive the full reward of his
troublesome labors for the temporal good of the community, our Lord said to her: ''His body, which is
wearied by so many labors for Me, is like a treasure-
house, in which I place as many pieces of silver as
his limbs make movements to fulfil the duties with
which he is charged; and his heart is like an ark in
which I place in reserve as many pieces of gold as he
has had thoughts of providing carefully, for love of
Me, for those persons who are under his care.''   Then
the Saint exclaimed, in surprise: ''It seems to me,
O Lord, that this man is not so perfect as to undertake all that he does purely for Thy glory; for I believe he also thinks of the temporal profit which he
obtains thereby, and consequently of his bodily convenience.   How, then, canst Thou, my God, find

such pleasure as Thou sayest, in his heart and in his body?" Our Lord condescended to reply thus: "It is because his will is so entirely submitted to Mine, that I am always the principal cause of his actions; and for this reason he will merit an inestimable recompense for all his thoughts, his words, and his works. If he applies himself to each action with a still greater purity of intention, he will increase his merit, even as gold exceeds silver in value; and if he endeavors to refer all his thoughts and anxieties to Me with a yet purer intention, they will become as much more excellent as refined gold is in comparison to that which is alloyed with a baser metal."[1]

Not less consoling and encouraging are the instructions of St. Francis de Sales on this subject. When asked whether one should not refuse or try to be freed from certain offices which cannot be exercised without many difficulties, distractions, and solicitudes, he answered: "It is a wrong opinion even of good and pious souls to imagine that it is impossible for them to preserve peace of heart and recollection of mind amidst pressing occupations. Where are there greater and more frequent motions than on the sea? Are ships ever free from being tossed about? And yet every passenger sleeps well, and the compass is always pointing to the North. Whoever seeks nothing but God in all his actions and refers them all to God's greater glory, will be content and happy everywhere, even in the most violent troubles and storms, because even in them he sees the Lord's will which

[1] Chap. 57.

permits and sends them. It is thus that he reaches his last end, to which all his desires are directed, and which consists in honoring God in all things, and under all circumstances. It appears strange to me to hear so many of those who have consecrated themselves to the service of God in a holy state, often complain when they are obliged to enter upon laborious offices, and call the duties thereof so many sources of distraction. Truly distracting occupations are those only which separate us from God. Now it is sin alone that separates us from Him; every lawful occupation far from separating us from God, only unites us to Him more intimately. We must belong to God even in the bustle of the most pressing worldly affairs. How can we exhibit ourselves as better and more faithful servants of the Lord than by undergoing for His sake, great hardships and troublesome labors? Is solitude not just as full of storms as the world of noise and cares? We must nowhere be discouraged, for the Lord is ready to assist all who hope in Him, and pray to Him with humility for His fatherly assistance. Take care that your cares may not turn into anxiety, perplexity, and disquietude; and no matter, how much your ship may be tossed about by the waves and storms of perplexing occupations, always look up to heaven and say to the Lord: My Lord and my God, for Thy sake I row on through these stormy waves; be my guide and my pilot! And then also console yourself with the thought that, when you arrive at the harbor, the joy and happiness which await you there, will be more, than an ample

reward for all the troubles and hardships which you
had to undergo to reach it. Now every storm drives
us nearer and nearer, provided our hearts be sincere,
our intentions constantly directed to God, and our
whole confidence placed in Him. Should, now and
then, the violence of the storm derange our stomach
a little, and make us, for some moments, suffer somewhat from vertigo, let us not be uneasy, but rather
take new courage to pursue our work the more man-
fully. Let us then not be cast down on account
of anxieties, perplexities and vexations that may befall us in the multiplicity of domestic affairs ; for
thus we shall be exercised in those very virtues which
our Lord Jesus Christ has recommended to us. Believe me, true virtue lives and grows just as little in
a heart never suffering any disturbance, as good fish
in stagnant waters. Whoever abandons occupations,
to which God calls him, that by means of prayer,
solitude, reading, silence, interior recollection and
meditation, he may unite himself more closely to the
Lord, instead of uniting himself more closely to Him,
he will only unite himself more closely to his self-
love. It is altogether a different thing to be separated from God, and to be deprived of sensible devotion
and the sweet consolation of the presence of God. In
the multiplicity of affairs and unavoidable occupations and troubles, which are inseparable from the
direction of a community, we cannot, it is true,
always enjoy these sweet consolations ; yet, if we suffer the privation of them for the love of God and refer
all our troubles to Him, instead of losing we do but

gain. We lose what is sweet, but we gain what is
strong. God, Who, according to the words of the
prophet, is always near those, who are in tribulation,
will never abandon one who works for the glory of
His holy Name. Let us rest assured that if obedience
obliges us to take care of many things, the Lord will
not fail to assist us in doing our work, if we do not
fail to co-operate with Him in doing His work. Now
His work is the sanctification of our soul. This is
our field. Let us work on it with humility, simplicity
and confidence, and unavoidable distractions will
never hurt us. That peace which is sought in avoiding labors, which serve for the greater glory of God,
is but false rest. God is accustomed to disturb the
peace of these souls by persecutions and tribulations,
as was experienced by the good brother Leonicius,
who was procurator of the Convent. God often visited
him with the sweetest consolations even in the midst
of hard labors, but withdrew them after his Superior
had yielded to his earnest request to retire into his
cell, there to give himself up to greater interior recollection and contemplation.''

Something similar happened to a holy religious
of the Order of St. Francis. After he had spent many
years very profitably in the conversion of the Indians,
he at last desired very much to retire from the world,
in order to prepare himself to die well. For this end,
he retired into a monastery of his own Order in Spain,
where he lived in a very austere recollection. As
often, however, as he went to prayer, he seemed to
see Jesus Christ crucified complaining tenderly to

him: "Why hast thou thus left Me upon the Cross, whilst thou seekest thy own repose and ease?" The good religious was so touched with this vision, that he returned again to the harvest which he had left and served God therein again for a very long time.

We ought to be persuaded that God hates the peace of those whom He has called to fight His battles. He is not less the God of hosts and battles, than the God of peace. He called the Order into existence for a two-fold end. As He blesses the means to reach the principal end, so He, likewise, blesses the means to reach the secondary end, viz: to contribute towards the salvation of others, and thereby towards our own at the same time. Hence religious do so much good— they enjoy what is called the grace of religion. As the Lord gives particular graces to the members of contemplative Orders, to lead a life of recollection and strict enclosure, to sing the divine office, and to keep certain fasts, and to undergo such other austerities, as are peculiar to them, so, in like manner, He gives grace to the members of Orders of a mixed life, to acquit themselves well of their duties and charities towards their neighbor, because it is for this that they are called, as others are to solitude and retirement. We ought then, always remember well, that our perfection consists in acquitting ourselves well of the duties of our state. The spirit of prayer and solitude ought to be a very laudable thing amongst us; but such a spirit of prayer and retirement as would induce us to withdraw from assisting souls and from other duties of charity, would be a kind of temptation and

illusion of the devil, who is wont to transform himself
into an angel of light to deceive us, in order to make
us withdraw from our vocation, under the pretext of
laboring for our own advancement, and of avoiding
the dangers met with in the exercise of the ministry
or charity.

We must give ourselves up to prayer according
to the spirit of our vocation, i. e. with the intention
of obtaining new lights and new strength in the performance of our duties. The better we shall find ourselves disposed for these employments when we leave
our prayer, the more we may rest assured of having
made a good prayer; and the more the love of God
has been enkindled in it, the more zeal and fervor
ought we to display on leaving it, for gaining souls
to God or for procuring the glory of God in the faithful discharge of the duties of our state.

Let us then have an unbounded confidence in the
grace of religion or of the Order to which we belong,
always remaining easy in the employments that God
and obedience have given us; let us be very careful
not to listen to our own inclinations in the choice
either of place or employments in which we are to be
put. Let us renounce entirely our own will and
abandon ourselves to that of God, and suffer ourselves
to be led to Him by the way of obedience. Nowhere
shall we be in greater security for our salvation and
the progress in perfection, than where God has been
pleased to put us.

Once Blessed Margaret Alacoque had to perform
a certain office which prevented her from assisting at

the meditation of the community. This made her a little uneasy, but our Lord blamed her for it, saying: "Know that the prayer of humble submission and self-renunciation is more pleasing to Me, than meditation and every other kind of contemplation, no matter, how holy soever it may appear." "No one," says St. Frances de Chantal of St. Francis de Sales, "could ever be more determined, more generous, and more courageous, than this Saint, when heavy burdens were to be carried, labors to be performed, and designs, inspired by God, to be executed. Nothing could dishearten him; 'for,' said he, 'we must never abandon an affair, with which the Lord has entrusted us, but should courageously overcome all difficulties.' In one of his letters he writes of pressing occupations as follows: 'All these things are, it is true, different in themselves, but the intention, with which they ought to be performed, must be one and the same. Love alone gives true value to all our good works and exercises. Our Divine Saviour is the well-beloved of His heavenly Father at the river Jordan, where He humbled Himself; on Mount Thabor, where He was glorified; and on Mount Calvary, where He was crucified, because, in all these circumstances, He honored His Father with the same dispositions of heart, with the same spirit of submission and love. In imitation of His example, we, too, must endeavor to acquire solid love, which prompts us to seek, in all things, nothing but God's good pleasure. This alone will render our works beautiful and perfect, no matter how trifling they may appear.'

He himself practised this lesson to perfection. For
several years previous to his death, he could not apply himself at all to meditation, on account of so
many almost overwhelming occupations. Once when
I asked him whether he had made it, he answered,
'no ; but what I did, was just as good.' The fact
was, that he was in constant union with God, and he
used to say, 'that in this life we must pray by good
works also.' Thus his life may be said to have been
a continual prayer. He loved God's will in one
thing as much as in another, hence in the latter
years of his life, the purity of his intention became so
great, that in all things he could not wish for, love
or see anything else than God alone. Being quite
absorbed in God, he would say: 'Nothing in this
world could give me any real satisfaction except God
alone.' Thus he lived, indeed, not he himself, but
Christ in him.''[1]

St. Vincent de Paul speaks in the same manner.
"Now let us," he writes to a Superior, "pass from
the spiritual to the temporal. A Superior must take
care of both. As his subjects consist of body and
soul, he must provide for either, imitating God Who,
besides His so-called action ad intra — the generation
of His Son and the procession of the Holy Ghost—
created also ad extra, as it is called by theologians,
the world, sustains it, and makes new fruits grow
every year. His most adorable Providence extends
to all things so much so that, without His knowledge
and will, not even the leaf of a tree falls to the

---

[1] Life of St. Francis de Sales, by Clarus.

ground, that He has counted all our hairs, and that
He feeds even the vilest worms of the earth. This
consideration is sufficient to convince you, that you
must take care not only of what is of greater importance, viz: the spiritual, but as a Superior who has,
in some manner, to imitate God's Omnipotence, you
must also take care of the temporal, even in the most
trifling things, never believing, that this is below
your dignity. At first, when the Son of God sent
out His disciples, He told them not to take any money
with them; but after they had become more numerous,
He ordered that every division should have their
procurator, who should not only provide for the wants
of the poor, but principally for those of His own disciples; nay, what is still more remarkable, He even
permitted women to follow them, that they might
provide for their necessities. If the Gospel says, we
should not be solicitous for to-morrow,[1] it intends
only to warn us against too great anxiety for the
temporal, but not to intimate, that we should no
longer labor for food and raiment, as otherwise it
would also forbid to sow."

"Disgust and reluctance, fretfulness, discontent
and whatever temptations occur in this sort of occupation, must be resisted and repelled by the consideration, that God's will is equally amiable in all things,
and that, like the guardian angels who are equally
happy, no matter, whether they have to guard good
or bad men, Catholics or heretics, Jews or infidels,
you, too, must, in imitation of those spirits, whose

[1] Matt. 6, 34.

happiness consists in doing God's will, seek and find, in all your affairs, no other than this angelic happiness and satisfaction. Often pray to your meek Jesus, that He may keep you meek, in order that, as St. Francis de Sales says, you may not only resemble a gentle dove flying up to the sky when you elevate your soul towards heaven in prayer, but may also be like it, when sitting in its nest, that is to say, in your conversations and dealings with your subjects. To be obliged to attend to a multiplicity of affairs is, indeed, a constant martyrdom; much patience is required for it, which God, however will not fail to grant to you, provided you ask it of Him most earnestly, and exert yourself to practise it faithfully. You must prepare yourself for it every morning by a special meditation, making the firm resolution to practise this virtue of patience throughout the whole day and renewing it as often as you forget yourself. Let no opportunity pass for showing your patient charity to every one. Moreover, do not imagine, that the good success of your affairs depend on your own efforts and care, but rather on God's assistance and blessing alone. Therefore trust in Him, believing that He will do your work, provided you do calmly your own part. I say *calmly*; for too great anxiety proves injurious, not only to our heart, but also to the good success of our affairs, and causes much uneasiness. When we were little children, how carefully did we collect bricks, small pieces of wood and the like for building little houses, and how did we not grieve, when some one destroyed them;

but now we laugh at these childish amusements. When once admitted into heaven, we shall think the same, seeing that all the affairs, which gave us so much trouble and uneasiness, were nothing but children's plays. By this I do not mean to say, that we should devote no time or attention to these children's plays and amusements, for God gave them to us in this world as pastimes, but that we should not suffer them to cause us unnecessary trouble and uneasiness. Let us not be disturbed, if some one should upset our little houses, or frustrate our insignificant schemes; for, in the hour of death, they will be of no use. Let us be persuaded, that our devotion and piety will be so much the better, and the more solid, the less we live according to our own liking, and the less our own choice is found in all our actions."[1]

§ 2. *Take Counsel of God and Men.*

"You must," wrote St. Vincent de Paul to a certain Superior, "show, in all things, your dependence on Jesus Christ, the Son of God; by this I mean to say, that, when you are about to do something, you must previously consider whether it is in accordance with the principles of Jesus Christ. Should it be so, then say: Let us do it in God's name! but should it not be so, then say: "No, I will not do it! Likewise when a good work is to be done, say to the Son of God: My Lord, what wouldst Thou do, shouldst Thou be in my place? In what manner wouldst Thou instruct this people, or console this

[1] St. Francis de Sales.

afflicted person, or encourage this despairing sinner?
Show this dependence also by your obedience to your
Superior. Rest assured that Superiors have learned
a good many things both by their own experience,
and by the grace of their state. I mention this in
order that you may not undertake anything of importance without having previously informed your
Superiors about it. Should this not be possible for
good reasons, that do not allow you to wait for our
decision, then go to another Superior nearest to you,
and ask him what he would do, were he in your
place? We know from experience, that God blesses
this manner of proceeding; but those, on the contrary, who did not act thus, entangled themselves in
affairs which caused great annoyance and embarrassment both to themselves and to us." When Vincent
himself was asked his advice, he would, in all humility and confidence, recommend himself to God and
then represent to himself the hour of death, considering what advice he would then give.

"A Superior," writes St. Alphonsus, "should
never think himself so wise as to be able to direct
a whole Institute by his own light and wisdom. He
always stands in need of prayer and advice. He
should never judge things rashly and without mature
consideration, but should well reflect over the matter
before he gives his decision." "In matters of importance," says St. Ignatius, "after long and deep
reflection, do not omit to consult others, and that the
matter may be well considered, limit these conversations to the space of one hour, during which time no

other topic is to be introduced. Let no one be a so-called decretalist, i. e. a man to whom a question has no sooner been proposed than he gives his decision. Look rather to the end and consequences of things, than to the principles thereof. Is the matter of great importance, take as much time as possible to reflect upon it, and that you may not be misled by passion, regard the affair as if it were another man's business and not your own. Whilst you thus dispose all things with foresight and prudence, acknowledge yourself as a useless servant, abandoning all to God, and looking only to Him for the success of your operations, and when any point has been determined by your counsellors and yourself, do not forget to retire, and then treat with God upon the matter in prayer, protesting before Him that you wish for nothing but the accomplishment of His holy will. Take the habit never to carry anything into execution, until it has been concluded in this manner."[1]

"In domestic affairs," it is said in the life of St. Vincent de Paul, "he even consulted his lay-brothers, not believing at all, that this was below his dignity, but rather calculated to inspire the subjects with greater love and esteem for their Superior, and to draw the blessing of God upon what had been determined upon in this manner." Hence Rodriguez remarks on this subject, that it is a great fault, even in Superiors, not to receive or ask for the advice of others; wherefore it is generally said, that a man of limited talents, but knowing his own defects, and

[1] Life St. Ignatius.

34

willing to listen to the good counsel of others, is more
fit to govern than another, who has greater talents,
but who is full of self-conceit, and thinks himself so
experienced in all things, that he feels offended when
he is admonished, or when an advice is given to him.

Holy Scripture abounds in passages, confirming
this truth. "Have you not seen," says Solomon,
"one who thinks himself a very able man? There is
more to be hoped for from a fool than from him.
The carriage of a fool appears very good in his own
eyes; but a wise man hearkens to counsel. I am
wisdom, that make my abode in counsel. Where
there is a gseat deal of good counsel, there salvation
is to be found."[1]

Although Moses was very wise and enlightened
himself, yet he failed not to take the advice of Jethro,
his father-in-law, who advised him to choose some
persons who would assist him in the government and
in the administration of justice. "You do not well,"
said Jethro to him, seeing him do every hing himself, "to consume yourself with imprudent labor;
what you undertake, is above your strength, and you
can never be able alone to sustain it."[2] Moses took
this advice in all humility, and put it forthwith into
practice, and did not act like those who, when advised well, seem to feel much displeased with the ad-
viser, thinking that no one less able than they themselves, should be so intrusive as to advise them.

St. Peter, the head of the Apostles, also yielded
to St. Paul in the question of the circumcision, and

[1] Prov. 11, 14.   [2] Exod. 18, 17--18.

when admonished by St. Paul, he did not despise
him for having persecuted the Church, nor did he
say: "I am the supreme head of the Church; it belongs to me to decide in this matter; to me every one
must listen!"

§ 3. *Avoid Precipitation.*

"We live in an age of untiring activity," says
Father Coffin, C. SS. R.,[1] "in an age which measures
success by immediate, visible, and palpable results,
in which no sooner is a work begun than men are at
once impatient to see its completion. The world cannot bear to work step by step, to watch the proper
place and time, and occasion, for its designs: all must
be done at once; to begin and finish must be, were it
possible, simultaneous; calmly to wait and let things
maturely grow, is considered a sign of weakness, is in
itself a failure. The patience and forbearance, and
the gentle providence of God, is forgotten; neither
do men remember how even Wisdom itself, though
"she reacheth from end to end mightily, yet ordereth
all things sweetly." The Saints enlightened and
guided by the Holy Ghost as they were, thought and
acted quite differently, knowing that too hasty desires
trouble and disturb the peace of the soul; confound
its thoughts; quicken its emotions; disconcert its actions; corrupt its will; destroy grace; prevent the
co-operation of God, and prove, that we are influenced
by nature alone."

In all his works St. Vincent de Paul would

[1] Preface to Mysteries of Faith.

always proceed calmly, noiselessly and considerately. In order to imitate the example of Jesus Christ, he would choose those means to reach his end, which were of a more gentle nature, and would excite less the attention of others. Thus he avoided many intrigues of those who were disposed to work against him. However, when it happened, that difficulties and obstacles were thrown into his way, he would not try to remove them by main force, although he could have done so very easily, his influence at court being very great; he preferred to wait patiently until God would incline the hearts of his adversaries in favor of his designs. For this very reason all his works became so much the more permanently established. Many would often wonder how a man, who was so slow and backward in carrying out his designs, could bring about so many astonishing works. But the wise and discreet servant of the Lord was thoroughly convinced, that the success of important undertakings was prevented by nothing so much as by precipitation and impetuosity. He often used to say, that precipitated affairs would generally turn out failures, but, on the contrary, to delay them would never prove disadvantageous, but always profitable; for by acting thus, we gain time to consider and examine carefully all difficulties and reasons to the contrary, to discover the best time and opportunity for success, to become more assured of the Divine Will, to keep better pace with God's Providence, and thus to have the great consolation, that the Lord Himself commenced and accomplished all works, which we undertook for the Divine glory. He was always afraid to encroach upon the course of Providence, and to get, as it were ahead of our Lord. God perfectly justified his manner of proceeding, by enabling him to accomplish more within forty years, than many others would have done within whole centuries. The best undertakings, he would say, often turn out bad by precipitation, because there is generally too much self-will in them, which considers good and practicable only what it approves itself as such. The issue of affairs will always show how false this is. The good designed by God, is brought about, as it were, by itself, even before we think of it.

Relying on the word of Christ: "Seek ye first the kingdom of God and His justice, and all these things shall be added unto you," he let Divine Providence manage his affairs, firmly believing that the members of his Society would never lack the necessaries of life as long as they would live up faithfully to their rules. But for that he would not be less industrious than God requires of us. His confidence in God was firm and unshaken, but not presumptuous. He did what was in his power. His principle which he often repeated to his brethren was, "commence every affair after mature reflection, then continue and finish it." If any one acted rashly and without consulting others he was sure to be punished by him. Hence he would depose from their office all those who, without previous permission, would tear down or build up something, notwithstanding the good intention they might have had in doing so.

"For," said he, "if every one wishes to follow his
own ideas, the dependence ordained by God would be
destroyed altogether, and in our houses we would see
nothing but constant changes and disorders." When,
however, the house of God and the salvation of souls
were in question, no expenses would be too great for
the Saint. But as to his own support and that of his
Society, he would permit nothing superfluous, but,
on the contrary, he would cut off from the necessaries
of life as much as discretion allowed, both to mortify
the desires of the flesh and to be better enabled to
bestow alms upon the poor. This was also his course
of action in the erection of buildings. He would
never without an evident necessity contract too heavy
a debt. "For," said he, "we cannot expect from
God more than is necessary; wherefore we must not
undertake anything superfluous." The Superior of
one of his houses most earnestly begged of him permission to commence a certain building, because the
Missionary priests, as he said, were dissatisfied with
their bad dwellings and could not keep up a regular
discipline. Vincent answered him as follows: "You
write to me for permission soon to commence your
new house; but, my dear Sir, we cannot think of
such a thing as yet. It is a great charity of the Lord
to have given us this house which is good enough until He is pleased to give us a better one. We are not
in fault for the evil consequences of which you speak,
because we cannot help them for the present. We
imitate the Lord in His conduct towards His people.
For whole centuries He permitted great disorders and

the loss of numberless souls, in order to establish an Order altogether Divine, and open the way of salvation for all by the life, sufferings, and death of His Son Whom He sent at the appointed time — when by so many exhortations, prophecies and longing desires, His people had been prepared for His arrival. Should I, perhaps, make a wrong application óf this, I beg for better instruction, and should you be able to give it, I most willingly accept it."

"Would we learn to be patient as God is patient," says Father Coffin, C. SS. R., in the above cited Preface, "to order things, as He does, *sweetly*, to be content with the knowledge that, when we have done our best, whether in the work of our own sanctification, or in our efforts for the good and salvation of others, we must after all wait patiently, and hope and pray, leaving the result to the good providence of God: would we cherish hidden ways, and humble, unpretending aims, and rest satisfied that we are only allowed to plant and sow, while it is for others to reap the fruits of our labors; — then let us try to live with Jesus in His Hidden life, and not be over-anxious to see the results and success even of our purest undertakings; for God Himself, after having waited four thousand years to redeem mankind, thought it not too long to wait even yet a period of thirty more, before He accomplished that work of love for which He had expressly come into the world."

§ 4. *Be Resolute in your Undertakings.*

"No difficulties," says St. Vincent de Paul, "should deter us from carrying into execution what has been determined upon after calm and mature deliberation." Had he, after mature reflection, resolved upon something, and finding it at the same time in accordance with the principles of Jesus Christ, nothing was able to shake him in his resolution; he would no longer mind any difficulty. He exhorted every one to be thus resolute. After we have recommended an affair to God, we must stick to what we have resolved upon, looking upon everything contrary as a temptation, and fully confiding that we shall not displease God, nor have to render Him an account for so doing; for we might tell Him in truth: 'I have recommended this affair to Thee, I have taken the advice of others; I could not do more to know Thy will.' The example of Pope Clement is a proof of what I have said. A very important affair was laid before him, in which a whole kingdom was concerned. Many a courier was sent, but a whole year elapsed, before he would come to a decision. Meanwhile he recommended the matter to God, and consulted and deliberated upon it with men of great discretion and experience. At last he gave his decision. Soon after he dreamed, that he saw Christ with an angry countenance, reproaching him, and threatening to punish him severely for what he had done. On awaking, he felt greatly alarmed. He related his dream to Cardinal Toledo, who, after having reflected upon the matter before God, answered the Pope, that he should not be alarmed at all, considering his dream as a delusion of the devil. After having recommended the affair to God, and consulted others upon it, he had no reason to be frightened. The Pope then felt quite easy.

A priest, remarking one day to St. Vincent de Paul, that a certain affair might have bad consequences, he replied: "We ought not to look so much to the consequences, as to whether the matter is in accordance with the doctrine and example of the Lord." St. Francis de Sales expresses the same opinion when he says: "After having consulted prudent and discreet men and come to a final decision, we must reject every thought, that could make us doubt its propriety. All we have to do is, to carry into effect what we have decided upon after calm and mature deliberation. No difficulties whatever must intimidate and prevent us from so doing. Instead of reflecting upon the difficulties which we may meet, we should rather think, that we might have met with greater ones, had we come to another decision. This is always a solid reflection; for, as we cannot see into the future, we know not, whether God has prepared for us consolation or affliction, peace or trouble, and temptation. Everything depends on our decision; if it be based on wise and solid principles, wise and good will be its execution. Should it prove a failure, it will be our fault." He himself after having maturely reflected upon a thing, especially if it concerned the greater glory of God

35

and the salvation of souls, was most resolute, braving all dangers and difficulties, no matter, to what height they arose. When there was question in the Council of the Duke of Chablais of removing all Calvinistic preachers and re-establishing the Catholic religion, he managed so as to have all heresies completely banished from the Province. For this end, he laid before the Council, first political reasons, then he cast a glance upon the religious side of the question, saying that, "when the honor and glory of God were concerned, something should be left to Providence. Had Constantine, Theodosius, and other princes, acted merely as politicians, and consulted human prudence only, heathenism, infidelity, and heresy, would still be prevailing. God supports and confirms on their thrones, those potentates who endeavor to make their subjects, subjects of the Most High. He pours forth His benedictions upon the dominions of those princes, who, by their zealous efforts, re-establish true religion and the fear of the Lord."[1]

§ 5. *Proceed with Circumspection.*

In order to treat every one right, observe and consider his manner of acting, his natural disposition and character, and then treat him accordingly, either with courtesy and affability, with earnestness, with frankness, or with reserve. If one be of a choleric disposition, if he speaks fast and likes to speak, be affable and sociable with him, not appearing

[1] Life by Clarus.

grave, phlegmatic, or melancholy. If any one be reserved, and slow and earnest in his conversation, act with him in the same manner, because he will like this method of acting. It is to be observed, that if one of a choleric disposition has to deal with another of the same character, and if both have not altogether the same spirit, there will be great danger, that they will misunderstand each other in their conversation. If one knows that he is of a choleric disposition, he should consider in advance all the details of his conversation with others, in order to enter upon it well prepared, being firmly determined to suffer rather, than to allow himself to be put out of humor by another, especially if he knows him to be of a delicate constitution. Should he, however, have to treat with a phlegmatic or melancholy character, he will not be in so great a danger to exasperate him by inconsiderate conversation. Be discreet in all your conversations, especially in mediations of peace and in spiritual conferences, as you must expect that, whatever you say, may possibly go before the public.

§ 6. *In Public.*

In public meetings be never too forward to speak ; above all, be discreet and amiable, especially when affairs are taken into consideration. Be calm and attentive in listening to what others say and endeavor not only to understand the meaning of their words, but also their inclination and intention, in order to see, whether it be better to answer or to be silent. In controversies, expose your reasons both for and against, in order not to seem to be attached too obstinately to your own opinion, and above all endeavor, that no one may feel hurt, or exasperated by what you say. If the points in dispute are of such a nature as to oblige you to speak, express your opinion in a most calm and modest manner. Let not your conversation be arranged according to leasure and ease, but according to the advantage and disposition of him, with whom you have to treat, in order that he may arrive where God wishes to lead him. Let your answers to questions be short, but very considerate; exhortations to piety, on the contrary, must be more lengthy, sweet, and calculated to touch the heart to the quick.

In all your business transactions, especially with your equals or inferiors, speak little, in proportion to their dignity and authority ; listen willingly to whatever they say, until they have finished speaking, after which give your answer to everything, and then take leave ; should they recommence to say something still, answer as briefly as possible. Be short but obliging in taking leave.[1]

§ 7. *Do not make use of Duplicity in your*
Dealings with others.

Be simple with the cunning, the deceitful, and the malicious. After St. Vincent de Paul had accepted a Mission-house in a certain Province, the inhabitants of which were said to be very cunning and malicious people, he gave the following advice to the

[1] St. Ignatius.

Superior of the house. "You are about to set out for a Province, the people of which are said to be very cunning. If this be true, you cannot gain them over to God in a better way, than by great simplicity of heart; for the principles of the Gospel are diametrically opposed to the principles of the world. Going as you do to make Jesus Christ known in these regions, you must act up to His spirit, which is a straight-forward and candid one." As he had, after some time, to send another Superior to the same Mission, he purposely chose a Father of great candor and simplicity, being fully persuaded, that simplicity and candor are the best weapons to overcome hypocrisy and the prudence of the flesh. He cherished the greatest affection for the candid and the simple of heart.

§ 8. *Avoid excessive Zeal in abolishing Abuses.*

Although what St. Alphonsus says, be true, namely, that on the day of judgment we shall see many religious of both sexes condemned to hell for having introduced bad customs, or for not having abolished them, when it was in their power, yet, in correcting them, great discretion is required. St. Francis de Sales would always proceed by slow degrees and in a very gentle manner, when abuses were to be reformed; being mindful of the Proverb: "Festina lente." He would blame indiscreet zeal, which goes to excess, not doing any good, because it wants to do too much at once. His motto was: "Step by step." He often repeated the words of the Wise man: "The path of the just, as a shining light, goeth forward and increaseth even to perfect day."[1] Hence it was his opinion, that we should endeavor to gain firm ground by slow degrees. "True progress," he would say, "is to pass from small things to greater ones. God Himself Who is altogether independent of time to bring His works to perfection, and would have it in His power to make everything reach its end at once, is, nevertheless, so slow in His operations, that they can scarcely be noticed." He would not imitate those who in the reformation of manners, commence with the exterior, thus to reach, as they say, the interior, troubling themselves with the former so long as to forget the latter, and thus neglect the essential for the mere accessory.

When he wished to re-establish religious discipline in a convent of men, he required but two things, spiritual reading with meditation, and the frequent reception of the Sacraments. "Thus," he would say, "we shall reach our end by and by, without creating any disturbance or using any violent means." In communities of nuns he also required but two things, viz: inclosure, and meditation twice a day for half an hour each time. "By these two means," he said, "nuns will be easily led back to their duties, and to the observance of their particular rules." He would not insist much upon exterior severity and bodily mortifications though very good and laudable in themselves, as they affected merely the exterior. Upon being asked, whether it would

[1] Prov. 4, 18.

be well to introduce walking barefoot in a religious community, he replied with his accustomed serenity: "Why strip the feet of the shoes." It is the head, and not the feet, which is to be reformed. We read in the life of St. Alphonsus, that he wished to introduce community life into every convent, and he would establish it wherever he could; but it was his opinion, that, if all the members of the community were not in favor of giving up all personal property, it would be better not to insist upon it any longer; "for a nun," said he, "who is not faithful in this, will make others follow her also, and then she will not only relapse into her former condition, but will be the cause of many quarrels and scandals." Under such circumstances he would be satisfied to induce them to the faithful observance of the rule, to the frequent reception of the sacraments, and to the practice of meditation. Having once informed the nuns of a certain convent, that he wished to introduce community life among them, they all rose up against him. Seeing that more harm than good would result if he were to insist upon carrying out his intention, he simply said: "Be easy; I had only your own good in view, but as you do not agree with me, forget whatever I have said about it." He was persuaded that, if one member of a religious community would not agree with the rest, he or she would get up a party, thus causing disorders and the final ruin of the convent. Far from showing himself offended by the opposition of the nuns, he paid them a paternal visit the next day.

At the time of St. Francis of Assissium there were some Fathers, Provincials of his Order, who were animated with the bad spirit of Brother Elias; and as he could not depose them without offending them grievously, and without causing great troubles and disturbances in their communities, he said: "Let them live as they please. They will one day repent of it. The loss of some few is a less evil than the ruin of many. The deposition of these officials would cause great dissatisfaction, and those good brethren who obey them now in all the simplicity of their hearts, might be greatly scandalized." Hence St. Augustine would say: "As the good man of the house did not permit his servants to gather up the cockle, lest by doing so they might root up the wheat also with it,[1] we must never try to remedy certain evils by opposing greater ones." Great minds, enlightened by superior wisdom, know this but too well and go by it, whilst officials of a limited judgment and urged by false zeal, wish to do away with evils by main force, no matter, what the consequences may be; not satisfied with the good already done, they insist upon more, without considering, that there are unavoidable evils, which must be patiently borne with, and that good is often destroyed by indiscreet zeal, which always aims at what is best.

For this reason, St. Vincent de Paul wrote to one of his Missionaries as follows: "In remedying disorders, do not go to excess, especially if you foresee that greater evils will ensue." "Evils which have

---

[1] Matt. 13, 25.

become general," says St. Augustine, "should not be attacked directly, because you not only fail to reach your end, but you moreover exasperate the minds of all to such extent as to make them unwilling to listen to any representation, no matter, how good it may be; this, however, will not happen, if you act more indulgently. I therefore beseech you to indulge human weakness as much as possible, and I assure you, that you will gain the affections of the guilty much sooner by compassion, than by rigor. I do not wish to say that you should approve of their faults, but I say only, that the means should be gentle and lenient, as well in consideration of the condition and the place of these unfortunate people, in which great discretion is necessary, as also of the great harm, which might arise from exasperating them.

When Mons. Fouquet, Bishop of Bayonne, was advised to forbid begging to certain Religious, who led a rather disedifying life and possessed personal property, he directed his Secretary to apply to St. Vincent of Paul to give his opinion upon the matter in question. The Saint answered as follows:

"My opinion is, that you must treat disedifying Religious as Jesus Christ treated sinners. Bishops and priests who, owing to their calling, ought to be more perfect than Religious considered as such, should first, for some time, work upon them by their good example, remembering that the Son of God did not follow any other course of conduct for the space of thirty years. After this, they should speak to them

in all charity and meakness, yet with firmness and
authority, without threatening with interdict, suspen-
sion or excommunication, chastisements, which our
Divine Saviour never adopted. What I say, may
perhaps appear strange to you, but I cannot help it.
This my opinion is the result of my meditations upon
the Gospel-truths which Jesus Christ has taught us
both by His Word and example. · According to my
observation, everything done in accordance with His
precepts, has always been blessed with remarkable
success. The holy Bishop of Geneva (St. Francis de
Sales) and others have sanctified themselves, and
many others, by following His doctrine. You will
object, perhaps, that a Prelate, for such a conduct,
will be despised. Let it be so for some time, nay, it
is even necessary, that it should be so, in order that
we may glorify the life of Jesus Christ in all its circumstances, not only by our temporal wants, but also
in our own person; for it cannot be denied, that having practised patience for some time, and as long as
our Lord is pleased, we shall, by His grace, do more
good in three years, than otherwise in thirty. Indeed, Sir, I do not believe, that there is any better
way of securing success in our undertakings. You
may make nice regulations, have recourse to punishments, to the privation of all power and rights, but
will you, by so doing, make them any better? There
is but little hope for it. Such means will neither en-
large nor preserve the kingdom of Jesus Christ in
the hearts of men. How often did not the Lord,
in the Old Law, arm heaven and earth against man?

Did He succeed in making him better? Was He not obliged, at last, to come down upon earth Himself, and humble Himself before man, to make His yoke agreeable to him? Do you think a Prelate will be able to effect by his power what God could not obtain by His Omnipotence? Hence it is my opinion, that Mons. Fouquet is right in not excommunicating those Religious, who possess property, and in not forbidding them to preach during Advent and Lent in parish-churches in the country, after having, upon due examination, given them power to do so. Should any one abuse this power, his Lordship's prudence and discretion will know how to apply a proper remedy.''[1]

Fenelon advised his parish-priests to extirpate superstitious practices with a gentle hand, showing no spirit of rigor, of harshness, or of domineering; that they should work against them more by way of instruction and exhortation, than by commands and threats. It will be very easy to banish certain disorders if, in their place, you introduce something useful, because men, in general, are disposed to give up something if they receive something else in its place. Before commencing to abolish an error, you must try to gain the esteem and affection of those you wish to benefit, because charity easily robs charity. In many cases it is more advisable to commence to redress disorders by individuals, than by many at once; because, in the latter case, some might not feel disposed to yield, and then they will prevent others also

[1] Orsini's Life of St. Vincent of Paul.

from doing so; but by trying to gain one after the other for your cause, you will succeed better in carrying your point, as the example of these will induce others to follow also. To ensure easier success, make use also of a simile or a history well calculated to convince the mind of the perverseness of an error or custom, and of the advantages flowing from its being given up.

In this spirit St. Gregory wrote to St. Mellitus, Abbot, as follows: "Whenever Almighty God shall bring you safe to our most reverend Brother Augustine, Bishop, acquaint him with the result of my long deliberation on the subject of England, which is this: that the idol-temples in that country ought not to be destroyed; but that after the demolition of the actual idols contained in them, some water should be blessed, and sprinkled in the temples, and that their altars should be raised in them, and relics deposited. For, if the temples in question have been well constructed, they ought to be transferred from the worship of idols into the service of the true God; in order that the nation, observing this tenderness in the treatment of its religious buildings, may be the rather led to put error from its heart, and when it comes to know and worship the true God, may the more readily resort to the temples with which it is familiar. Moreover, since it is their practice to slay numerous oxen in the sacrifice of their devils, for this solemnity some corresponding one should be substituted; on the day of the dedication of the church, therefore, or of the martyrs whose relics are deposited in it, they may construct tents out of the branches of the trees in the neighborhood of these same churches, into which the old temples have been converted, and celebrate their festival with religious joy, no longer sacrificing their animals to the devil, but killing them for their own use to the glory of God, and giving thanks of their abundance to the Giver of all things, and thus being the rather disposed to inward satisfactions by how much their innocent festivities are more indulgently promoted. For it is an undoubted fact, that to mould hard minds into shape all at once, is impossible. He who strives to reach the highest place ascends thither by slow steps, not by vaulting. Thus did our Lord make Himself known to the people of Israel in Egypt, while the honor of the sacrifices which were formerly offered to the devil He reserved to Himself, when He appointed the slaying of animals as a part of religious worship ; that in this way, as their hearts were changed, they might partly give up and partly retain the use of sacrifices ; offering indeed the same animals as before, but with a different object, and so not as the same sacrifices."[1]

§ 9. *Be an Enemy of Differences.*

Let a Superior, moreover, be an arch-enemy of differences, law-suits, and of whatever may be calculated to alienate the hearts of his fellow-men, even with the loss of temporal advantages, as nothing temporal can equal peace and harmony. "Blessed are the peace-makers!"[2] St. Vincent de Paul, not being left

[1] Epist. xi. 26.   [2] Matt. 5.

in quiet possession of a foundation in a certain diocese, wrote to the Superior thereof as follows: "After having settled your accounts with the grand-vicar, and returned every article contained in the inventory, and having obtained a receipt for everything, you will beg to take leave without complaining in the least, or saying anything to indicate that you unwillingly leave the place. You, however, will beseech the Lord to bless the city and the diocese. Above all, I beseech you not to say anything either in public or in private, that might lead others to think that we were dissatisfied. Finally, ask the blessing of these Rev. Gentlemen, both for yourself, and for your subjects, even for myself who prostrate myself in spirit at their feet."[1]

St. Francis Xavier was one day informed that a very learned priest of the Society, lived at variance with the Vicar of the place, or at least that their opinions did not coincide. Although he was an aged Father who had lived with St. Ignatius for a considerable time, he wrote to him a very serious and sensible letter. After having reprimanded him for having profited so little by his intercourse with, and the example of, St. Ignatius, he thus continues: "You, like so many others who resemble you, are greatly mistaken, when you fancy that, without possessing deep humility, and without showing the same by your works and manner of life, you could follow your opinions and judgment, simply for the reason that you are members of the Society, regardless of the virtue of our holy Father Ignatius, who, for his eminent

[1] Life.

virtue, was raised by the Almighty to such repute
and authority. And do you ambition authority without the virtues, which alone can grant it? Remember,
it is better to do a little with peace, than a great deal
with turbulence and scandal. In the latter case, we
destroy more with one hand, than we build up with
the other. If we grasp at too much, we lose all. By
the love and obedience which you owe to our Father
Ignatius, I beseech you, on the receipt of this letter,
to repair immediately to the Vicar, to throw yourself
at his feet, most humbly asking his pardon for what
has occurred, and then kiss his hand. It would even
please me still more, if you were to kiss his feet,
promising him never more to oppose his will in the
smallest degree. Believe me, on your death-bed, you
will rejoice at having done this. Trust in the Lord,
and rest assured, that, when His Divine Majesty, and
men too, shall have witnessed your submission, the
very fact of it will draw upon you, the blessing of
heaven so abundantly, that you will succeed in whatever you undertake for the glory of God and the welfare of your neighbor. My dear Brother, would to
God, you could but see the great love and affection
which dictate these words, you would think of me day
and night, and perhaps this love for you would make
you shed tears of tenderness. Were we permitted to
see one another's hearts, believe me, you would see
yours enshrined in mine."[1]

St. Francis of Assissium, whose eyes were ever
fixed upon the supreme peace, gave to his friars the

[1] Life of St. Francis Xavier.

following advice: "We are sent, dearest brethren," he says to them, "to assist the Clergy for the salvation of souls; that what is found less in them may be supplied by us. Every one will receive his reward, not according to authority, but according to his labor. What, above all, pleases God, is the gain of souls; . and this we shall better accomplish by keeping peace with the Clergy, than by being at discord. But if they impede our effort, vengeance is God's, and He will repay in proper time. Therefore be subject to prelates, and as far as is in you, let no evil zeal arise. ˙ If you be the children of peace, you will gain both Clergy and people; and this will be more acceptable to God than if you gained the people alone, and scandalised the Clergy. Conceal their faults; supply their multiplied defects; and so doing, you will be more humble."[1]

"I recommend to you," writes St. Alphonsus to a Superior, "to keep peace as far as possible. Should you see that things do not go according to your ideas, it will be better to be indulgent, even at the loss of some temporal advantage, rather than to endanger the spiritual by violating charity. St. Ignatius severely punished those, who disturbed peace and undermined charity. Do everything with peace, and leave to Providence whatever you cannot change."[2] "You have been advised," St. Francis de Sales wrote one day to the nuns of the Visitation, "to commence a law-suit for the sake of one hundred dollars; but I advise you not to do so even for a

---

[1] Wadding, an. 1219.   [2] Letters Apr. 22.

thousand. Scarcely a Saint can remain wise in a
law-suit. 'Litigare et non insanire vix sanctis conce-
ditur.' Our Saviour never went to law, although He
was wronged in a thousand ways. I do not wish to
blame those, who go to law, provided it be done for
justice' sake; but I say, nay, I even write, and were
it necessary, I would write it down with my own
blood, that whoever wishes to be perfect and a disciple of Jesus Christ crucified, must adopt this
doctrine. Avoid law-suits, let the world gnash its
teeth, let the prudence of the flesh be scandalized and
cry aloud; we must prefer what Jesus Christ says:
"Him that taketh away from thee thy cloak, forbid
not to take thy coat also."[1] Peace is a valuable and
holy article worth being bought at a high price."

The officials of St. Francis de Sales had one day
gained important law-suits. His steward, whose
purse was rather poor, insisted upon having refunded
by the opposite parties, all the expenses of these law-
suits. But the holy Prelate would not agree to this.
"But these expenses," said his steward, "are very
considerable." "And do you think it but little profit
to win over those hearts which may, by these law-
suits, have become alienated from us? I, for my part,
consider this a greater gain than everything else.
I am a Father, I must treat them as my children. You
must go and tell them on my part, that I do not require anything from them, neither for old debts, nor
for the expenses incurred in these law-suits, provided
they acknowledge, for the future, the episcopal rights,

[1] Luke 6, 29.

proved, established, and confirmed by the Senate. Having gained the law-suit to keep up the rights of the Church, we must try to win back the good feelings of our neighbor, which become so easily alienated in law-suits; if we have lost them, we should go to law, if necessary, to regain them; for a father must make himself beloved by his children.''

"I, for my part," says St. Vincent de Paul, "admire Christ our Lord Who, it is true, never approved of law-suits, yet wished to have one Himself and lose it." The more favorably the law pronounced for this Saint, the more readily was he disposed for a compromise, and if a considerable loss for his opponent was in question, he managed that the execution of the juridical sentence pronounced in his favor, might be mitigated and put off, in order that his adversary might lose as little as possible. To act in this manner, requires a heart completely detached from the goods of this world. St. Vincent was a perfect model of this detachment. A valuable country-seat was offered to him as a present, which he accepted only after long reflection and re-iterated requests of the owner, as well as of another great benefactor. After many very expensive improvements by which the Society saved the estate from total ruin, the donor died, and his heirs went to law to reclaim the donation. The law pronounced in their favor without any compensation for the improvements. Thus the Society suffered a loss of thirty thousand Livres. This blow came quite unexpectedly, as the Society believed their title well established. Even one of the judges came to Vincent to indicate the means and ways to elude this sentence. He thanked him for his kind advice, but declared, that he willingly adored the disposition of Providence in this affair. But to his own he said: "God forbid, that we should elude this sentence! It is Thou, O Lord Thyself, Who hast pronounced it; consequently we acquiesce in it; and in order that its execution may not be put off, we now already sacrifice this estate to Thy Divine Majesty! My brethren, let us still add another sacrifice to this, one of praise and thanksgiving! Let us praise the Supreme Judge of the living and the dead, for having visited us on the day of affliction! Let us thank Him for having delivered us not only from every affection to earthly goods, but even from the goods of this world themselves and for having given us the grace even to rejoice at their loss. I readily believe, that this joy is a general one for us all; for as Christ chastises those, whom He loves, we must look upon this chastisement as a proof of His love for us; truly, we must rejoice at it. O my God! who else than Thou couldst give us this grace! Thou art the source of all joys, and without Thee, there is no true one. It is Thou, then, Who grantest it to us! Yes, Reverend Gentlemen, let us rejoice at having been found worthy to suffer something. But how can we be joyful in sufferings, they being so bitter and unwelcome to human nature? They are like bitter medicines, which would promote health much less, were they sweet. Their being bitter does not prevent us from taking them. Why is this? Because we appreciate health, which we hope to recover by taking them. It is the same with afflictions, disagreeable as they are, they contribute so much the more towards the spiritual welfare of the soul or of a whole society, purifying it like gold in the fire.   On Mount Olivet and on the Cross Jesus Christ our Lord suffered a most painful agony; He was abandoned not only by men, but even by His heavenly Father; but in the height of His excruciating pains and sufferings, He rejoiced in doing the will of His heavenly Father.   We, too, must be filled with joy, when we see how the good pleasure of God is accomplished in our humiliations, temporal losses and contradictions.   Let us, as St. Paul writes, "look on Jesus the author and finisher of faith, Who having joy set before Him, endured the Cross, despising the shame."[1]   Why, then, should not we, too, rejoice at the loss of our goods? Ah, my beloved brethren, how well is God pleased to see us here assembled, exhorting one another to rejoice. On the one hand, we have become a spectacle for the world, for the angels and for men, because by this sentence of the law, we were represented as unjust proprietors of this estate; but, on the other hand, "count it all joy when you shall fall into divers temptations."   Let us rest assured, that we have made a great gain by this loss.   For by depriving us of this country-seat, God deprived us at the same time of the pleasure, which we might have derived from an occasional visit to it; but such a pleasure for our human nature, would have been, for our souls, a sweet,

[1] Heb. 10, 34.

but deadly poison, a two edged sword and a consuming and destructive fire. Behold now our merciful Lord has delivered us from this danger, and by having become poorer by this loss, His Divine Bounty wished to increase our confidence in His Providence, nay even to force us to abandon ourselves altogether to Him both in regard to the higher gifts of His grace, and to the necessaries of life. Would to God, that in compensation for this temporal loss, we all would receive an increase of confidence in the Lord, of resignation to His holy will, of detachment from this world and ourselves ! My God, how great would our gain then be! I hope, His paternal bounty, which disposes all things to our good, will grant all these graces.''

Let us draw the following conclusions from what has been said :

First, that we must offer to God in sacrifice all our goods, both temporal and spiritual, and consolations with everything that we may have or wish for; we must do this with full earnestness so as to be ready at any moment to abandon everything, in order to follow Jesus Christ in His poverty, patience and humility.

Secondly, that we should never go to law, no matter, 'how justifiable may be our reasons for doing so, and that, should we be forced to do so, we should not do it before all means for a compromise have been tried and our right be perfectly well established. We should as much as possible follow the advice of our Lord. ''Him that taketh away from thee thy

cloak, forbid not to take thy coat also,"[1] for God will
return to us what men take from us. St. Vincent
followed this advice. Many persons of high standing
and several skilful lawyers felt sorry for Vincent, and
one even offered to take up again this law-suit at his
own expense. But Vincent did not wish to hear
about it any longer, and this for the following
reasons:

First, because from the very beginning he would
have been willing to give up the said estate, had the
lawyers not declared that the title and claim of his
Society were indisputable; but as the law had pronounced otherwise, contrary to their expectation,
God had released him from the obligation to urge his
right any longer.

Secondly, as it was the duty of his Missionary
priests to settle differences among the people, they
would have reason to apprehend, that God would
withdraw His grace, should they be determined to
make any further appeal in their behalf.

Third, because the Society would give scandal by
t to the people, who would accuse us of being too
much attached to earthly goods, of which the Clergy
are anyhow too often accused.

Finally, he said, it has always been very hard
for me not to act up to the advice of Jesus Christ, no-
matter, how plausible the motives may be for not doing so; and if in the beginning I did not follow His
advice, it was for no other reason than because
I thought, I could not give up an estate, which we

[1] Luke 6, 29.

had lawfully acquired, and because it belonged to a Society, of which I was but an unprofitable steward.

In conclusion to all that has been said let us, as St. Vincent de Paul says, rest assured that the merit and success of our actions will be proportionate to the purity of our intention and to our exertions. The Lord will reward us according to our labor, not according to the success thereof, says St. Paul. Let us do what is in our power, says St. Alphonsus, but with case of mind, abandoning to Jesus Christ what we cannot change.

In order to secure, in a more special manner, the Divine blessing and assistance, especially in affairs of importance, let us, in imitation of St. Alphonsus and other Saints, add to all our exertions, most fervent prayers, masses, alms for the poor and necessitous, and beg others to do the same for us.

For, according to St. Augustine, the Holy Ghost will assist in all affairs him who endeavors to relieve the necessitous. Hence it is said: "Blessed are the merciful, for they shall obtain mercy."[1]

[1] Matt. 5.

CHAPTER XIX.

SOME REMARKS CONCERNING THE DIRECTION OF SOULS.

O man can come to Me except the Father Who hath sent Me draw him.[1] From these words of our Lord Jesus Christ it is evident that it belongs to God to attract souls by His grace to a supernatural life. Many, are the means and ways which the Lord makes use of for this purpose. In most instances He avails Himself of the ministry of His servants, to induce souls to love their Creator and aim at perfection. The Lord cannot confer upon His servants a greater honor than to make them His assistants in the salvation and sanctification of souls. "It is for this reason," says St. Francis de Sales, "that the ancient bishops and fathers of the Church, notwithstanding their numerous occupations of importance, never declined to superintend the particular conduct of several souls who had recourse to their assistance, as appears by their epistles; in which instance they imitated the apostles, who, amidst the general harvest of the world, picked up certain remarkable ears of corn with a special and particular

---

[1] John 6 44.

affection. Who is ignorant that Timothy, Titus, Philemon, Onesimus, St. Thecla, and St. Appia, were the dear pupils of the great St. Paul as St. Mark, and St. Petronella were of St. Peter? And does not St. John write one of his canonical epistles to the devout Lady Electa?

"It is painful, I confess, to direct souls in particular; but it is a pain that gives a comfort, like to that which is felt by the laborers in the harvest and vintage, who are never better pleased than when they have most to do, and when their burthens are the heaviest. It is a labor which refreshes and revives the heart, by the sweet delights it brings to those who are engaged therein. It is said that when the tigress finds one of her whelps, which the huntsman leaves in the way to amuse her, whilst he carried off the rest of the litter, she loads herself with it, be it ever so big, and yet feels not herself more heavy, but rather more light, in the course she makes to secure it in her den, natural love making her burden more easy: how much more willingly, then, will a fatherly heart take charge of a soul in which he has found a desire of holy perfection, carrying it in his bosom as a mother does her little child, without being oppressed by so beloved a burden! But this must be indeed a fatherly heart; and therefore the apostles, and apostolic men, call their disciples not only their children, but still *more tenderly*, their *little* children."

Hence, the success of a Superior to promote souls to perfection, will be so much the greater, the more he succeeds in winning the hearts of his subjects by

37

his affectionate conduct for them ; for then they will behave towards him with perfect confidence, and it will be easy for him to work upon the reformation of their hearts, to which he should direct his principal attention; as the exterior man easily follows the interior, but not *vice versa*.   In this reformation of their hearts, he must have in view nothing but the glory of God and the good of souls, dealing with them according to the mode observed by God and His angels, leading them by inspirations, suggestions, illuminations, remonstrances, entreaties, solicitations, in all patience and doctrine, knocking like the spouse at the door of their hearts, gently pressing against them that they may open; if so they be open, introducing salvation into them with joy ; if they refuse, bearing the denial, with gentleness, according to the example of our Lord Who bears with resistance and rebellion against the light He gives.

He must not expect to see at once the fruit of his efforts.   Many souls are a very barren ground, from which, he will gain in proportion as he persevered in laboring with cordiality to promote their spiritual welfare.   He must, of course, openly speak his mind when it becomes necessary, and then, wait in peace a successful issue.   The divine Samaritan did not direct that the patient should be healed, but that remedies should be applied.   The Superior must have patience with souls and leave to God the care of healing them. He requires no more.

He must be aware that all will not take the same rapid flight, in the career of perfection, but that some will soar higher than others, while not a few will make but inconsiderable advances. Each one must be treated according to his capacity. Hence what he requires of his children must be, neither too much, nor too untimely, nor too much at once; he should teach them to elevate themselves towards heaven by slow degrees, to make a low flight like hens if they cannot take the lofty flight of eagles, to walk on the common road if unable to follow a more perfect one. "If you cannot pray," says St. Frances de Sales, "like a soul enjoying the gift of contemplation, you can at least make a spiritual reading and reflect on the same; if you are not strong enough to fast, you may at least deprive yourself of a delicate morsel; if you cannot quit the world, you may at least guard against its spirit; you cannot love God with a pure love; but you may love Him at least out of gratitude; you do not experience a lively sorrow for your sins; but you can make efforts to obtain it by asking it of God; you cannot bestow many alms, but you can give at least a drink of water; you cannot bear great insults, but you may bear at least a little reproach without murmuring; to be despised is beyond what you can endure, but you may bear with that little coldness manifested by your neighbor in his behavior towards you; the sacrifice of your life is not required of you, but you can put up with some inconvenience and preserve patience under some little trying circumstances."

Let a Superior also be aware that there are certain little souls of whom nothing can be expected but that they should walk at a quiet and easy pace, without being urged; for should they be pressed, they would stumble and be filled with disappointment and disgust.

Souls deficient in courage must be managed as a General disposes of his troops. They are not to be placed in the front ranks, lest they should be seized with a panic and occasion disorder, that is to say, they are not to see all their wounds, for fear they should deem them incurable; they are to be encouraged to proceed at an easy pace, according to their strength. The conduct of the great Apostle is here to be copied, who, in all his proceedings, kept in view, the various degrees of weakness or strength which he discovered in his spiritual children. Whenever they are to be tried for their advancement in virtue let it be done with an amorous zeal and with a sweet spirit of charity, without forcing their hearts and without overwhelming them with any uncalled-for severity. This conduct must be observed especially in regard to souls of real good will and also in regard to weak and timorous souls, who by, a little hard treatment would be at once altogether disheartened.

Discouragement and diffidence being one of the most frequent temptations for souls trying to advance on the road to perfection, the Superior must know how to raise their courage, invigorate their spirits, and inspire them with unbounded confidence, that they may walk with ardor in the performance of their duties, and may pursue their course without murmur and without disgust. He must perpetually inculcate the fear of God, not only to beginners, but to all persons whatever progress they have made in christian virtue and perfection. Religious souls, unless possessed of that fear which belongs to the spouses of Christ, will soon stumble on their road.

There are certain souls of superior endowments who both advance themselves and others; these are not to be spared but must be vigorously urged on to the practice of true humility, of self-abnegation, with a degree of steadiness that unites sweetness and force.

There is but too common a failure in the direction of souls, which contributes rather to divert them from God, than to lead them in the right path, namely if a spiritual director recommends to souls his peculiar taste and brings into action his favorite methods of proceeding in the spiritual life. What he must attend to is, the discovery of the particular attraction which God imparts to each soul in order to manifest it to those under his direction and see that they follow it faithfully.

He must be sagacious and discreet to discern the attractions of God from those of self-love. There are certain unmortified characters who are led by their airy imaginations and vainly suppose themselves to be in a certain way of holiness to which they have no pretension. These are to be peremptorily diverted from pursuing their empty fancies, whatever they may allege in extenuation of their conduct; for it is the only mode of withdrawing them from themselves and leading them to God. On the contrary, one possessed of solid virtue is not to be disturbed in his course, as that would have a direct tendency to impede the operation of God. This, therefore, is a matter of extreme delicacy ; the virtuous and steady character is to be encouraged and supported, whilst the light and airy disposition, in which dissimulation forms a prominent feature, is to be tried and carefully scrutinised.

Let the Superior lay but a slight stress upon extraordinary and transcendant gifts, as it must be his purpose to conduct souls more by the solid mode of self-denial, profound humility, sweet charity, cordial support and sincerity, prompt and simple obedience, candid accusation of their faults, tranquil modesty, sweet and devout conversation and attraction to the presence of God, than by any other method of a more elevated nature, as it is but too true that the human mind is so easily led by the imagination, is so prone to credulity, and so much attached to its own devices, that where there is no appearance of pure and solid virtue, little hopes can be entertained. To set much value on extraordinary occurrences, or to hold one way of sanctity in less estimation than another, would be a mark of great ignorance, since no state or way is low or despicable but that of sin and imperfection.

Hence if the Superior observes a soul gifted with a higher and more sublime degree of prayer, he must not on that account set more value on her, unless he discovers in her at the same time a solid foundation of unfeigned virtue. What he should love to witness is, the appearance of those courageous souls, who form the most absolute and efficacious purpose to pursue the right road in spite of every obstacle and without examining whether they have to experience relief or disgust, pleasure or pain, consolation or desolation. His direction must be that in every occurrence, whether of interior peace or commotion, the soul should go straight to God by an unconditional surrender and a complete denial of her will, sweetness of heart and equality of mind.

As to the relative importance of the virtues conducing to perfection, he should teach his children—

1 — To prefer those the practice of which is the most frequent and common, to such as are seldom called into exercise, for instance: Patience exercised in the midst of injuries, sufferings, and contradictions; true and profound humility, practised in the midst of humiliations, abjection and scorn; sweetness and equality of humor amidst an inequality of sentiments and events and a multiplicity of business and bustle; ready and simple obedience practised under the influence of repugnances, disgusts and difficulties.

2 — Not to judge of the comparative supernatural merit of a virtue by the greatness of its external act; in as much as a virtue apparently small may be practised with much grace and charity, and a more splendid one with a very feeble degree of the love of God, which nevertheless is the rule and the measure of their value in His sight.

3 — To prefer the more universal virtues to such as are more limited in their reach, charity always excepted. For instance, to have a higher esteem for

prayer, which is the torch of all the rest; for devotion which consecrates all our actions to the service of God; for humility, which makes us have a low opinion of ourselves, and of our actions; for gentleness, which makes us yield to every one; for patience, which makes us endure all things; than for magnanimity, magnificence, or liberality, both because these virtues have respect to fewer objects and because they have less scope.

4 — To regard the shining virtues with a little suspicion; for their splendor gives a strong handle to vain-glory, which is the very poison of the soul.

5 — Not to esteem virtues according to the value set upon them by the generality of men, who are very bad judges of that kind of merchandise; thus, they will prefer temporal to spiritual alms; hair-shirts, fasting and bodily austerities to meekness, modesty and mortification of the heart, which are nevertheless far more excellent.

6 — Not to practise those virtues only which are more conformable to their taste, without troubling themselves about those which belong more particularly to their office and the duties of their state, serving God according to their own fashion, not according to His will, which is so frequent an abuse that we see numbers of persons, even among the devout, who are carried away by it.

7 — To keep their hearts detached from everything created, from place, time, persons, even from the practice of particular virtuous acts, in order to attach them to none but to God alone without reserve,

and to seek no consolation, no rest, no honor and glory except in the Cross of our Saviour at Whose feet every one ought to sacrifice all his caprices, affections, aversions, passions, inclinations, in a word, his entire self; for, we must suffer and sacrifice much for God, if we wish to enjoy Him.

8 — To love particularly three kinds of crosses: First — those which on account of their long durance, become in the end annoying and irksome. "Those crosses which we meet with in the public streets," said St. Francis de Sales, "are excellent, but those which we find at home are far more excellent, because they are heavier. They are better than iron-chains, disciplines, fasting and everything that has been invented by the spirit of austerity. In this the magnanimity of the children of the cross is manifested."

Secondly — those which come without being sought for. These come from God; they are all filled with the perfume of the place from which they come. Wheresoever there is less of our own choice, there is more of the good pleasure of God. The cross which our Lord lays upon us is far preferable to the one which we lay upon ourselves. To carry our cross, means to embrace, with perfect submission to the divine will, all pains, troubles, contradictions, and mortifications of this life, the little ones as well as the great ones, no matter whether they are according to our liking or against it. We like to choose our own cross and leave another, we prefer a heavy one which strikes the eyes and is noticed by others, to a light one of which we become tired because it lasts

so long.   Illusion! We must carry *our* own cross —
the one which presses upon us at present, — and not
another.   And its merit consists not in its quality,
but in the degree of perfection with which it is borne.
There is often more virtue in not saying an unlawful
word, or in not casting a curious glance than in wearing a hair-shirt.   Condescension to the humors of
others and sweet but most reasonable forbearance
with our neighbor, behold, what ought to be our
cherished and special virtues.   "O how much shorter
work it is," said St. Francis de Sales, "to accomodate ourselves to others, than to wish to bend every
one to our own humors and opinions."

A third kind of crosses which must be dear to
us, are unjust vexations and persecutions.   "Blessed
are they that suffer persecution for justice sake."
They bear more resemblance to our Saviour and lead
with Him a hidden life in God ; they are considered
wicked, poor fools, though they are good, rich, and
wise ; they are held in abomination by the wicked,
but loved and blessed by the Lord.   Persecutions are
relics of our Saviour's Cross ; we must not lose even
the smallest particle.

9 — To choose from among the different spiritual
exercires one for more frequent practice, such as the
presence of God, an exercise so highly commended by
the Saints, and so easily to be kept up by frequent
but fervent ejaculations ; or purity of intention ; or
submission to the divine will in all things, an exercise which cannot be too highly esteemed ; or self-
abandonment into the hands of God, and self-re-

nunciation, as any of these exercises includes gener- ally all christian perfection.

10 — In the same manner to choose, one particu- lar virtue, such as humility, gentleness, patience, mortification, prayer, mercy and the like, for special practice; this is something peculiar to all religious Institutes which cultivate some particular virtue which constitutes their spirit without neglecting the others. Upon these principles the Saints would not augur well of those persons whom they saw fluttering from one exercise to another, from one look to an- other, from one practice to another; comparing them to drones who alight on every flower without extract- ing honey from any, ever learning without ever attaining to the true science of the Saints; always gathering, collecting and heaping up, without becom- ing rich, because they put everything into a bag with a hole; restless spirits who, seeking peace in spiritual riches, find it not.

11 — Our law in everything must be the will of God; but it is not sufficient to will what God wills, we must also will it in the manner He wills, and in every one of its circumstances. For instance, when ill, we must will to suffer this particular complaint and not another, in this special place and at this time, as well as among such persons as it shall please God.

CHAPTER XX.

ON MENTAL PRAYER.

THE exercise of mental prayer is the regular method of sanctifying souls. On this account, mental prayer has always been the favorite and delightful occupation of the Saints; they devoted to it as much time as possible. It is the faithful practice of this exercise that leads to the reformation of life and manners. The exhortations of the Superior of a religious Community should be zealous and unceasing.

Mental prayer, it is true, is not absolutely necessary; but it certainly is morally necessary. It is by reflecting on the eternal truths that we come to understand the importance of salvation, the means which we should adopt, and the impediments which we should overcome in order to be saved. Now he who neglects meditation, neither sees his spiritual wants, nor the necessity of asking aid from God to overcome temptations and work out his salvation. It is for this reason that such a one either neglects prayer, altogether, or if he prays now and then, he prays at random, as it were, not knowing how to pray according to his spiritual necessities ; or he prays without being in earnest to obtain something in prayer. Now to neglect prayer is to be lost; and not to understand how to pray with fervor and according to one's spiritual wants is, to remain in the state of mortal sin, and to be in constant danger of damnation. How many are there, who say the rosary and other vocal prayers, and yet for all that, continue io live in mortal sin. Experience, however teaches, that he who is regular in making his meditation, will either give up sin or give up meditation.

Mental prayer contains three parts : the preparation, the meditation, and the conclusion. In the preparation there is to be made an act of faith in the presence of God, an act of humility, and a prayer for light. These acts may be made in the following manner : O my God, I believe, that Thou art present within me ; I adore Thee from the depth of my nothingness ; on account of my sins, I ought to be in hell ; I am sorry for having offended Thee; forgive me all my sins ; enlighten my understanding, in order that I may profit by this meditation. Say a Hail Mary to obtain this light. Let the preparation be short but made with fervor.

In meditation we bestow our attention upon divine things, in order to excite our hearts to produce holy affections, petitions and salutary resolutions. We are bound to form ourselves upon the divine model which our Heavenly Father has given us in Jesus Christ; and we can have no better intention in all our actions, than to perform them, because our

Lord has shown us the example, that is to say, to practise virtues, because our Father has practised them. Now to do this well, we must consider them in meditation; for a child who loves his father, endeavors to acquire a conformity of dispositions and inclinations with him, and to imitate him in all his actions. This method of entertaining our mind in prayer is the most secure, and leads to the reformation of life. It is for this reason, that the mysteries of the life, death and passion of our Lord are the most useful subjects of meditation. Seldom does it happen that we do not profit by the considerations of the actions of our Lord.

Besides the consideration of the mysteries of the life of our Lord is best calculated to produce, in our hearts, the three principal fruits of mental prayer, that is pious affections, fervent petitions for all the graces necessary for our salvation, and firm resolutions to avoid some particular fault, and to practise some particular acts of virtue.

The *first fruit* of mental prayer consists in exciting our hearts to produce *pious affections*. After we have sweetly and simply considered our first point, we should pass to the colloquy by tender words of affection on the proposed subject. These affections consist in acts of adoration and praise of the divine Majesty; in acts of confidence in God's goodness and power, in acts of confidence in the merits of Jesus Christ, and in the intercession of the Bl. V. Mary; and above all in acts of confidence in God's promises to save all who pray to Him for their salvation.

These affections, moreover, consist in acts of love of God's infinite goodness and perfection; they consist in desires to love Him as much as He wishes and deserves to be loved; they consist in acts of acknowledgment of our unworthiness to receive from Him anything but hell. Again, these affections consist in acts of thanks for God's infinite benefits; in acts of sorrow for our past sins; in acts of resignation to the Divine will in all things; they consist in acts of oblation of ourselves to God, that He may dispose of us as He pleases. Of these acts there are three which should never be omitted, that is, the acts of sorrow for our sins; the acts of resignation to the Divine will and of oblation of ourselves and of all that we are and have, to the love and glory of God for time and eternity; and lastly the acts of the love of God, and desires to love Him as much as the Angels love Him. Although these acts may be expressed in words, yet it suffices to make them with the heart.

The *second fruit* of meditation consists in fervent petitions. Our affections should be followed by fervent prayers for all the lights and graces necessary to salvation. This is, perhaps, the most important part of meditation; for the prayer of petition is of all other kinds of prayer the most indispensable. As no infant can enter the kingdom of heaven, without baptism; so in like manner, no adult person shall obtain life everlasting, without asking of God the graces necessary for salvation. This is the common teaching of all Theologians.

The rebel angels were pure spirits; they were

more perfect than we are; they had not to contend with the corruption of the flesh; for they had no bodies; but our flesh is constantly rebelling against the spirit. They were not subject to the evil inclinations of concupiscence; all their natural inclinations led them to love God above all things: our inclinations constantly draw us away from God, and lead us to sin. The rebel angels had no temptation from the world; for all creatures only served to inspire them with sentiments of admiration of the power and goodness of the Creator: but every object around us fixes our heart on the world, and takes away our thoughts and affections from heaven and God. Neither had they any devil to tempt them; but all the devils in hell are leagued against us; they are constantly going about like roaring lions, seeking whom they may devour.

Now, if in spite of all their perfection, if in spite of their being free from all the attacks of the enemies by which we are constantly assailed, the angels fell, and could not but fall, because they did not pray, shall we who are all weakness and corruption, be able, without continual prayer, to persevere till death in victoriously repelling the unceasing assaults of the world, of the flesh, and of the devil? No; unless in our meditations and other spiritual exercises, we make use of frequent petitions to God for his graces, in order thus to acquire a habit and a facility of turning to Him for help against our enemies in all difficulties and temptations, it will be at least morally impossible for us, to persevere till death in the faithful discharge of all the difficult duties and obligations that shall fall upon us, and in escaping all the dangers of perdition to which we shall be exposed. And this is especially the case with those charged with the care of others.

God, it is true, gives us grace to do what is easy without our asking it, but not what is difficult. Even to the Saints He only promises to give grace to pray for strength to do what is difficult, that is, to conquer violent temptations and to discharge hard obligations. Now all Christians, have difficult duties to perform, but the obligations of religious and especially of those who have charge of others, are peculiarly difficult; they have often to combat violent temptations to neglect their duties, and to offend God. In order to enable weakness and sinfulness like ours to overcome till death all difficulties and the enemies that are constantly opposed to us, God must impart to us His own all-powerful grace, and that He will not do unless we ask it continually. But how shall we offer to God frequent petitions for His assistance, unless in our meditations, we acquire, a habit and facility of asking His graces. This part of mental prayer, which consists in asking of God all the graces which we stand in need of, is of the greatest importance. It is by attending to it well, that we acquire a habit and facility of turning to God for help in all difficulties, dangers and temptations. Without attending to it, we shall scarcely ever acquire this habit and facility. Now without this habit it will be impossible to avoid mortal sin in the discharge of our duties, and in the

38

difficult temptations by which we are often assailed.
It is on this account, that St. Alphonsus says, that
every preacher should, in almost all his sermons, exhort his hearers to the practice of prayer; that he
should admonish them never to cease to call for aid in
all their temptations, at least by invoking the holy
names of Jesus and Mary as long as the temptation
lasts; he says, that no Confessor should content himself with simply endeavoring to excite his penitents
to sorrow for their sins, and to a firm purpose of
amendment; but that he should also be careful to
impress upon them the necessity of praying for grace
in order to remain faithful to their resolutions, and of
asking the Divine aid as often as they are tempted to
offend God. He concludes his book on prayer in the
following words: "I say, and I repeat, and I shall
repeat while I live, that our salvation depends altogether on prayer, and that, on that account, all writ-
ers in their books, all preachers in their sermons, and
all Confessors in the tribunal of penance should continually exclaim and repeat: 'Pray, pray, and never
cease to pray;' for if you continue to pray, your salvation is secure; if you give up prayer your perdition
is inevitable." In our meditations, we should ask
not one, nor two, nor a thousand graces, but all the
lights and graces, without a single exception, which
are necessary to bring us, and to bring us *efficaciously*
and infallibly to eternal glory. "All things, whatsoever you ask when ye pray, believe that you shall
receive, and they shall come unto you."[1] Jesus

---

[1] Mark xi. 24.

Christ was not content with saying, "all things," or "whatsoever;" but, to exclude the possibility of a single grace being excepted, He said: "All things, whatsoever you ask when ye pray, shall come unto you." Prayer then is a universal means, by which every single grace necessary to bring us infallibly to eternal life, may be obtained with infallible certainty since the Son of God cannot be a liar. In this respect it differs from the sacraments, from penitential works, and the other means which God has given us in order to obtain eternal life. These are particular means, each producing or procuring particular graces; baptism produces one grace, and penance another; it is the same for the other sacraments or means of salvation. But to none of these, nor to all put together, without prayer, has God promised all the graces necessary for eternal life. Prayer is the only means to which He has promised all the *efficacious* helps and graces necessary for our salvation. It is a means given to all without exception; for God gives the grace of prayer to the most hardened sinners as well as to the most holy of the just; and He has given it to every adult that ever lived from the time of Adam to the present day. By making a good use of this grace of prayer, the worst sinner may obtain, as *infallibly* as the greatest Saint, every efficacious grace necessary for his salvation, and may thus *infallibly* secure everlasting glory. For Jesus Christ has promised to hear the prayers of all, — of sinners as well as of Saints. "For every one that asketh, receiveth."[1]

[1] Luke xi., 10.

He who says every one, excepts none. On the day of judgment, then, the reprobate shall be without excuse; if they say, they had not strength to resist temptations, Jesus Christ shall answer: if you had not strength, why did you not ask it? Had you asked for it, I should certainly have given it to you.

If they say that, after they had fallen into sin, they were unable to rise from it, He will answer: Had you had recourse to Me, I would have raised you from the state of sin; I would have clothed you with My grace, and would have brought you to eternal glory.

Hence in meditation, when the heart is excited to fervor by the consideration of the eternal truths, we should make frequent and fervent petitions in the name of Jesus Christ, for all the efficacious lights, helps and graces which are necessary to secure *infal_libly* our eternal happiness. These petitions should always be made with the heart, but they may also be expressed in words. The celebrated Father Segneri said of himself that, until he studied theology, he was accustomed to spend the greater part of the time of his meditations in reflections and pious affections; but that afterwards God enlightened him, and thenceforward he employed himself generally in asking God's graces. He added: "If there is anything good in me, I attribute it to this practice of recommending myself to God."

Although it is very important for us to ask, in our meditations, all the graces we stand in need of, and especially for the graces suggested by our reflections, we should be very careful to pray, in every meditation, for three graces in particular : first, for the pardon of all our sins ; secondly, for the gift of the love of God, and thirdly, for the gift of final perseverance, and for the grace to persevere till death in praying for this great gift. We should be careful to ask these three graces also at Mass, after communion, and in all our other spiritual exercises.

First we should pray for the forgiveness of all our sins, because we do not know, and shall not know till after death, whether they have been pardoned or not. We read in Holy Writ, that we do not know whether we are worthy of love or hatred.[1] And though God had revealed to us that our sins were forgiven, we should still continue till death to beg of Him, "to wash us still more from our sins and to cleanse us from our iniquities ;" for after the guilt of sin has been forgiven, the temporal punishment due to it, frequently and generally remains. Among the temporal punishments due to sin, after the remission of its guilt, the Saints count the withholding of many of God's graces. From eternity God prepared for us all abundant graces to work out our salvation. Some of these graces were necessary to lead us to a high degree of perfection, and to make us Saints ; others were so necessary, that without them we should not be saved. In punishment of sin, even after its guilt has been remitted, God sometimes withholds both of these kinds of graces, and therefore, our past sins, after they have been forgiven, may be the cause of our

[1] Eccl. ix.

damnation, by preventing God from bestowing upon us certain graces without which we shall be certainly lost. On this account the Holy Ghost tells us not to be without fear about sin forgiven.[1] In order then to secure not only the pardon of all our past sins, but also the graces which may be with-held in punishment of them, and particularly the graces without which we should be lost, we must pray frequently and fervently in our meditations for the complete and entire remission of all our sins, and of all the penalties due to them. By frequent and fervent petitions for these objects, every one, even the most abandoned sinner, however enormous his crimes may have been, can easily and *infallibly* avert the chastisement of sin, which consists in the with-holding of God's graces ; and he may thus infallibly prevent the danger of his past sins being the cause of his damnation, after their guilt had been remitted.

Secondly, we must ask with fervor the gift of God's love. This gift should be the object of all our prayers, because it brings with it all the other gifts of God. "He that loveth Me," says Jesus Christ, "shall be loved by My Father."[2] Acts of love are made by desiring to love God and to see Him loved by all men above all things, for instance: "My God, I love Thee with my whole heart; I desire to love Thee as much as the angels love Thee, and as much as Thou wishest me to love Thee ; I desire to see Thee loved by all men as much as Thou deservest to be loved. Make me love Thee more and more, and assist

[1] Eccl. v. 5. [2] John 14, 21.

me always to overcome every obstacle that might prevent me from loving Thee as much as Thou deservest
to be loved. Let me seek nothing but Thee; make
me live for Thee alone.''

We can also make acts of love by resigning ourselves in all things to the Divine will, saying : My
dear Saviour, make known to me what is pleasing to
Thee ; I am ready to do it, whatever it may be.

Again, we can make acts of love by offering ourselves to God without reserve, saying : O my God, do
what Thou pleasest with me, and with all that belongs to me. St. Teresa used to make such offerings
of herself fifty times in the day.

Thirdly, we must above all, pray with great
fervor in our meditations for the grace of final perseverance. This grace is the grace of graces; this is
the grace on which our salvation depends; if God
give it to us, we shall be saved ; if He does not give
it, we shall be lost. The grace of perseverance is the
gift which distinguishes the elect in heaven from the
reprobate in hell; if the elect had not received it,
they would be lost; and if this grace had been
bestowed upon the damned, they would now be in
glory. This grace crowns all the other gifts of God ;
without it they will be a source of greater damnation.
God gives this grace to infants without any co-operation on their part ; He takes them out of life before
they lose their baptismal innocence.

This grace of perseverance, however, God never
gives to any adult who does not ask for it. This
grace is a special gift, which we cannot merit. We

cannot merit it by the sacraments, nor by penitential austerities, nor by alms-deeds. God has given us *one means of infallibly obtaining it*, and this means is, to pray for it continually till our last breath. It is not enough to ask this gift once or twice, nor for a year, nor for ten years; our petitions for it must cease only with our life; they must be frequently made for it in meditation, since this is the fittest time to pray for God's graces. Whosoever asks for it to-day, obtains it for to-day; but he who does not pray for it to-morrow, may fall to-morrow and be lost. In his history of the martyrs of Japan, St. Alphonsus relates, that an old man condemned to a slow and painful death, remained for a long time firm and steadfast in his torments; but when he was on the point of breathing his last, he ceased to recommend himself to God, denied his faith and instantly expired. "In order then to obtain perseverance," says St. Alphonsus, "we must recommend ourselves continually to God, morning and evening, in our meditations, at Mass, communion, and at all times, but particularly in time of temptations, saying and repeating continually: 'Assist me, O Lord, assist me; do not abandon me; have mercy on me.'" If we then wish to secure the grace of final perseverance, we must not cease till death to pray for it.

But in order to persevere to the end of our life in praying for this great gift, we must also unceasingly ask of God the grace that we may continue to our last breath to ask of Him this grace of perseverance. If we wish not to be forsaken by God, we must never

cease to pray that He may not abandon us. If we
continually beg His aid, He will most certainly assist us always, and will never permit us to lose Him,
or to be separated from His love. In order to secure
this constant aid and protection of God let us be careful to ask without ceasing, not only the gift of final
perseverance, and the graces necessary to obtain it,
but let us also ask of the Lord the great gift of prayer.
Oh! how great a gift is the spirit of prayer, or the
grace to pray always! If we persevere to the end in
prayer we shall certainly obtain the gift of perseverance and every grace we stand in need of; for God
cannot violate His promise to hear all who invoke
Him. Christians and more especially Religious,
should endeavor to raise their hearts to God every
quarter of an hour. By this practice we shall fulfil
the obligation of praying always; because, by offering all our actions to God through Jesus Christ in
order to obtain eternal glory, we make every act of
our life a prayer for the grace of eternal life.

The third fruit of mental prayer consists in making a firm resolution to do some particular good acts,
or to avoid some particular faults. It is always
necessary to ask God's help to be faithful to our
resolutions; otherwise we shall certainly violate them.

The conclusion contains three acts: first, an act
of thanksgiving to God for the lights received in
meditation; secondly, a firm purpose to practise the
resolutions made; thirdly, a petition to the Eternal
Father, through the merits of Jesus Christ and the
prayers of Mary, for grace to be faithful to them.
39

Let the meditation be closed with a Pater and Ave to recommend to God the souls in purgatory, the prelates of the Church, all sinners, and all our relatives, friends and benefactors.

At the end of meditation we should call to our mind, some sentiment which we should remember during the day, and thus excite our fervor in God's service. After meditation, we should endeavor to fulfil, as soon as possible, the resolutions which we have made.

This is the first method of meditation, in which many Saints spent several years before they were admitted to a more simple and sublime spirit of prayer called contemplation. Those who enter religion must begin here, if they have not already been habituated to this holy exercise; for it is of great consequence to imprint well on their minds, in the beginning, the truths of faith, by the sweet and simple consideration which they ought to make of them.

The second method is to make no use of the imagination, but simply and purely meditate on the Gospel and the mysteries of our faith, and entertain ourselves familiarly and simply with our Lord, on all He has done and suffered for us, without any representation. This method is better, more holy and secure than the first. It may easily be adopted, if the soul feel any attraction for it; but we must in every degree of prayer preserve a holy liberty, to follow the lights and emotions which God may impart.

A soul however that is faithful in the practice of virtue which is the true fruit of prayer, will not stop here. The Lord will conduct her to the prayer of a most simple union, and holy simplicity of the presence of His divine Providence. "There are some souls," says St. Francis de Sales, "who cannot confine their minds to any particular mystery, as they are drawn to a certain sweet simplicity, which keeps them in great tranquillity before God, without any other consideration than that they are in His presence and that He is their only good. In this state the soul is led by the sweet invitation of her heavenly spouse to enjoy His holy embraces; to forbear any studied efforts to excite holy affections and resolutions by the usual mode of attentive consideration of some religious truth; she exchanges her natural activity for a delightful and amorous repose; the soul is sweetly attracted to view the divine perfections in a more distinct and simple manner, to unite her pious desires with the divine will. In this state, the mind is enlightened with a simple and clear view of God's amiable perfections; the heart is inflamed with an ecstasy of love and the whole soul with all its powers, is absorbed in the contemplation of the beloved object. In this manner the prayer of the soul becomes continual by her attention to God in all things, by her invariable desire to please Him, by perpetually embracing His adorable will on all occasions, even under the severest strokes of adversity; moreover her spirit of recollection becomes so constant and uninterrupted, that she finds great difficulty in bestowing a due attention on such exterior occupations as demand her care. She may truly say with the sacred spouse:

"I sleep, but My heart watches;" that is, in every action of life such a soul can say: I am waking, but my heart reposes; I am speaking, but my heart loves ; I am performing the duty of recreation, but my heart prays ; I am enjoying necessary repose, but my heart speaks to God. In this state, the pious soul entrusts all her concerns, with perfect security to the care of her heavenly spouse, she leaves to Him exclusively the choice of His own favors, and the degree of holy contemplation He chooses to bestow ; and in every instance, receives with the same simplicity interior comfort or spiritual dryness, overwhelming joy, or the most distressing desolation of mind, in accordance with the gracious designs of Divine goodness in completing the work of her sanctification.

In order to make any advances in holy contemplation, it is ever necessary to be singularly attentive to the presence of God and to be extremely assiduous in withdrawing the soul from vain, superfluous and distracting thoughts and reminiscences; for the Divine spouse manifests His favors in proportion to the attention which He receives, and indicates His will where there is a disposition to lose sight of created objects, in order to communicate with the Creator. The predominant qualities which are required in this exercise of heavenly contemplation are, great simplicity of intention and extreme purity of heart, without the studied and elaborate efforts of the creature. If distractions divert the soul from the calm performance of this holy duty, she is required to exercise perfect patience and make use of the most amorous aspirations. "My God, Thou art the only support of my soul, my rest, my repose, my consolation; though I should cease to live, I will not cease to love."

We must not force ourselves to the prayer of contemplation, but wait with humility and patience the hour which our Saviour has destined to introduce us to this happiness. For to go to God we must let ourselves be conducted by His spirit. His choice is always best for us; some possess this simplicity and repose in a greater degree than others; and find there much light. It seems God makes use of this means to conduct souls to the end of their journey, and we receive there all necessary lights and strength. This attraction is so good that souls drawn from it, seem to lose their centre, and liberty of spirit, and enter into a restraint and perplexity, which robs them of their peace, and greatly retards their progress.

Souls thus absorbed in God should not strain themselves to make acts and reflections, because then God supports them in union of love with Himself. "Then," says St. Teresa, "God occupies with His light the understanding, and prevents it from thinking of anything else. When God thus wishes that our understanding should cease to reason, He occupies it and gives it a knowledge superior to that which it can arrive at, and keeps the intellect suspended." "When therefore in prayer," says St. Alphonsus, "God makes us feel that He wishes to speak to us, and does not wish that we should address Him, we should not try to do anything ourselves, lest we impede the divine operation in us ; we should only apply our loving attention to the voice of God, and say: "Speak Lord, for Thy servant heaieth." This repose of the soul in God, includes in an excellent manner all the exterior acts which we could make to satisfy our inclination. It is better thus to sleep in the arms of the Lord, than to watch elsewhere.

When God, however, does not speak to us, then we should address Him in prayer ; we should not lose our time in doing nothing, but should make acts of contrition, of love, purposes of advancement in perfection. These acts, however, should be made calmly and sweetly; and those acts to which the soul feels more attracted, should be made in preference to others.

This kind of prayer, in which the soul is absorbed in God, seldom lasts long ; the effe ts of it, however, last, and so, when the soul returns to the active state, it ought to return also to labor to preserve the fruit received in contemplation, by reading, reflecting, offering up pious affections, and performing similar acts of devotion, because, as St. Augustine confesses, he always felt himself after being exalted to some unusual union with God, drawn back again, as it were by a weight, to the miseries of this life, so that he felt obliged again to assist himself by acts of the will and the understanding, to a union with God.

Those who are conducted by this way, are obliged to a great purity of heart, self-debasement, submission and total dependence on God. They ought to be simple in mind, retrenching all reflections on the past, present and future, and instead of considering what they do, or will do, they ought to look up to God, forgetting as much as possible all things for this continual remembrance, uniting their mind with His goodness in all that happens at each moment, and this most simply.

It often happens that souls which are in this way, are tried by many distractions, and left without any sensible support, our Lord withdrawing the sentiment of His sweet presence, and all interior light, so that they are in a total inability and insensibility, but sometimes less so than at others. This astonishes souls which have not much experience. We always love the sweetness and delight of consolations; nevertheless the rigor of aridities is more rich in fruit; and though St. Peter loved the mountain of Thabor and fled from that of Calvary, yet the latter is the most profitable, and the Blood shed upon the one is more desirable than the brightness which environs the other. It is better to eat bread without sugar than to eat sugar without bread. When the Lord deprives us of those consolations and of the sense of His presence, it is in order that our heart should cleave to nothing sensible, but to Him only and His good pleasure. Jacob certainly was able to take off the skin with which his mother had covered his neck and hands, because it did not adhere to him; if any

one had tried to tear off that of Esau, the operation
would have been very painful, so as to make him
cry out. So, in the same manner, when we cry out
upon God's withdrawing sensible consolations, it is a
sign that they cleave to our heart or that our heart is
attached to them ; Jesus then reveals Himself for a
little while to those who enter His service, to detach
them from the false pleasures of the senses, and
attract their love more strongly to Himself ; then He
hides Himself, and withdraws His consolations, to
try them, purify them, humiliate them, to make them
understand their poverty and misery, and place a
proper guard on His divine favors ; to oblige them to
pray with faith and seek Him with submission, that
they may merit His graces. The soul in the absence
of Jesus, is sad and afflicted, but if she continue faithful He will console her. Like the disciples, she rejoices on seeing the Lord, and having learned wisdom
by the vicissitudes which she has experienced,
disposes her to lead an interior life, and love God
purely, without attaching herself, inordinately to
His consolations.

The ways of God are admirable. They are ways
of grace, unknown to nature ; ways of wisdom, incomprehensible to human reason, ways of peace, that
ensure tranquillity to the mind ; ways of love, that
charm and delight the soul.

God works for us, when He seems to be against
us. He is drawing near unto us, when He seems to
be afar off. He advances our affairs, when His
providence seems to have abandoned them to ruin.

He enriches, when He seems to impoverish us. He
saves us at the moment, when He seems to have forsaken us. He gives us life, when He seems to give
us death. He leads us to peace by warfare; to perfection by the way of imperfection; to glory through
ignominy; to the promised land through frightful
deserts; to heaven by the road which seems farthest
from it, and which appears to lead to hell!

"Blessed are the poor in spirit: for theirs is the
kingdom of heaven." This way is that of the Saints,
and the most secure; but it is poor, deprived of
sentiment, relish, knowledge, power, affection, desire and love. In fine, it is poor, and destitute of
all, but the resolution not to offend God wilfully, and
to please Him in all things, and especially to belong
to Him. This is all that this poor soul has, and this
in such a manner, that she receives no satisfaction or
sentiment, saying, only, though without feeling, that
she does not wish to sin, and that she desires our
Lord to fulfil His good pleasure in her; she does
good and refrains from evil, through reason; remaining in all, without any satisfaction, but this, which is
better than a thousand others, and with which she
should be content, which is to wish te remain willingly and sweetly in this privation, for the good
pleasure of God, Who wishes her to be so; esteem-
ing more His holy will, than all His consolations,
and her own satisfaction. This is to be poor in spirit,
it is in this state, that our Lord wishes the soul to be,
and to remain in it willingly and cheerfully. A soul
in this state should practise as many acts of virtue as

she can; saying sometimes to our Lord, though without relish: Lord I am all Thine, and I wish to do everything for the love of Thee.

A soul under aridity, may still make all the acts of prayer; if it be without relish or affection, it will not be without profit; for the prayer of patience, submission and abandonment to the good pleasure of God, which they ought to practise on this occasion, will not be less agreeable to the divine Majesty, but far more so, than if they enjoyed much sweetness. They should continue to keep themselves before God with profound reverence, and a devout exterior, amorously suffering this their painful trial.

It is a solid rapture to go out of our inclinations, to live according to the rule, which is the way of God for us, and in which we will find every means of perfection and union with God and our neighbor. We should, with great simplicity, leave to our Heavenly Father the care and conduct of our prayer and our interior, and be careful to keep close to Him, and practise faithfully the solid virtues which His goodness will present to us at each moment, without looking further.

It is certain, that when this aridity is great, the poor soul can only suffer. But this poor suffering is a prayer most agreeable to God, if accompanied with humility, submission and confidence; and if she is content with the will of God, and with the honor of remaining in His presence, as a slave before her Lord, as a mendicant before her rich Sovereign, a helpless wretch before the Omnipotent, a disciple near her good Master, a daughter at the feet of her Father, and in the exercise of similar affections as the Holy Ghost shall suggest, repeating a few words to our Lord, according to her situation. When these affections are entertained, with sweet submission, they are profitable, and they can always be uttered, though without relish. Besides, it is not our satisfaction which we ought to seek, but that of God Who wills it thus.

Such a soul will say, that, in the midst of her darkness, she cannot make these considerations, that she cannot, it seems, even say a word to our Lord. She does well to say: "it seems;" for this is not really so. The sacred Council of Trent declares, we are obliged to believe, that God and His grace never so far abandon us, as that we cannot have recourse to His bounty, and protest, that in spite of all the trouble of our soul, we wish to belong to Him. But remark, that all this is in the superior part of the soul, and because the inferior part does not see it, it remains in trouble; this afflicts the soul, and makes her think herself miserable, and then she begins to pity herself, as if it were a thing very worthy of compassion, to see herself without consolation.

A soul in this state should never make any useless reflections on what she does, has done, or will do, or what are her temptations, pains and inclinations for such curiosity would not only be useless, but dangerous. Instead of this, she should look to God in doing good, and flying from evil, as much as she can ; and if she fail, return to God with an humble

mind, full of sweet confidence, trusting that God will
aid her, and that she will do better. "The most
miserable," says St. Francis de Sales, "should have
the most confidence." She must do this and be
cheerful, suffering the cross of our Lord patiently,
without desiring to quit it; she must try to advance
blindly in simplicity and obey faithfully what she is
counselled.

Ah! let us consider, that our Lord and our
Master was pleased to be exercised by these interior
disgusts, but in an incomparably greater degree. Let
us listen to the words which He uttered on the cross:
"My God, my God! why hast Thou forsaken Me?"
He was reduced to extremity; for it was only the
highest point of His mind that was not overwhelmed.
But remark, that He speaks to God, to show us that
it is not impossible.

Which is better, the soul will ask, at this time
to speak to God of our pain and misery, or to speak
to Him of something else? I say, that in this, as in
all other temptations, it is better to divert our mind
from its pain, with a sweet violence, speaking to God
of something else; for if we speak of our trouble, it
will truly serve to increase our pain; our nature being such, that we cannot see our trials without being
moved to compassion.

But such a soul will say, that, if she do not pay
attention to it, she will not remember to tell it to her
director. And what matters it? We are certainly
like children, who are glad to go and tell their
mother that they have been stung by a bee, so that

their mother may pity them, and blow upon the wound, which is already healed. For we wish to go and tell our director or superior that we have been afflicted, and to increase our affliction, relating it all in detail, without forgetting the least circumstance, which can excite pity. Now behold great childishness! If we have committed some infidelity, well, let us tell it; if we have been faithful, we must also mention it, but briefly without exaggerating either.

To be without light, taste, sentiment, the enjoyment of all knowledge and without any satisfaction, or assistance from creatures, oh! how good this state is! what can the soul do in this state, but like a bird without plumage, hide under the wings of her good mother, Providence, and remain there in safety, not daring to come out, for fear that the hawk might catch her.

Whatever trial may happen to her, she must never relent in her duty, not considering, whether she perform it with her ordinary fervor and joy; for truly, that is not in our power, but fidelity is.

Blessed are those who suffer interior pains, provided they remain faithful to God, and continue constant in spite of these contrary winds.

Let us not be astonished at the combats between the inferior and superior part of the soul. Such attacks are ordinary for those who serve the Lord. These temptations are a fire in which God wishes to purify us. They will all pass away at the hour that divine Providence has marked. Let us be joyful in this trial, as much as possible. We advance more by this way, if we be faithful, than if we enjoyed consolation. God will easily pardon faults of weakness, for which we should not be afflicted, but which we should let serve to nourish the love of our abjection, the practice of which is dear to God.

It is a good practice, when we fail in the fidelity which we owe to God in the practice of virtue, to try to regain by humility, what we have lost by our tepidity, annihilating ourselves before God peaceably and tranquilly, then returning sweetly to our ordinary duties with new confidence in God. If we fail fifty times a day, let us rise as often in this manner with simplicity, without useless reflections about ourselves ; for generally a greater fault is committed by examining and reflecting on what we have done (especially when this has been forbidden us) than our first fault is. I wonder, that some souls make more account of a little fault, that is but a trifle, than they do of failing in the advice given them for their perfection. We must despise the attacks of the devil ; we must not dispute with him, nor answer anything but : God be blessed ;—and this two or three times a day. Let us make positive acts of renunciation of his wicked suggestions ; let us not be disquieted, for the wicked spirit devises only to disturb and trouble us. Let us bear humbly this cross, without considering it. If we cannot help being disquieted, at least, let us not be troubled at being disturbed. We must learn how to live in peace in the midst of war, and to remain content in the midst of agitations, and all sorts of temptations. "What does he know, who has not been tempted," says Thomas a Kempis.

Although we neither feel, nor see in the midst of desolation and darkness, it matters not. The Lord is with us, and upon this ground, as it is arid, we must build solid faith, firm confidence, and the efficacious love of a perfect submission. We must say, though without feeling: I believe, I hope more firmly, than if I abounded in lights and sweetness. I am well pleased not to have any, and to say to Thee, without taste or sentiment whatsoever Thou art my God; I am all Thine. Then we must remain in peace.

Perfect annihilation of self and complete submission to the will of God, is a great happiness. Alas! it is the only glory of souls dedicated to holy love. Let us be faithful to this practice, and do nothing according to our humors and inclinations, but all according to reason, and true piety, both in acting and suffering.

In order to ascertain clearly, whether in any instance, the practice of contemplation or sweet repose of the soul in the Lord, come from God, the following marks are given. The first is, that the devout soul in taking up a point of meditation, should, without any artificial efforts on her part or that of creatures, find her heart, her mind, and all her powers sweetly attracted to this sacred repose.

Secondly, amidst all the delights of this holy prayer, the soul thus favored must feel drawn to a more perfect obedience to God and her Superiors, to an entire dependence on God's Providence and a complete attachment to the divine will.

Thirdly, this sweet repose must have the effect of detaching the soul from all created objects and uniting it more perfectly to its Sovereign Good; for it is not reasonable to suppose that a soul which begins to taste the unalloyed sweets of heavenly things, should bestow her attention on objects beneath her regard.

Fourthly, this practice of contemplation must render the soul more sincere and candid in the declaration of her faults, and fill her with a child-like simplicity, humility and self-annihilation.

Fifthly, this practice must be followed by a strong determination to bear with unconquered patience all dryness, desolation, and a total absence of comfort which may eventually happen.

Sixthly, this spirit of prayer must render the soul more desirous, ever eager to suffer all things without any alleviation but what arises from the good pleasure of the beloved.

The seventh, and most certain mark is, when this sweet repose of heavenly contemplation contributes to render the soul more humble, inspires her with an utter contempt for the world and herself and fixes her esteem on the lowliness, the humiliation and the sorrows of the cross.

These are decisive landmarks to ascertain the boundaries which distinguish real contemplation from fanatical illusion.

www.ingramcontent.com/pod-product-compliance
Lightning Source LLC
Chambersburg PA
CBHW031812270326
41932CB00008B/395

* 9 7 8 3 7 4 4 6 6 0 1 0 5 *